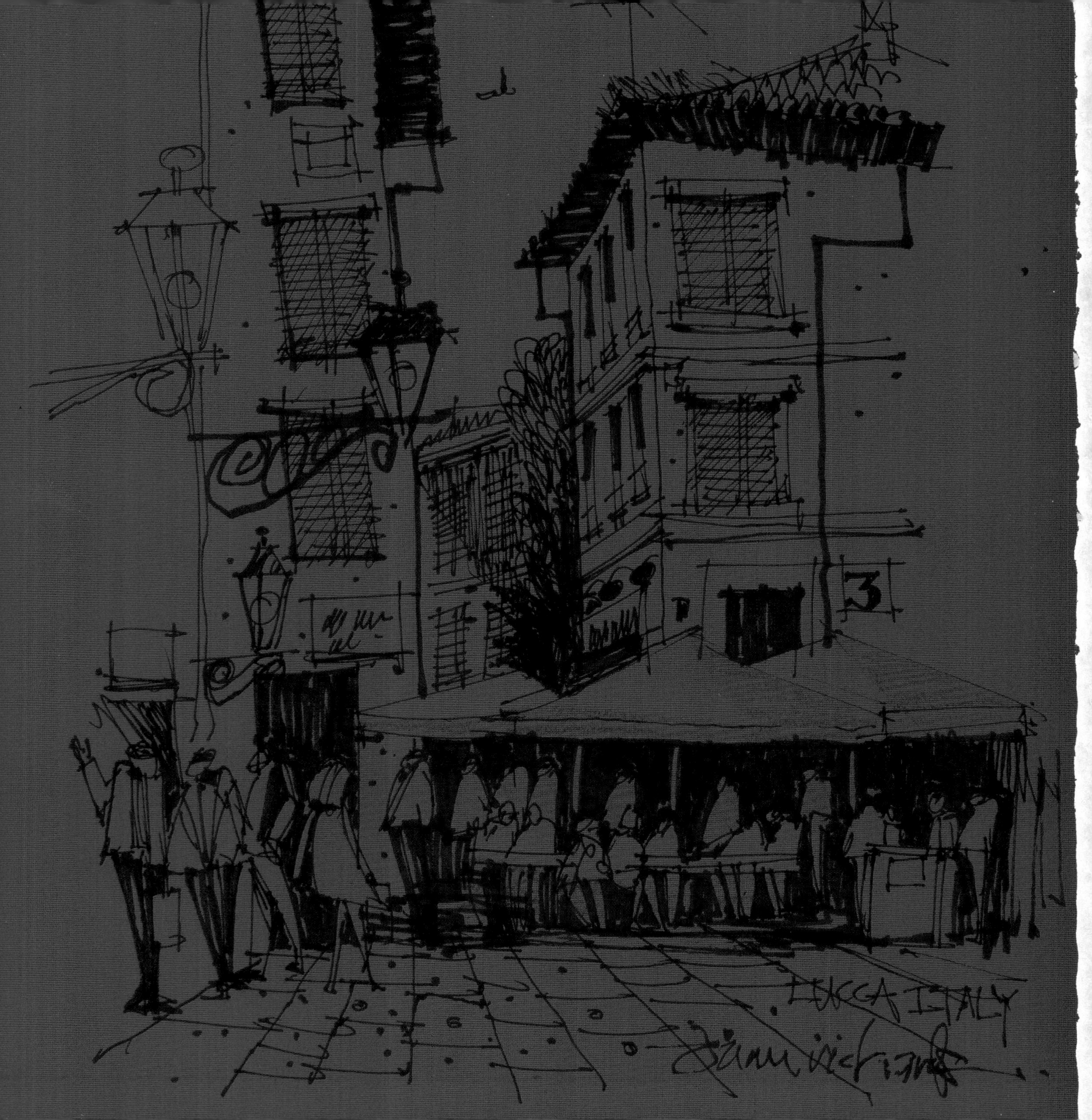
3
LUCCA ITALY

ORO Editions
Published by ORO Editions
Executive publisher: Gordon Goff.

www.oroeditions.com
info@oroeditions.com

ORO Editions Project Coordinator: Kirby Anderson
Graphic Design: Pablo Mandel, typestting by Micaela Carraro / CircularStudio

Typeset in Masqualero and Lyon Text

10 9 8 7 6 5 4 3 2 1 FIRST EDITION

Library of Congress data available upon request. World Rights: available.

ISBN: 978-1-961856-54-7

Color separations and printing: ORO Group Ltd.
Printed in China.

International distribution: www.oroeditions.com/distribution

ORO Editions makes a continuous effort to minimize the overall carbon footprint of its publications. As part of this goal, ORO Editions, in association with Global ReLeaf, arranges to plant trees to replace those used in the manufacturing of the paper produced for its books. Global ReLeaf is an international campaign run by American Forests, one of the world's oldest nonprofit conservation organizations. Global ReLeaf is American Forests' education and action program that helps individuals, organizations, agencies, and corporations improve the local and global environment by planting and caring for trees.

TRAVEL ARTIST

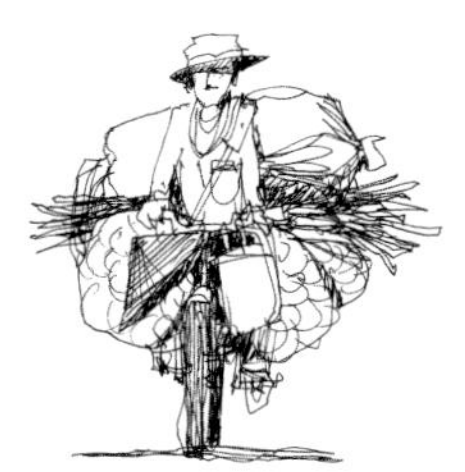

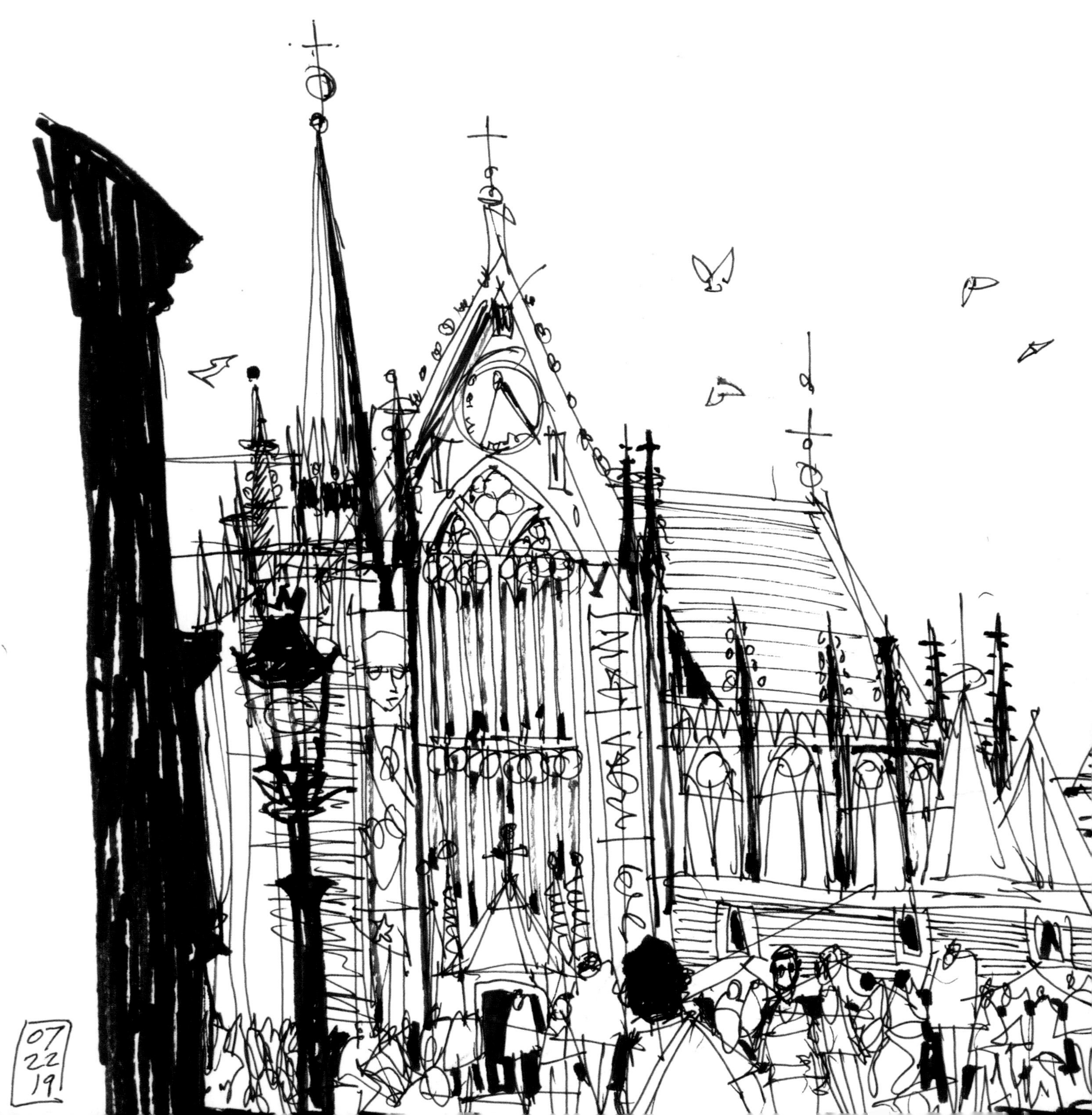
07
22
19

James Richards

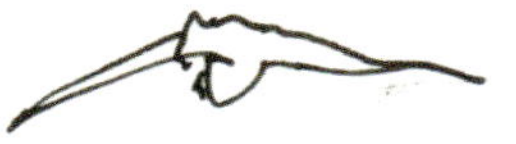

TRAVEL ARTIST

Sketchbook Drawings and True Stories from the Road

Foreword by Paul Heaston

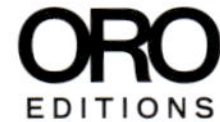

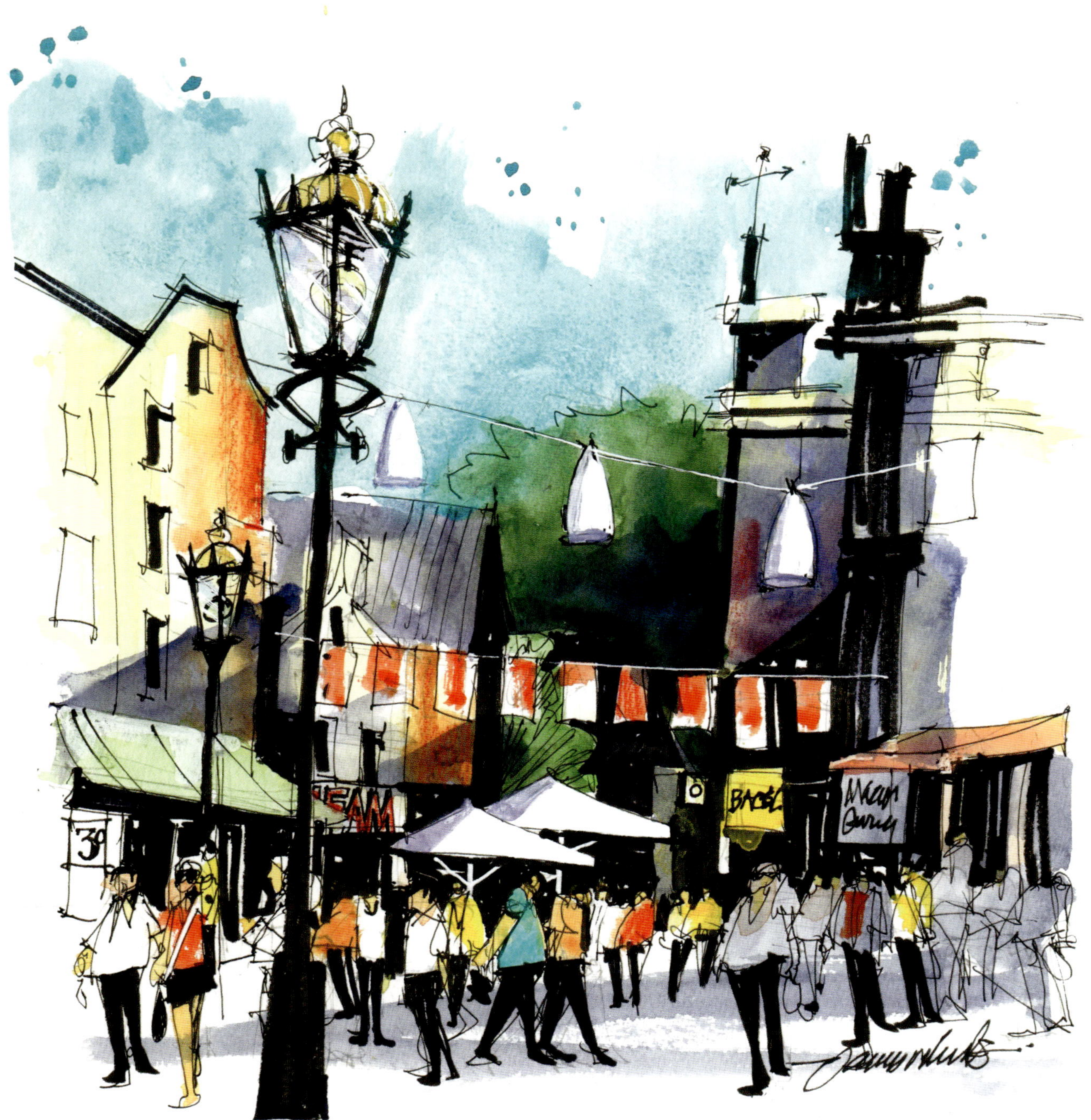

Amsterdam street life.

Dedicated to my professor, mentor and friend,
Max Z. Conrad, who taught me to travel.

CONTENTS

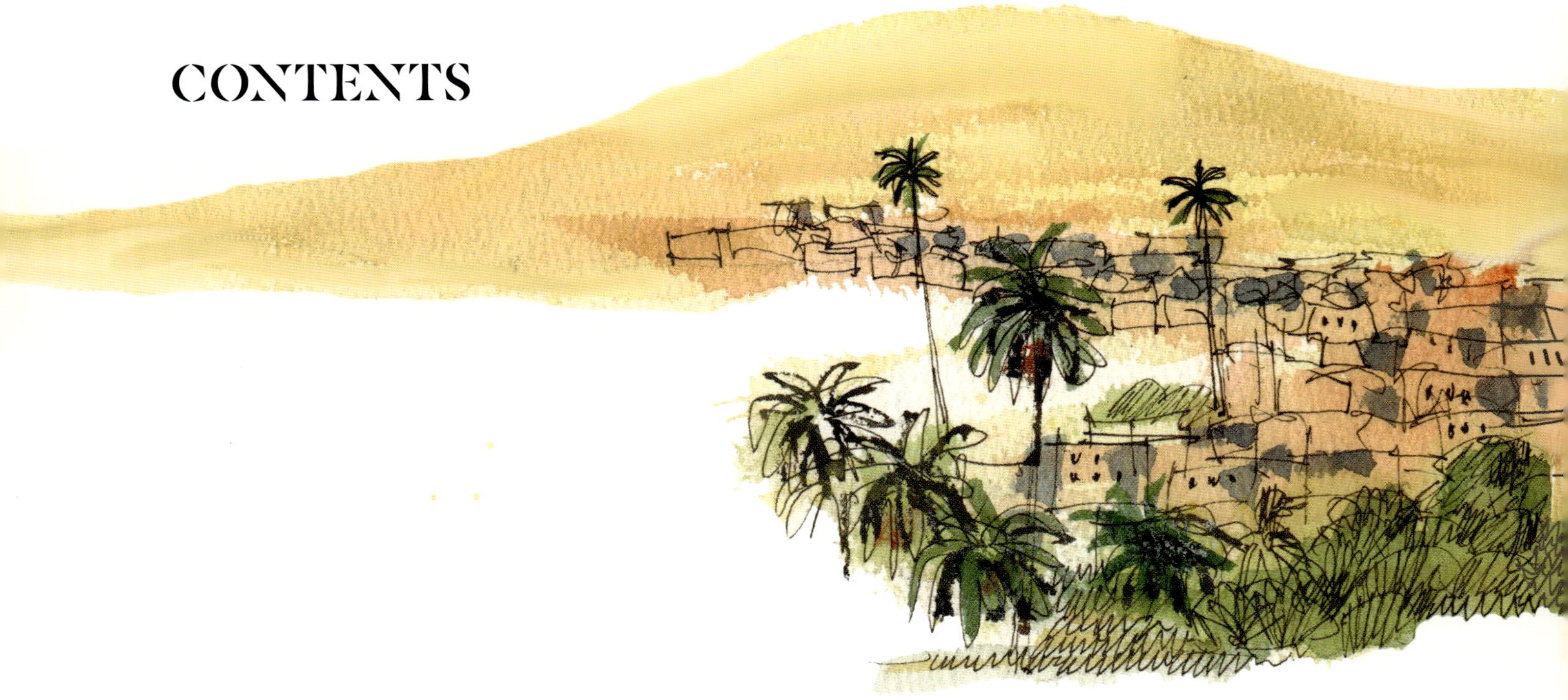

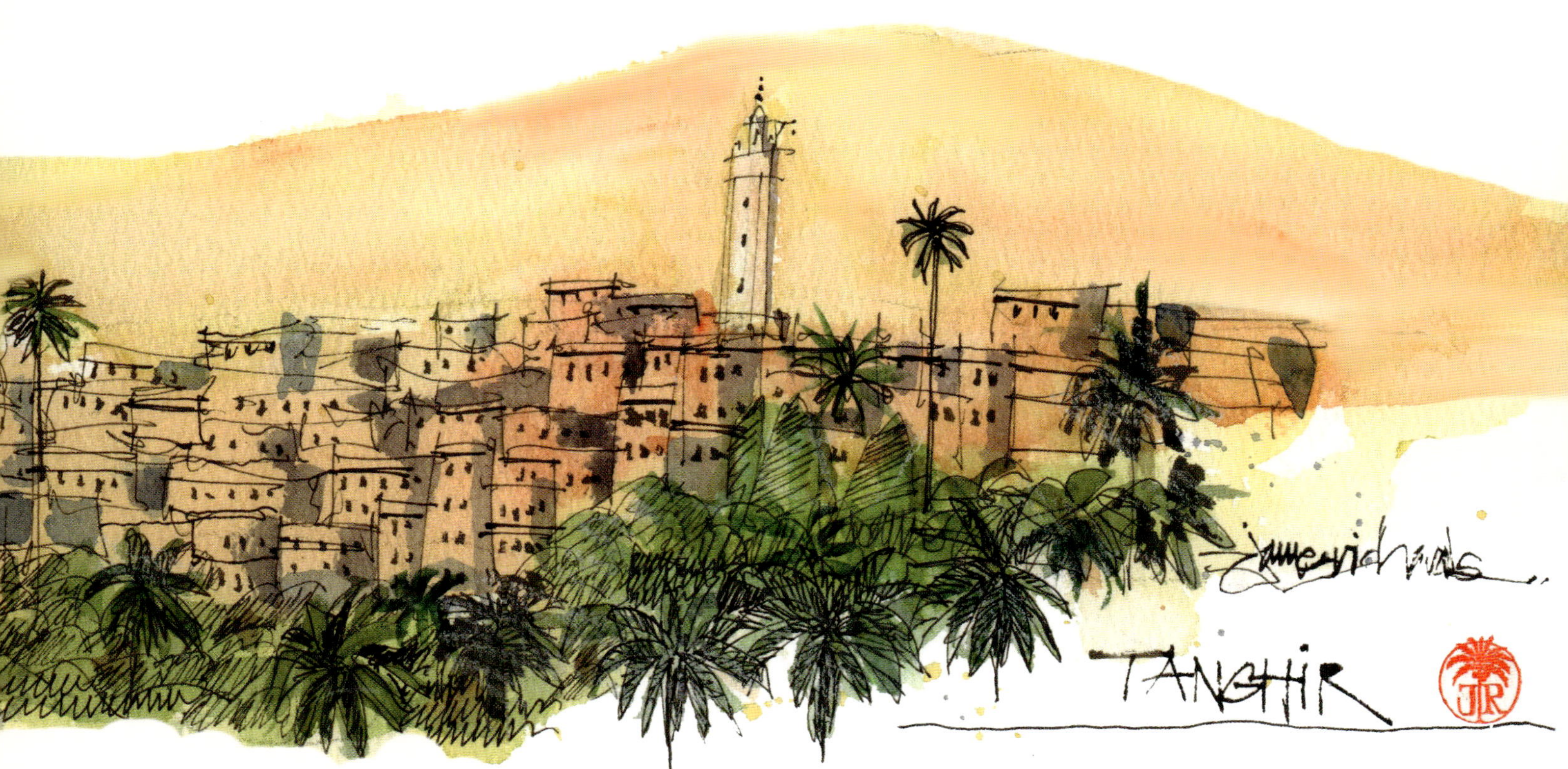
TANGHIR

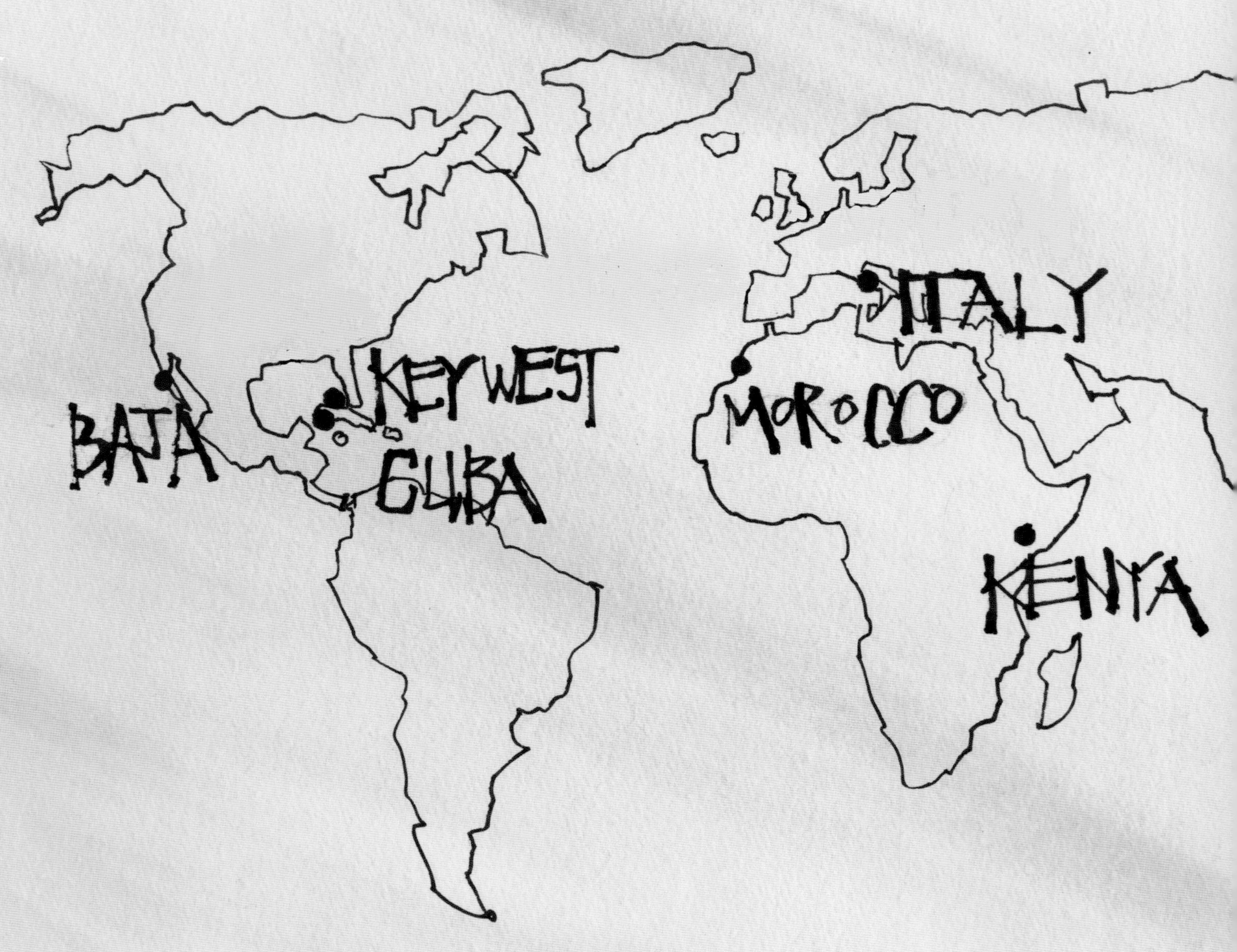
ITALY
KEY WEST
MOROCCO
BAJA
CUBA
KENYA

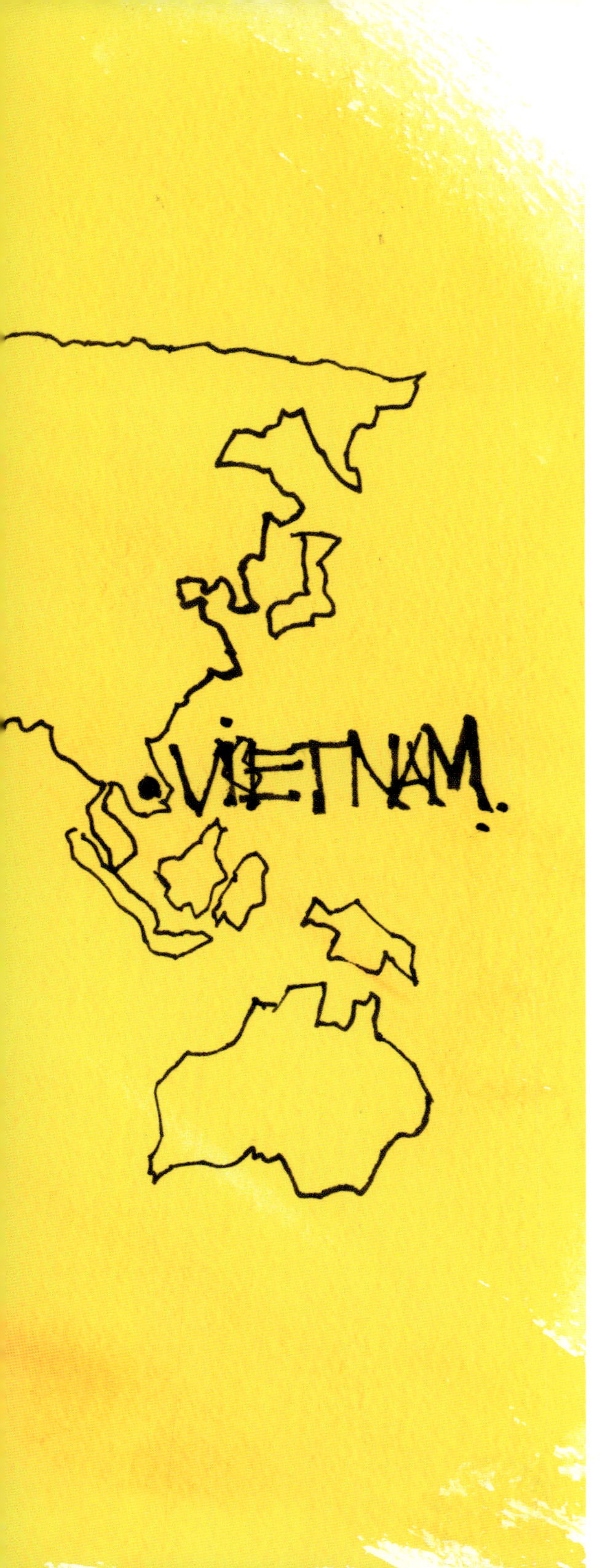

Is it Art?
Doesn't matter.
I never saw myself as Monet in the studio.
I wanted to be Anthony Bourdain
with a sketchbook.

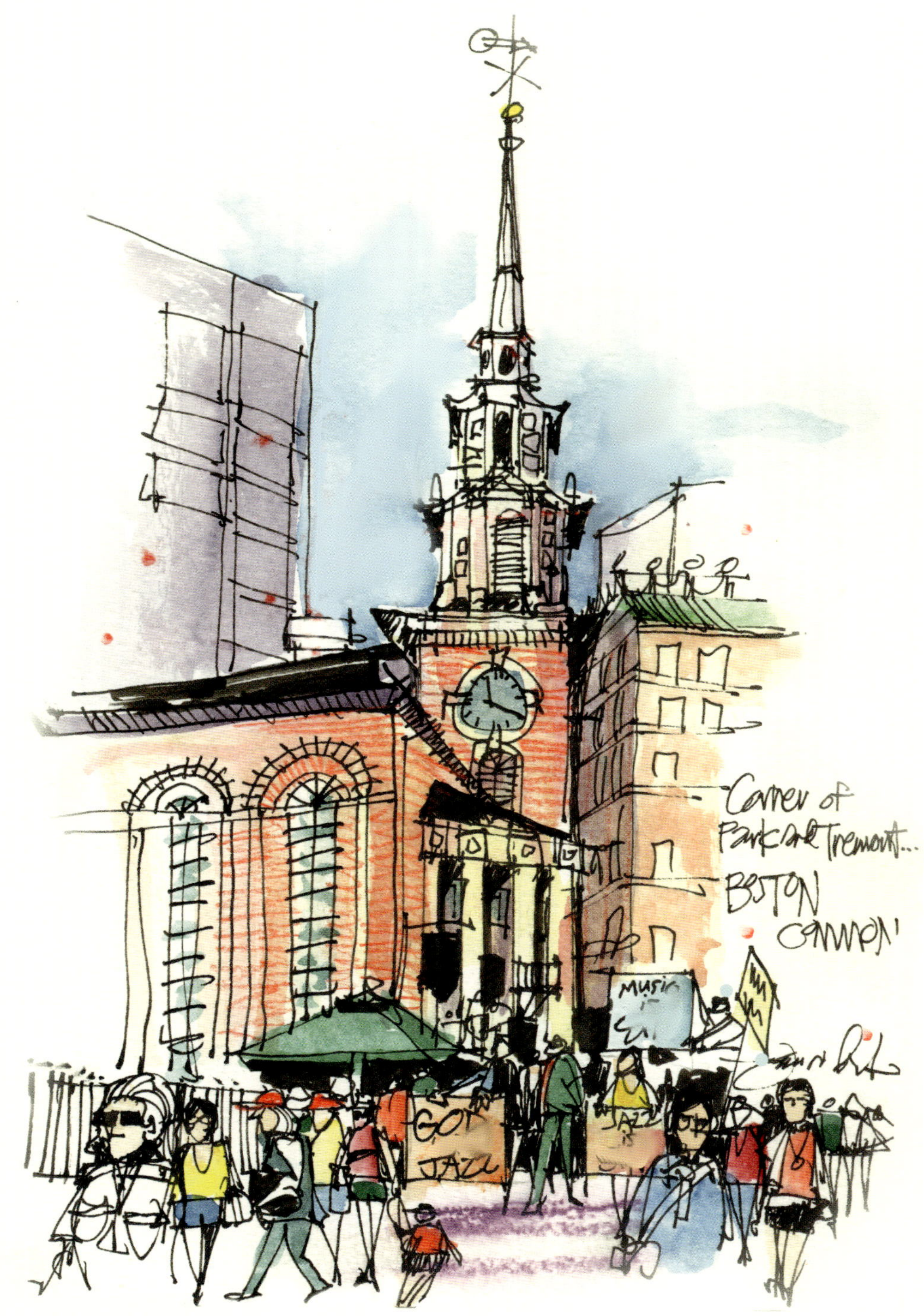

Boston, Massachusetts

FOREWORD

I'VE HAD THE GOOD FORTUNE to spend a bit of time with James Richards in some of the most beautiful places on the planet. He's one of those people you just instantly like. To his friends he's Jim. He's smart, funny, incredibly generous with his time, and one of the finest storytellers you'll ever meet. Jim's Louisiana drawl and easy laugh instantly puts you at ease and he has a way of spinning a yarn that leaves you hanging on his every word. You walk away after meeting Jim feeling like you made a friend for life. He's that kind of guy. And this is before you even see the sketches.

The sketches!

If you're lucky enough to be in the room when Jim pulls out his sketchbook and lets you flip through each page, it's pure magic. There's no other way to describe it. As I write this I find myself looking at his sketches for inspiration and getting lost among the scribbles of cobblestones, the paint splatters in the sky, the chaotic details of some ornate church facade. His sketches can be quiet or loud, but they always get your attention. A James Richards sketch has love in every mark, every brushstroke.

Jim and I met years ago because we both share a similar fondness for sitting in the street and drawing whatever is around us until our butts go numb. Lucky for us there are enough other people who enjoy doing the same thing that we feel a little less weird. Urban sketching is a very public affair. Chances are if you do it for long enough, people will notice. They'll come right up to you, look over your shoulder, ask questions.

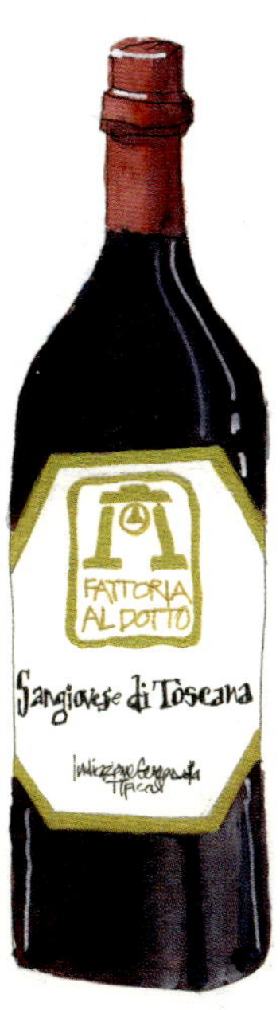

If you're not comfortable with close encounters of the curious kind, sketching in public can be a bit daunting. I've never gotten entirely comfortable with it and I've been doing it for nearly 20 years. Over time I have mastered the art of giving curt but polite answers to any questions I might get so as to discourage people from asking more of them.

But then there's Jim. Jim will take the time to answer every question. He'll show you his sketchbook. He'll show you his materials. He might even let you try them out. I'd wager Jim has created nearly as many urban sketchers as urban sketches. His warmth and generosity is contagious. Whether he's sharing his sketchbook with a stranger on the streets of Saigon who speaks no English or speaking to a roomful of enthusiastic urban sketchers who have traveled thousands of miles to learn from him, Jim finds a way to connect with everyone he meets. His passion for sketching is palpable and infectious.

I need to mention that being friends with Jim is really a package deal. Jim's constant travel companion, the one he calls "The Grownup in the Room," is his wife Patti, and when I say she is every bit as charming and delightful as Jim I may be underselling it. Business manager, travel planner, spiritual guru, motivational speaker, student wrangler are just a few of the hats I've seen her wear. But Patti isn't only support staff; she and

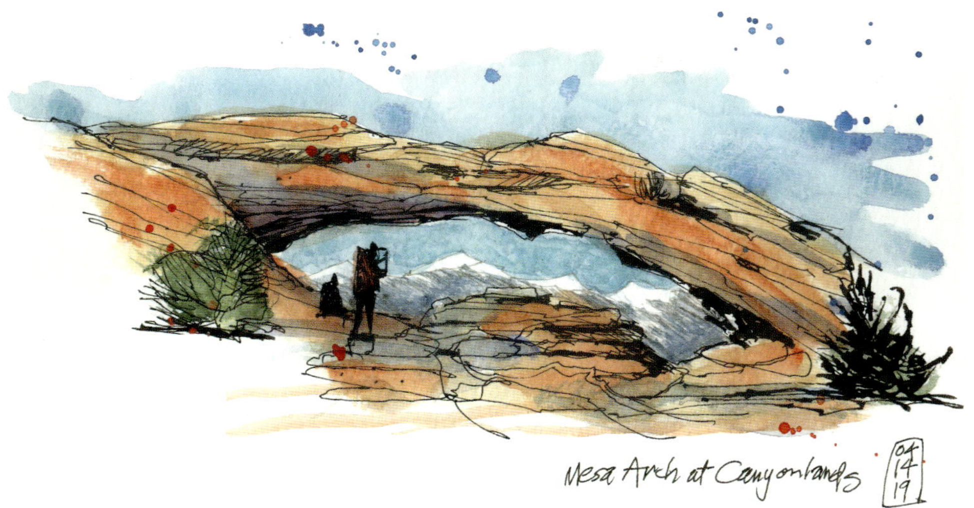

A bottle of fine San Giovese from Fattoria Al Dotto near Lucca.

Jim are a team in every sense of the word. There's no Jim without Patti and he'd be the first to tell you. Jim and Patti are really a powerhouse couple, and they also make for excellent breakfast conversation.

Whether or not you're a sketcher yourself, you are in for a treat. Every page is filled not only with colorful sketches but stories about the process of making them that are every bit as colorful. Sketching is more than the physical act of sitting down with a sketchbook and a pen. The sensory experience--the sounds, the smells, the heat on the back of your neck or the chill in your fingers--return every time you look at a sketch. So do the people you meet. The conversations with locals, the curious kids and the incredulous adults. The act of sketching reveals a place to you in every sense of the word. And Jim's sketches demonstrate this as skillfully as anyone who has ever sketched.

I'm excited for anyone getting to see Jim's art and read his stories for the first time. This book is like getting to know Jim the way I know Jim, minus the jetlag. In fact, if you're an artist, a word of caution: you will be tempted to immediately book a ticket to Portugal or Morocco, and I really can't offer you a good reason not to. As Jim is quick to point out, sketching changed his life. And what a life it's been.

Paul Heaston
September 22, 2024

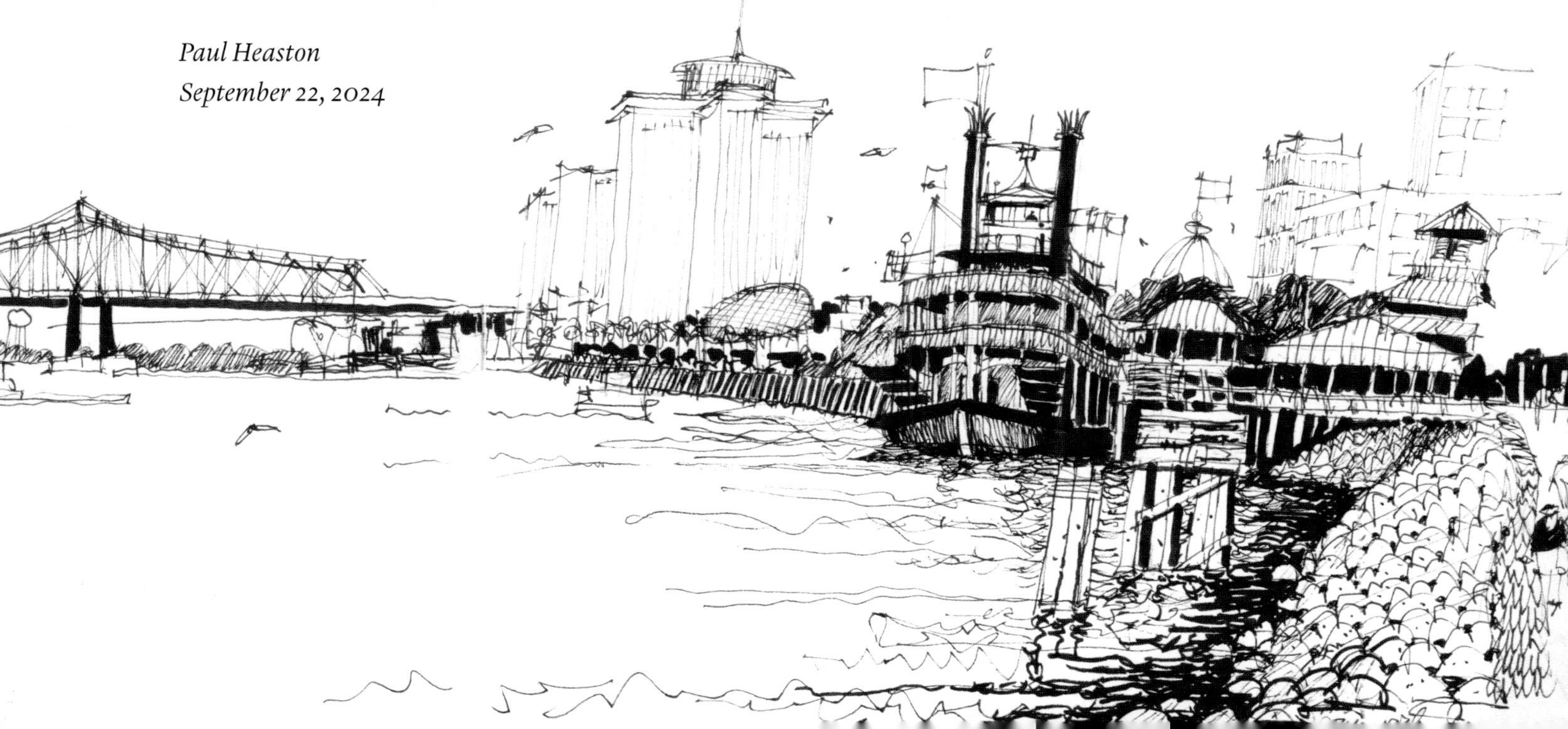

New Orleans: The Mississippi River seen from the top of the levee immediately adjacent to Jackson Square.

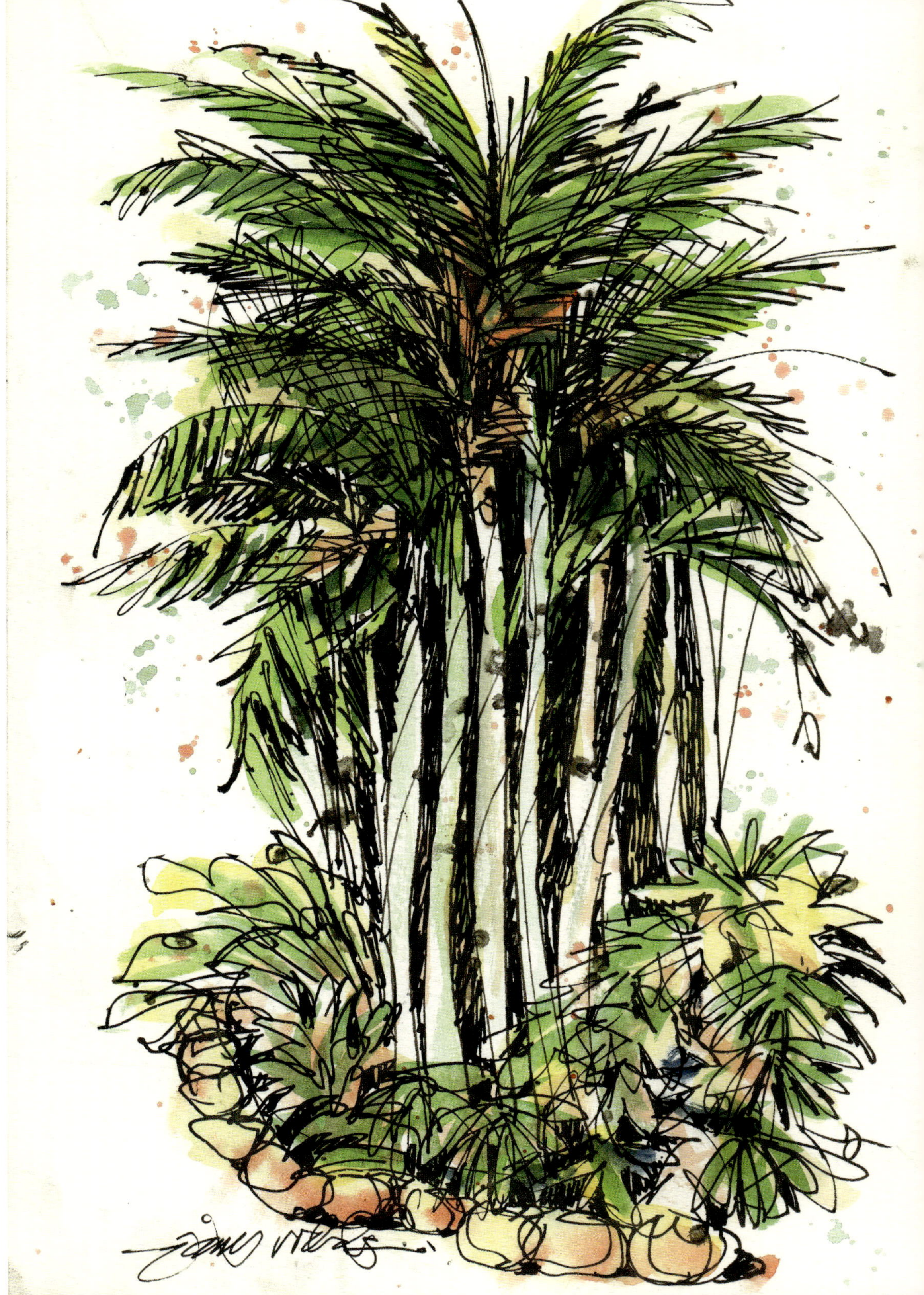

Palms, Cuba.

ACKNOWLEDGMENTS

UNDYING GRATITUDE, maximum love and respect to the tribe of inspirers, prodders, managers and muses who've brought me to the point of writing this page. And I probably wouldn't have gotten here without the patient and generous coaching of artist, writer and New York Times bestselling author Amy Stewart, who took up a torch and guided me through the dark and secretive catacombs of the publishing business, and who shepherded me from self-indulgent and pseudo-academic gobbledygook to writing in my own voice. And thanks to coach Gabi Goulart, who insisted I contact Amy. I'm very grateful to my friend, the incredible artist, impromptu harmony partner and occasional roommate Paul Heaston for writing the foreword. And many thanks to visionary publisher Gordon Goff and his team at ORO Editions who pushed this thing over the finish line, from files on a laptop to the beautiful volume you hold in your hands.

There are families you're born into and families you choose, and no one's been more inspiring and joyful in this journey than our Tuscan family, Karolina and Dawid Lenart. Big thanks as well to their team at Follow Your Senses in Tuscany. Patti and I are forever indebted. Many thanks to our clients and hosts around the world: Charles Meech, Annie Sumner and the Madeline Island School of the Arts, Kari Delany, Anna Barnes, Mayra Crespo, Ada Rosa Alfonso and Museo Hemingway, Adam Long, Rosanne Cash, Noga Grosman, Gathogo Githatu, Arthur Adeya, Dennis Mukuba, William Cordero Hidalgo, Stef Thelwell, Marissa Swinghammer, Meagan Burns, Tim Oliver, the captain, crew, naturalists and bartender of the ship National Geographic Seabird, all of our cherished workshop guests, the landscape architecture programs of 27 universities and many private design firms.

I'm grateful for the inspiration and friendship of Bill Johnson, Chris Flagg, Jeff Williams, Gabi Campanario, Chien Bau, Rob Sketcherman, Alvin Wong, Tracey Holden, Jenny Freidooni, Sandra Belegi, Kathryn and David Seay, Stephen Reed, Jean Bono, Mark Engelien, Duane Blossom, Keith Jones, Kate Stedman, Peggy Dean, Celestine Sahli, Oksana Kornelyuk, Buck Abbey, Bruce Hearn, the Usual Suspects (you know who you are), and all the amazing artists who inspire me daily. You guys rock.

Very special thanks to the boys in the band (Chip, Bob, Richard) and our guiding spirit Susan Apollonio.

Thanks to the Rum Runners for always having my back.

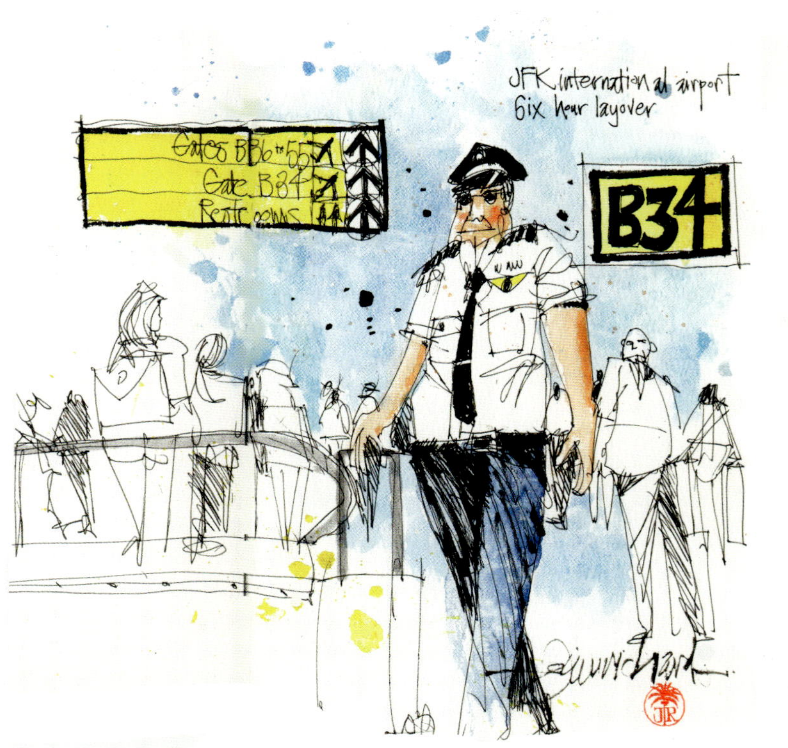

JFK Airport, New York.

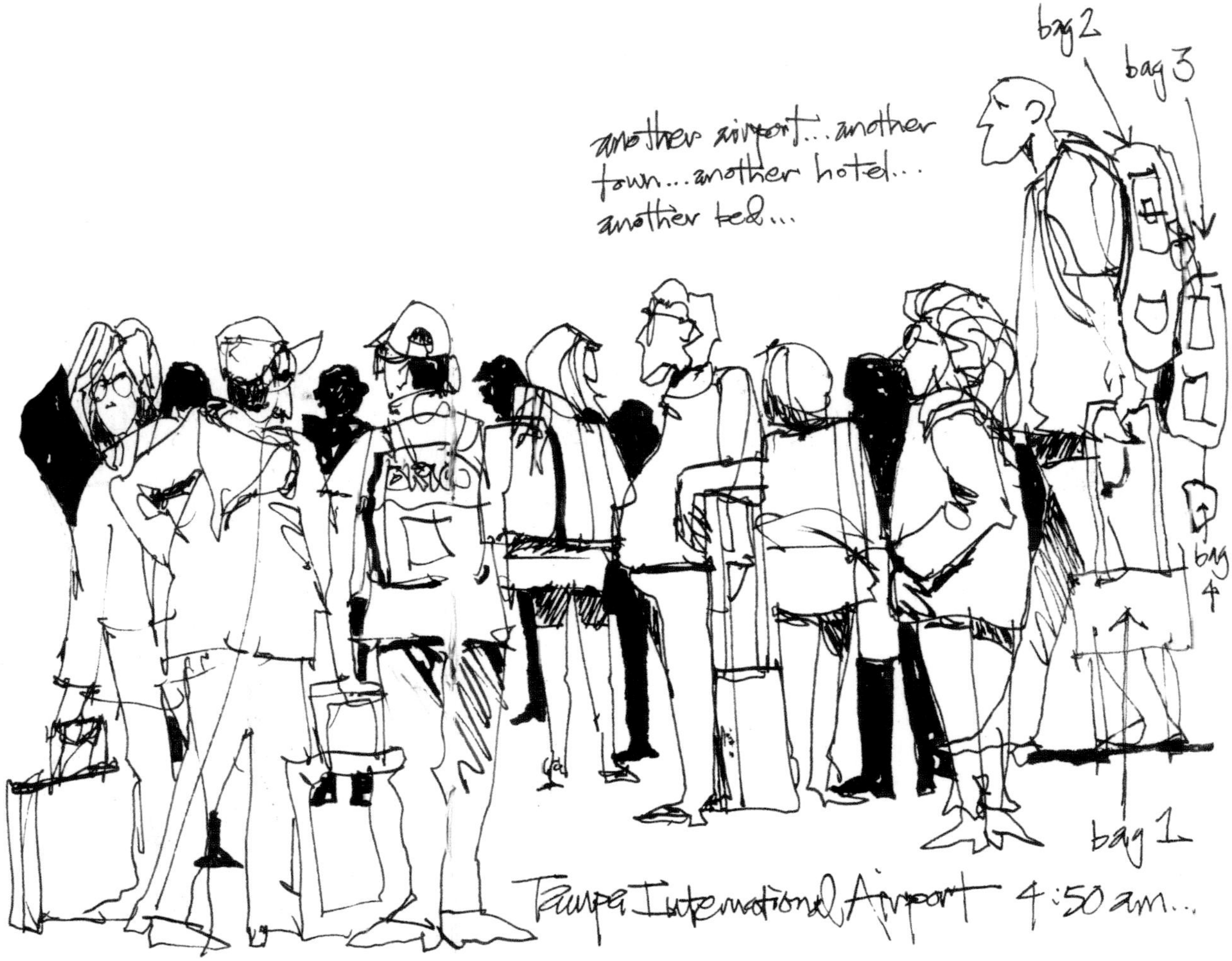

None of this is possible without my business manager, driver, wife and Grownup in the Room Patti. I'm not kidding, just ask around. Nor without the love and inspiration of Jessica, Cassie, Sebastien, Dave, Mick, Reid and Charlie. Thanks to my brothers and love all y'all. Larry, you were right. The book was too long.

Very special thanks to Mojo Risin' Coffee Company for allowing me to nurse cappuccinos over a couple of years to get this book written. See you tomorrow.

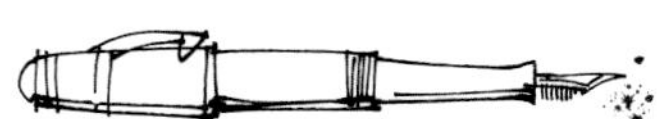

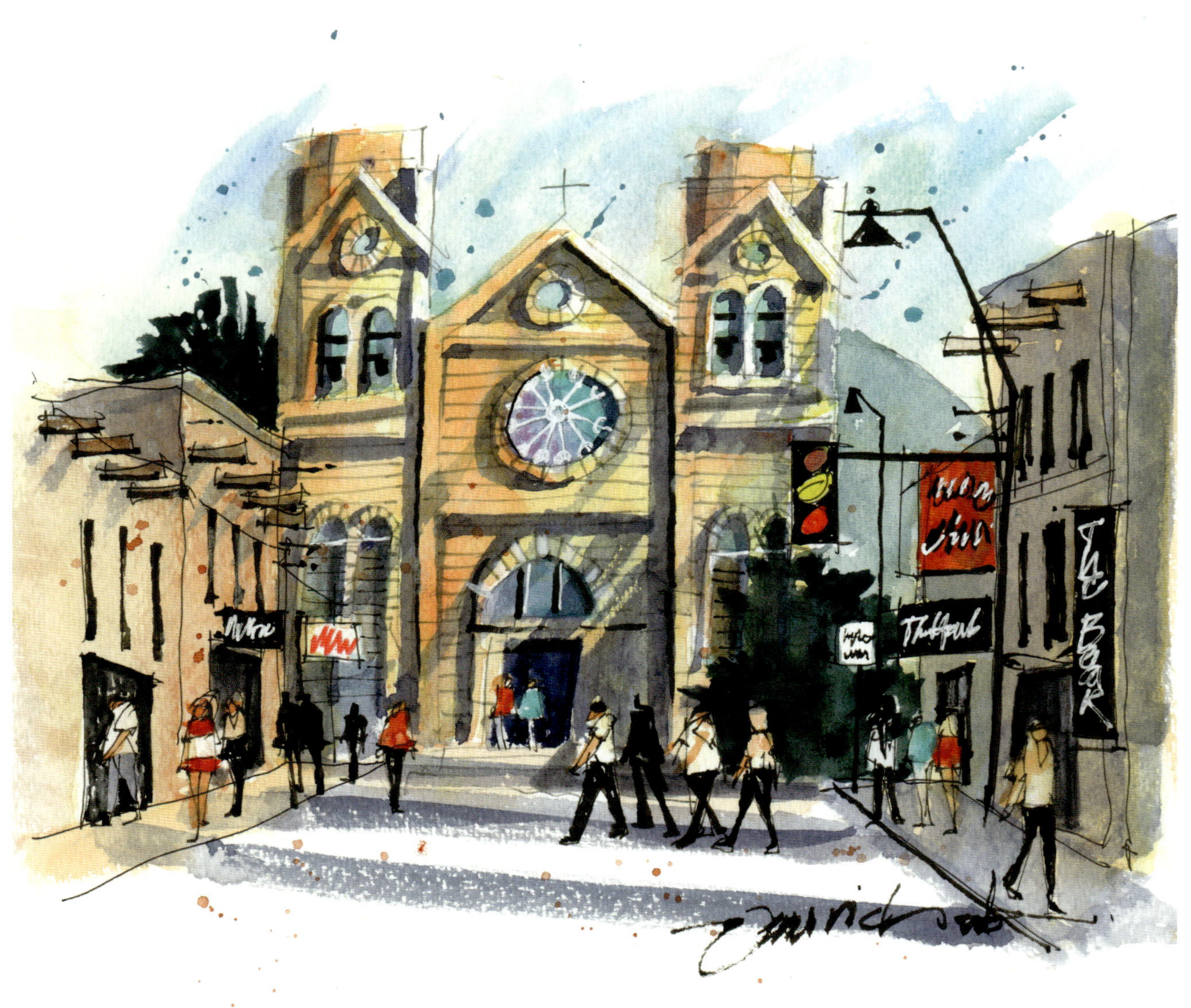

Top: St. Francis Cathedral,
Santa Fe.

Opposite: Bayfield,
Wisconsin.

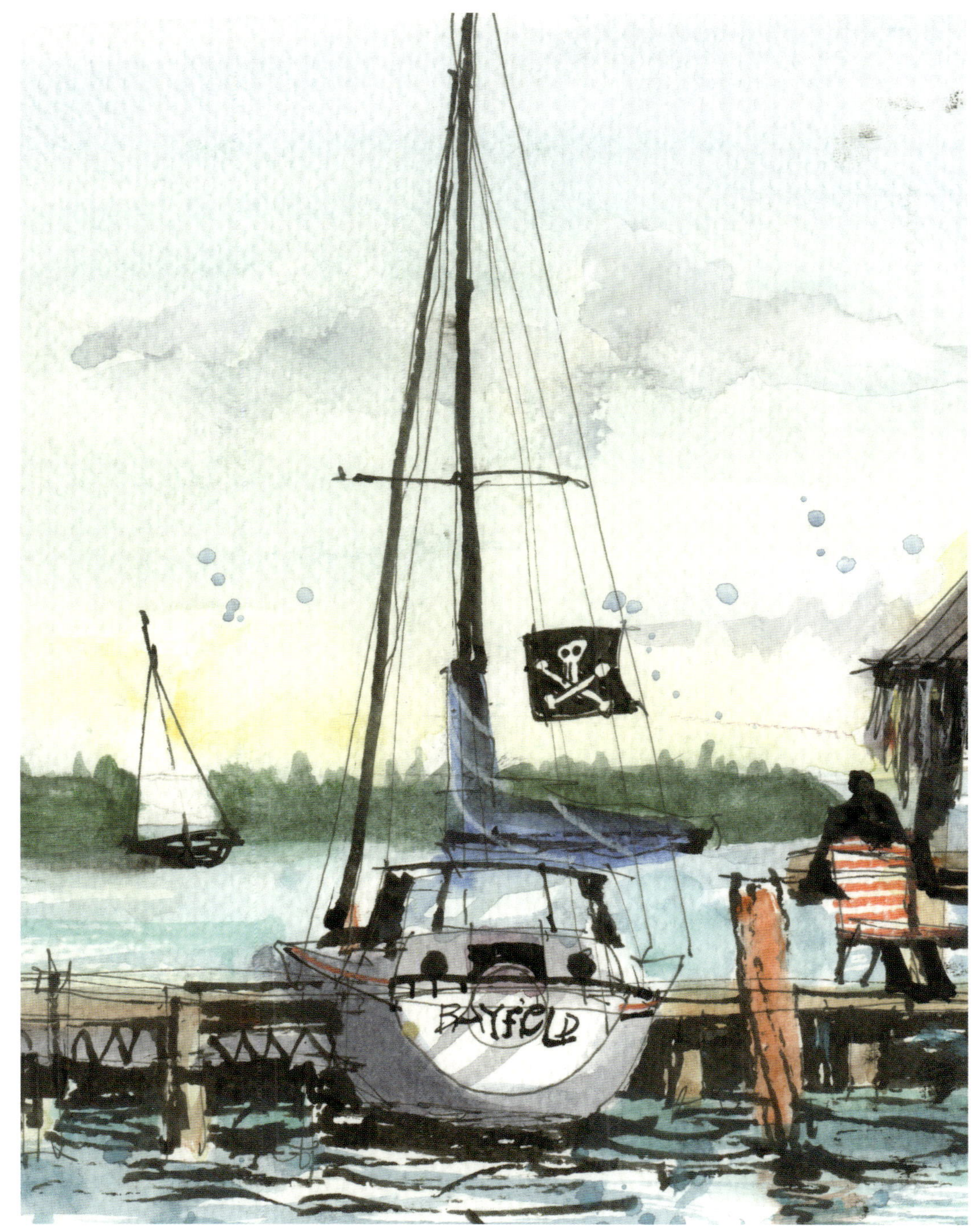

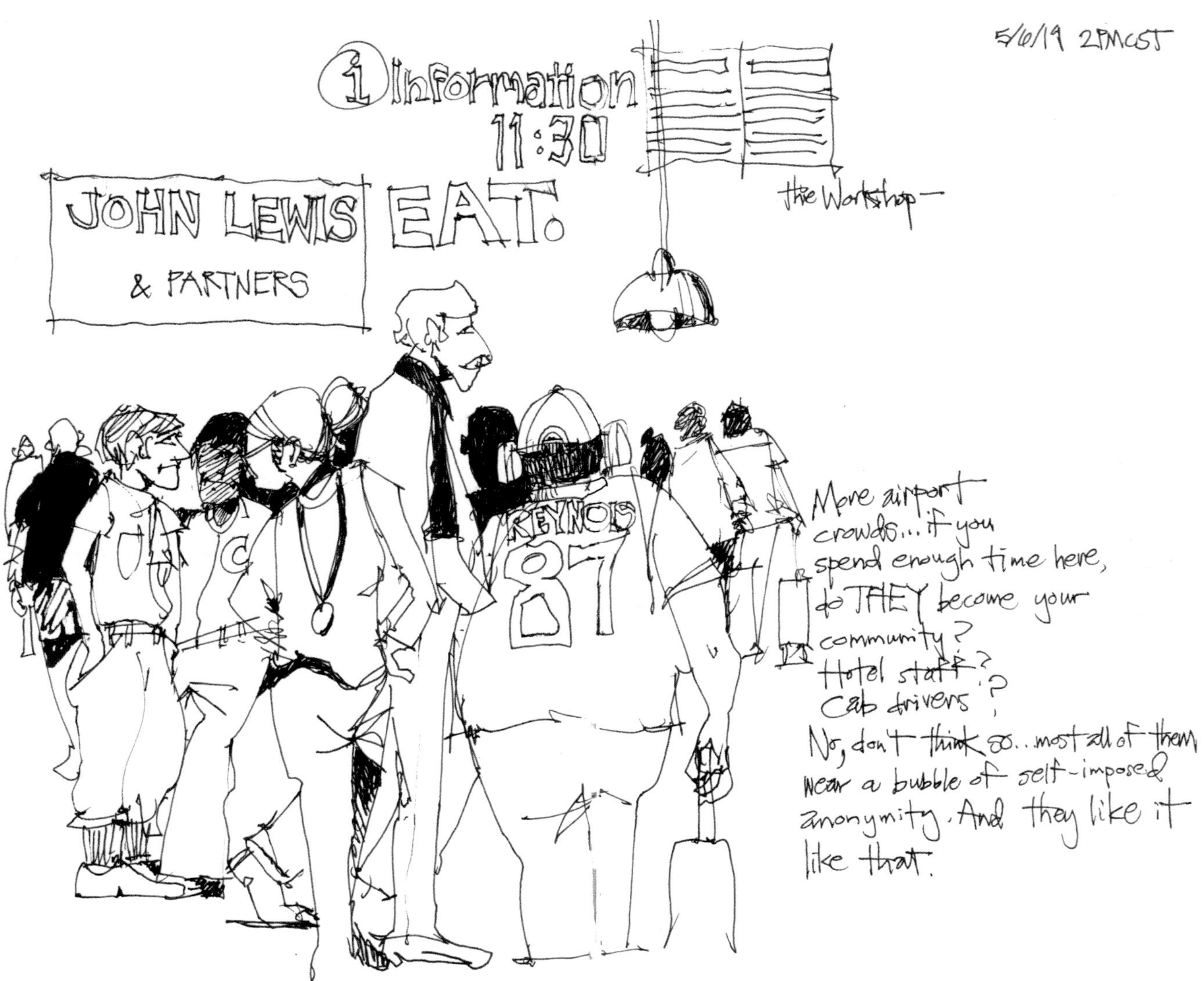
5/6/19 2PM CST
i Information
11:30
JOHN LEWIS
& PARTNERS
EAT.
the Workshop
REYNOLDS
87
More airport crowds... if you spend enough time here, do THEY become your community?
Hotel staff?
Cab drivers?
No, don't think so... most all of them wear a bubble of self-imposed anonymity. And they like it like that.

INTRODUCTION

I'VE CLAIMED SQUATTER'S RIGHTS on a favorite little piece of French Quarter sidewalk at the corner of Royal and St. Peter. It's prime real estate for street musicians, but I'll be gone before they wake up. For now, it's mine. My back's against the brick wall of the historic LeBranche House, drawing in the sketchbook on my lap. It's one of those mornings when my brain is engaged, eyes and hand are in sync, and the lines and tones seem to draw themselves. I'm liking this one, and I'm surprised at how quickly it's coming together.

I picked this spot because it has a great view of Royal Street in the very early morning—the Royal Street tourists never see. Locals of every description mill in and out of the neighborhood grocery store in the historic building across the street. The studio apartment above, with its ornamental iron railing dripping with carnival beads, lush collection of potted plants and a funky, life-sized sculpture of a pink flamingo looking down on happenings below can't help but make you grin. Delivery guys are pushing hand trucks up the street, and local shop owners are hosing down their sidewalks. Residents who live above the ground-floor shops and galleries are walking their dogs. See, this is really a neighborhood. That's what I hope to capture in this sketch.

I feel someone behind me. "Whoa! Did you just do that?"

"Uh, yeah."

"I mean, you drew that while you're sitting here?"

"Yeah."

"Man, how long did it take you to do that?"

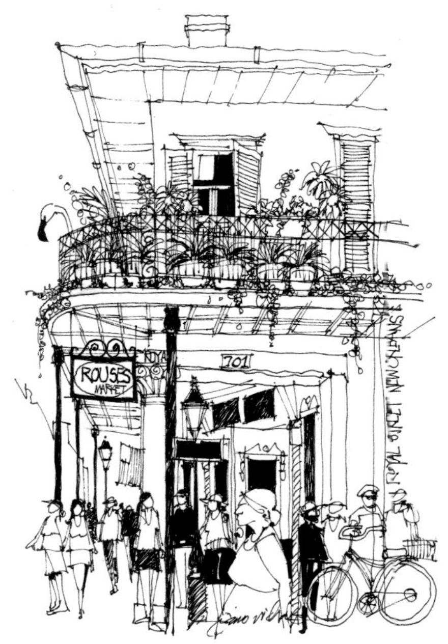

Opposite: Heathrow Airport, London.

Top: Royal Street, New Orleans.

"Fifty years."

"What? Wait, oh yeah, I get it. No, really, how long? You know, it's weird. I've never paid that much attention to that building before. I mean, I've never seen it like I'm seeing it here. That's cool! Know what I mean? Hey, do you know where I could get a good breakfast?"

"Half a block this way on your right."

This was New Orleans, but it could have been Rome, Istanbul, Rio or a village in Vietnam. One more real place is in the sketchbook. One more person is looking at a place a little differently. That's my job.

It didn't start with the idea that becoming a vagabond artist was a shrewd career move. It started with a sketchbook and a cheap pen. Now, 20 years later, I'm unpacking from 13 days in Morocco, with dog-eared pages of drawings and stories, and wondering how my grown-up and respectable career somehow morphed into visiting 50-odd countries, drawing in sketchbooks, and how I became someone different in the process.

Over the previous two weeks, my adventurous cadre of sketchbook artists and I had experienced a Morocco that a tourist with a camera would never see. That's because drawing changes travel. It turns up the intensity and pulls you fully into the moment. We look more deeply and see more clearly. And because we're looking for scenes that, when drawn, collectively tell a story, the journey becomes more purposeful.

Conversely, travel changes drawing. It becomes much more than an attempt to make a recognizable facsimile of what you're seeing. Travel sketching becomes a doorway for discovery.

It helps us discover places. It forces us to get out of the hotel or bus, to pay attention and become more aware of the particulars of our surroundings. Your trip becomes less about an itinerary with boxes to be checked, and more about exploring, noticing and sketching your personal take on the busy streets, the funky signs, the lively plazas, fascinating buildings and the life between buildings where people move, converse in groups, perform, pass the time on benches, and mostly watch other people. Travel with a sketchbook helps you see beyond the tourist's Instagram photo op to eke out the essence of the place, to get

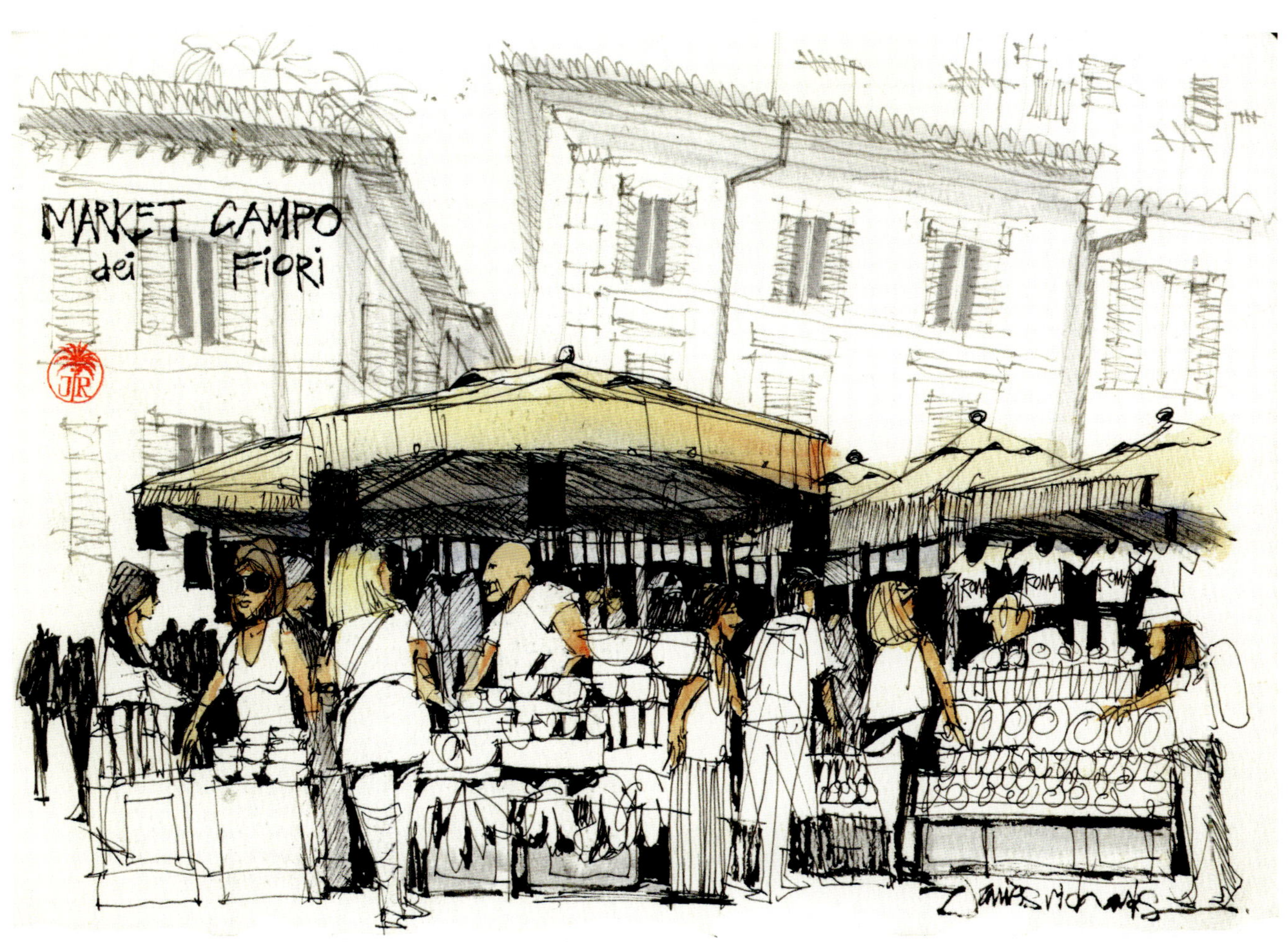

Morning market, Rome.

under its skin and know it on more intimate terms. The world becomes your studio, your sketchbook is your passport.

Travel sketching helps us discover connections. Where a stranger with a camera on a local street away from home may raise suspicion or resentment, a sketchbook raises curiosity. It opens doors to conversations with locals and other travelers. They may share insights into the place. They may share personal stories. They may comp your mojito or buy your cabrito taco from the street cart. These personal encounters expand the experience of travel beyond what any tour guide can tell you. That's because drawings are a universal language that can transcend normal barriers of distance, language and ideology. It's drawing with a mission. Many times, I've been told by locals, "You've made me see my own place with fresh eyes!" That's really cool. And it's a very good reason to draw.

Now, twenty years later, I'm unpacking from 13 days in Morocco, with dog-eared pages of drawings and stories, and wondering how my grown-up and respectable career somehow morphed into visiting 50-odd countries, drawing in sketchbooks, and how I became someone different in the process.

Finally, travel sketching helps us discover something of ourselves. If you let it, sketching changes you. You may tap into a latent talent. You may reconnect with that kid inside you that drew just because you felt great when you did it. Certainly, you see places differently. You notice more, and the more you sketch, the more you see. You become more aware, and awareness is everything. You start to pay attention to the aged stone in the architecture, the details in ornamental ironwork, patterns in the tile paving, dappled sunlight through the trees. You quickly sketch the accordion player serenading anyone who will allow him to. You doodle the noisy red tuk-tuk at the stop light. You learn to see the remarkable in the everyday. It's all around us, all the time, but you have to be tuned into it. Sketching helps you do that.

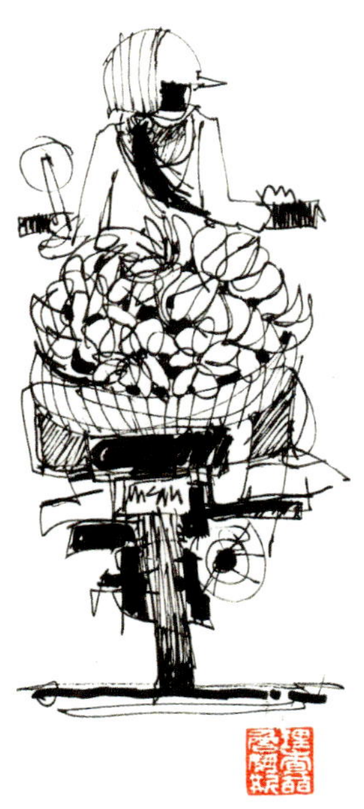

Hanoi, Vietnam.

As your informal drawings accumulate, your sketchbook becomes a priceless, self-illustrated retelling of your travels. Some drawings may be small, quickly scrawled thumbnail sketches made with a ballpoint pen, or informal freehand maps of the day's itinerary. Others may have been done with more detail, maybe even with watercolor washes. There may be notes, and a streetcar ticket or beer label glued onto the page. Taken together, they tell a personal story of what you saw and how you saw it, captured to best of your ability at the time. And because they've been drawn in your own hand, they're uniquely yours in a way that a camera's snapshot can never be.

So, Morocco is in the books. It's currently the latest stop in my version of what Bob Dylan calls his "Never Ending Tour"—fifty countries so far, more to come. The seven chosen for this volume represent some variety of experiences, some geographic diversity, and frankly, are the ones I thought would make a good book. Now, it's time to clean the fountain pens, replace the watercolor tubes that are squeezed dry, look over the maps with my wife Patti (henceforth known here as "The Grownup") and start thinking about the next one.

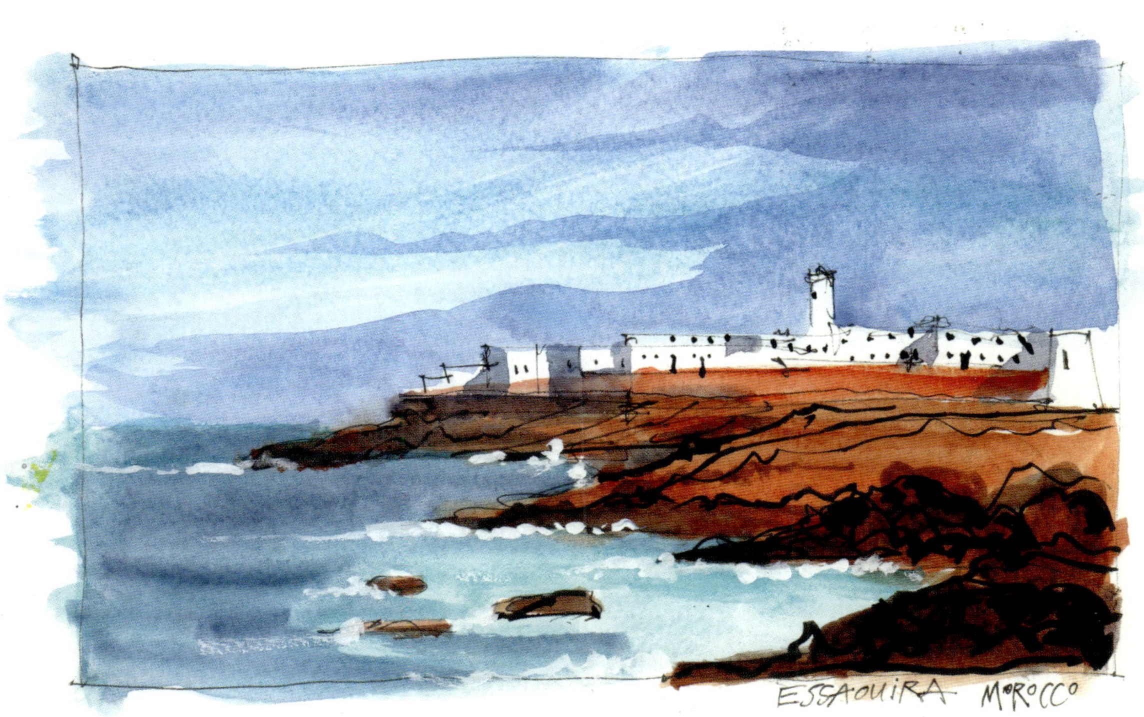

Essaouria, Morocco.

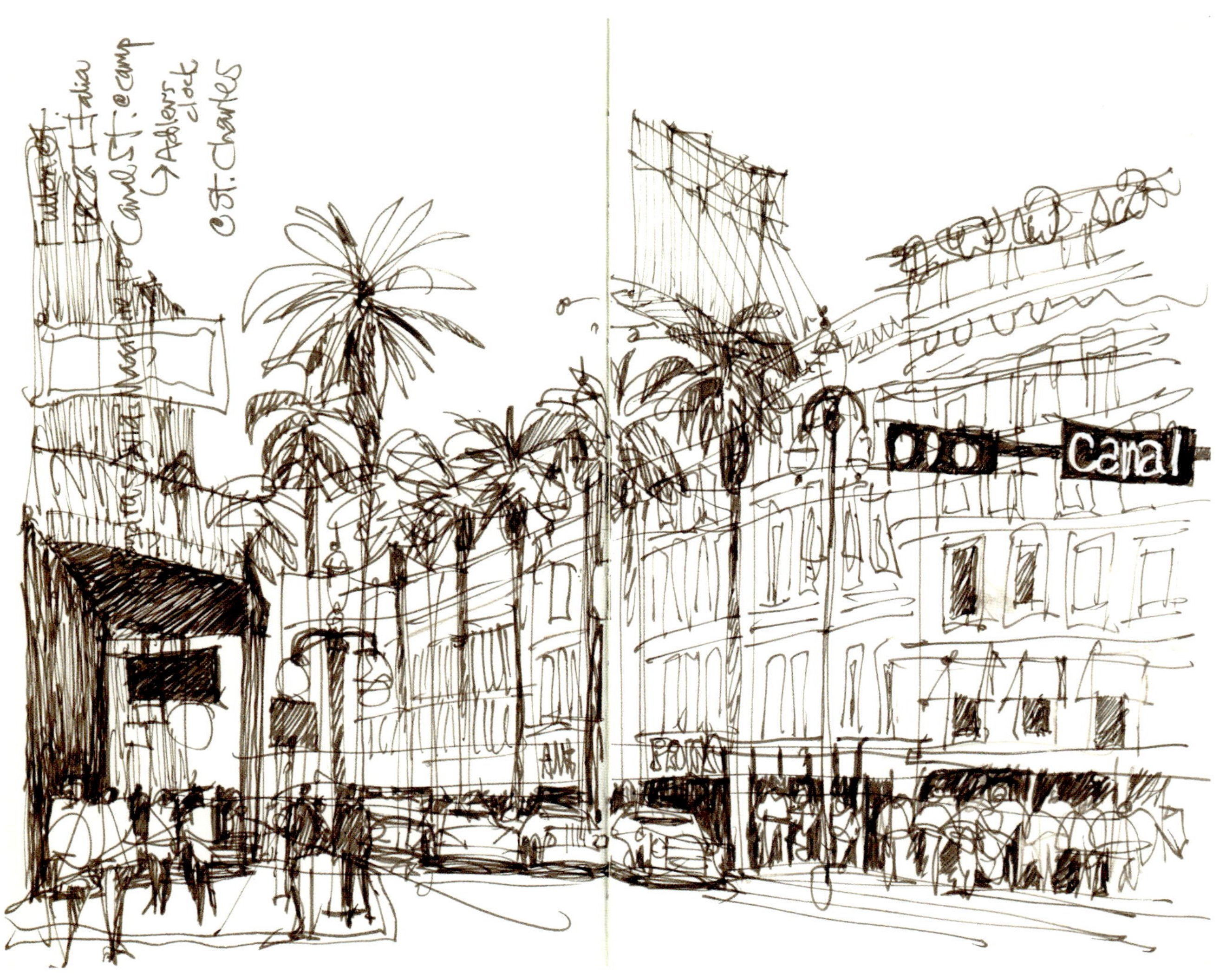

Canal Street, New Orleans.

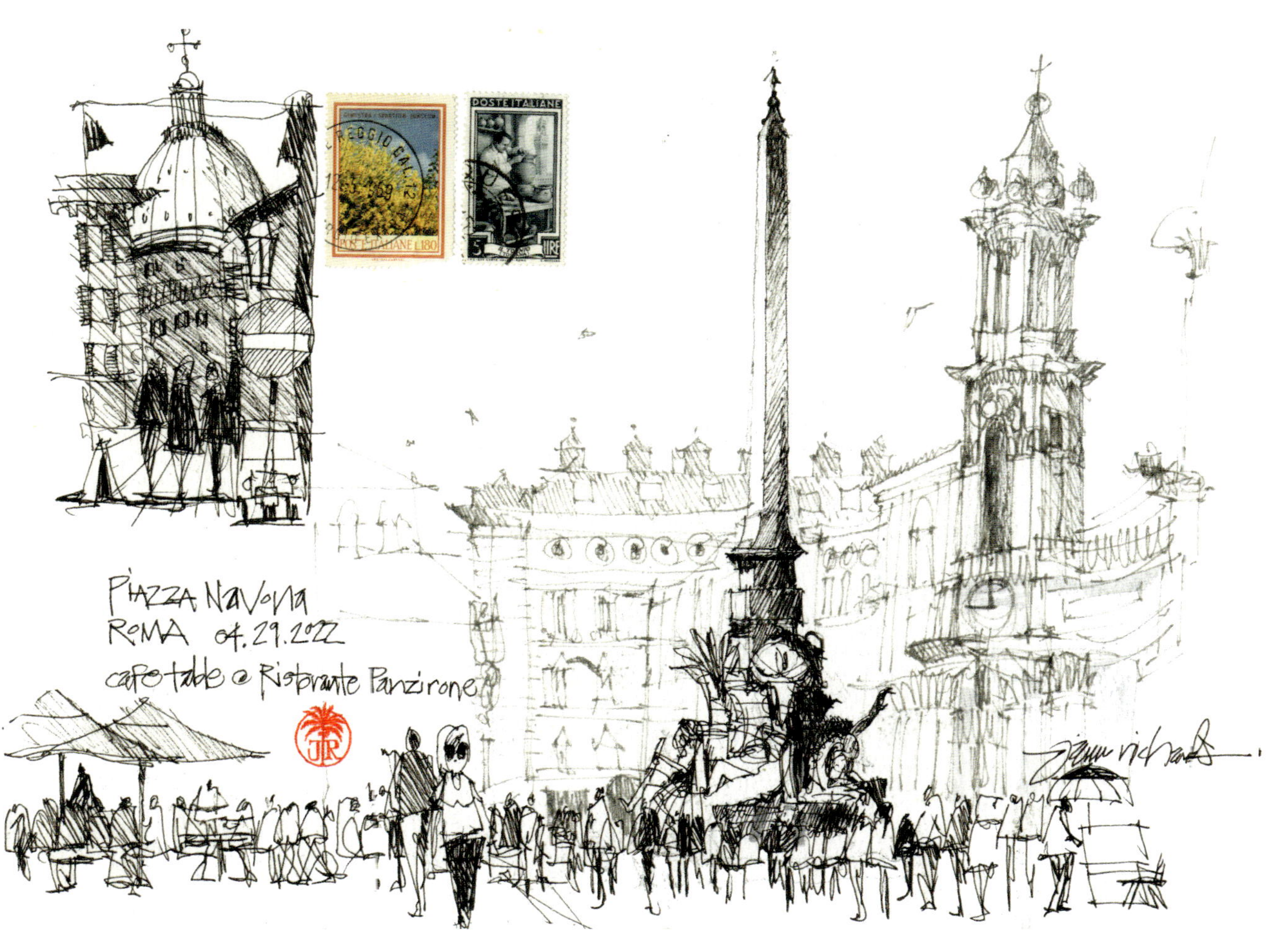

Piazza Navona, Rome, drawn on location during breakfast at a sidewalk table.

Road-Worthy Tools

These are my must-haves for a trip:

- An Etchr Perfect Sketchbook, size B5 (roughly 7 × 10 inches), portrait format.
- Fine line pen with waterproof ink
- A fude nib fountain pen with waterproof ink
- A .07 mechanical pencil for line sketching
- Gray Polychromos colored pencil for heavier line sketching
- White gel pen.
- Brush Pens in light, medium and dark gray
- Metal travel watercolor palette filled with my own color choices:
    - Cobalt Teal Blue, Ultramarine, Jadite Genuine, Deep Scarlet, Azo Yellow, Cobalt Blue, Deep Sap Green, Mayan Orange, Hansa Yellow Deep, Burnt Umber, Burnt Sienna Light, Opera Rose, Naples Yellow, Prussian Blue, Alizarin Crimson.
- Travel brushes, nos. 3, 6, 12 round.
- Small hand-held pencil sharpener.
- A few random colored pencils.
- Glue stick for pasting in ticket stubs, stamps and other "found objects"
- A few folded paper towels
- Small leakproof plastic container for water
- Lightweight folding stool
- Ecuadorian Panama Fedora
- cool sunglasses
- corkscrew

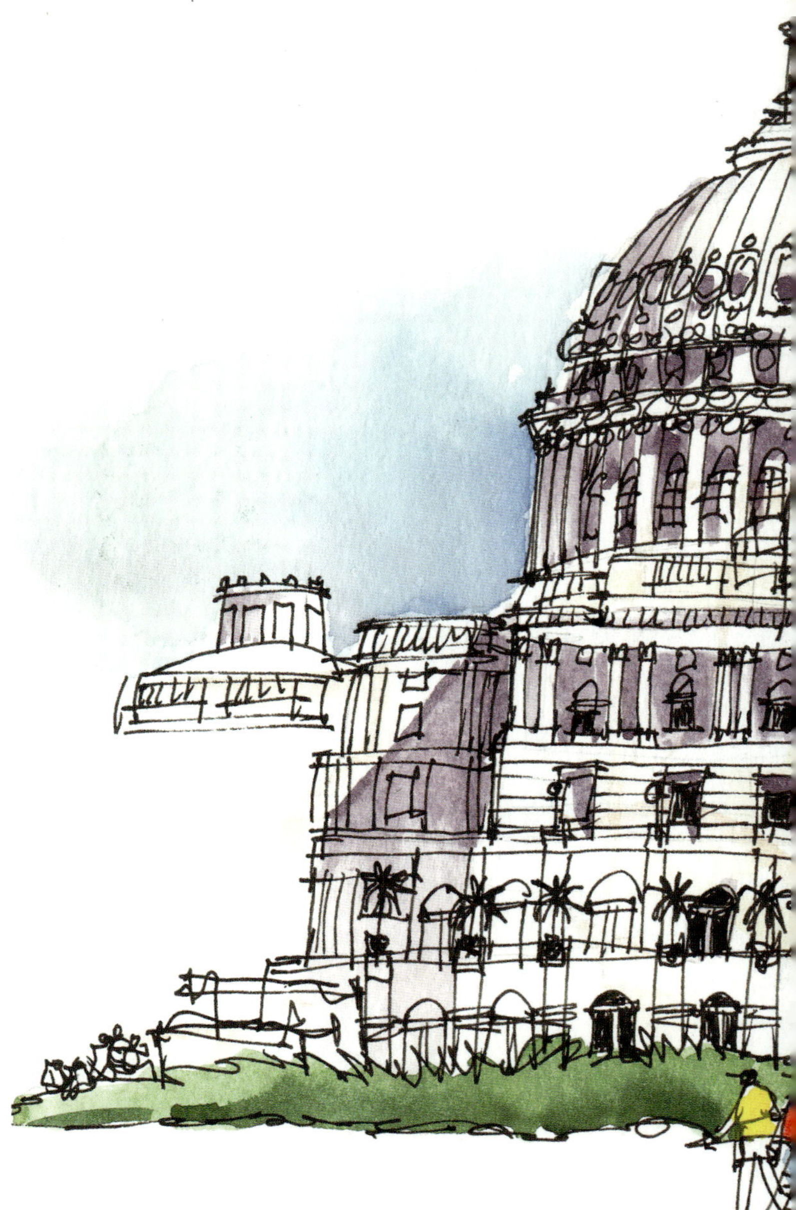

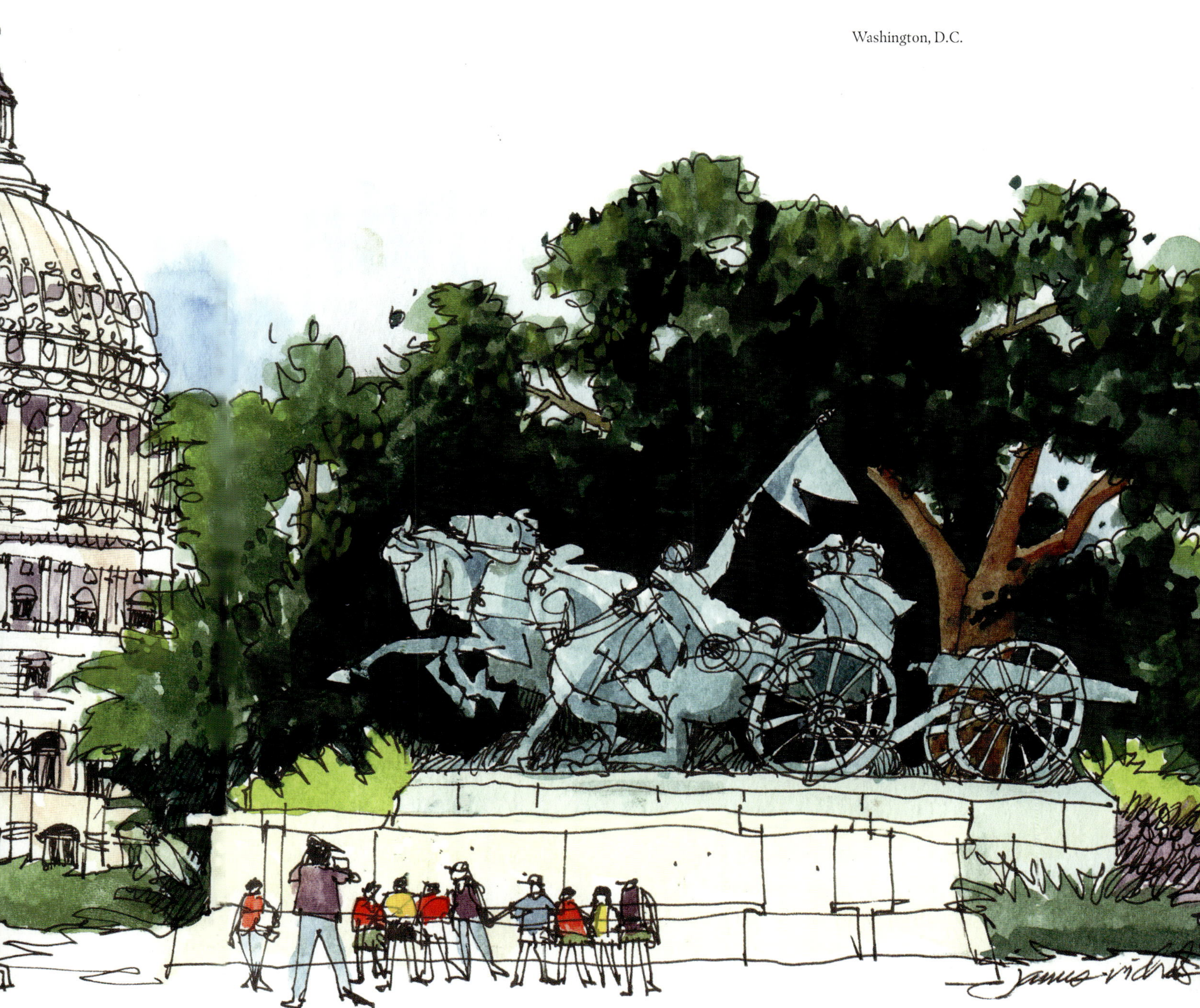

The Sketcher's Code

Don't aspire to be great. Aspire to be prolific. If you're prolific, becoming great takes care of itself.

That's right. Want to get good? There's a secret. Do it all the time. Period. That's it.

Carry a sketchbook and pen with you. Commit to drawing in it every day.

Draw in ink. No erasing.

Draw anything. Draw a shelf of books, the view out the window, a tree in the park, your own hand. Tell yourself, "This is just for practice" to nip perfectionism in the bud.

Repeat.

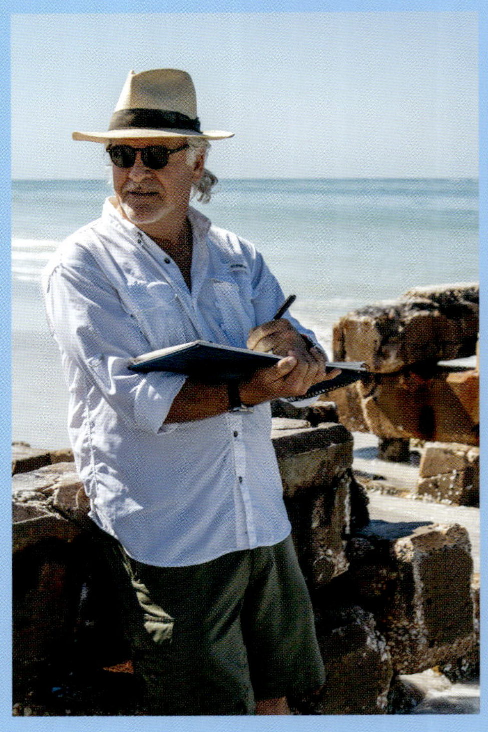

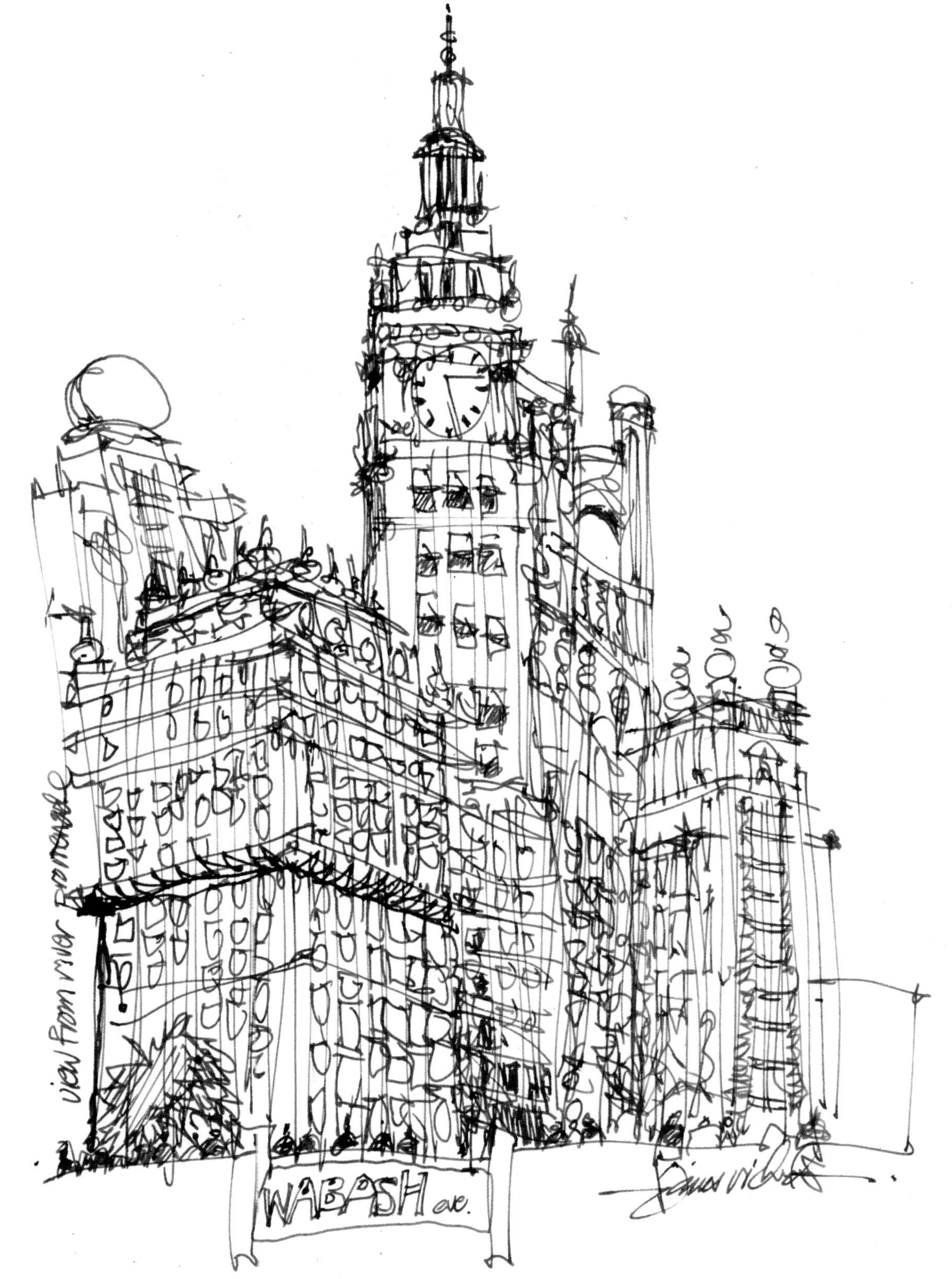
view from river promenade
WABASH ave.

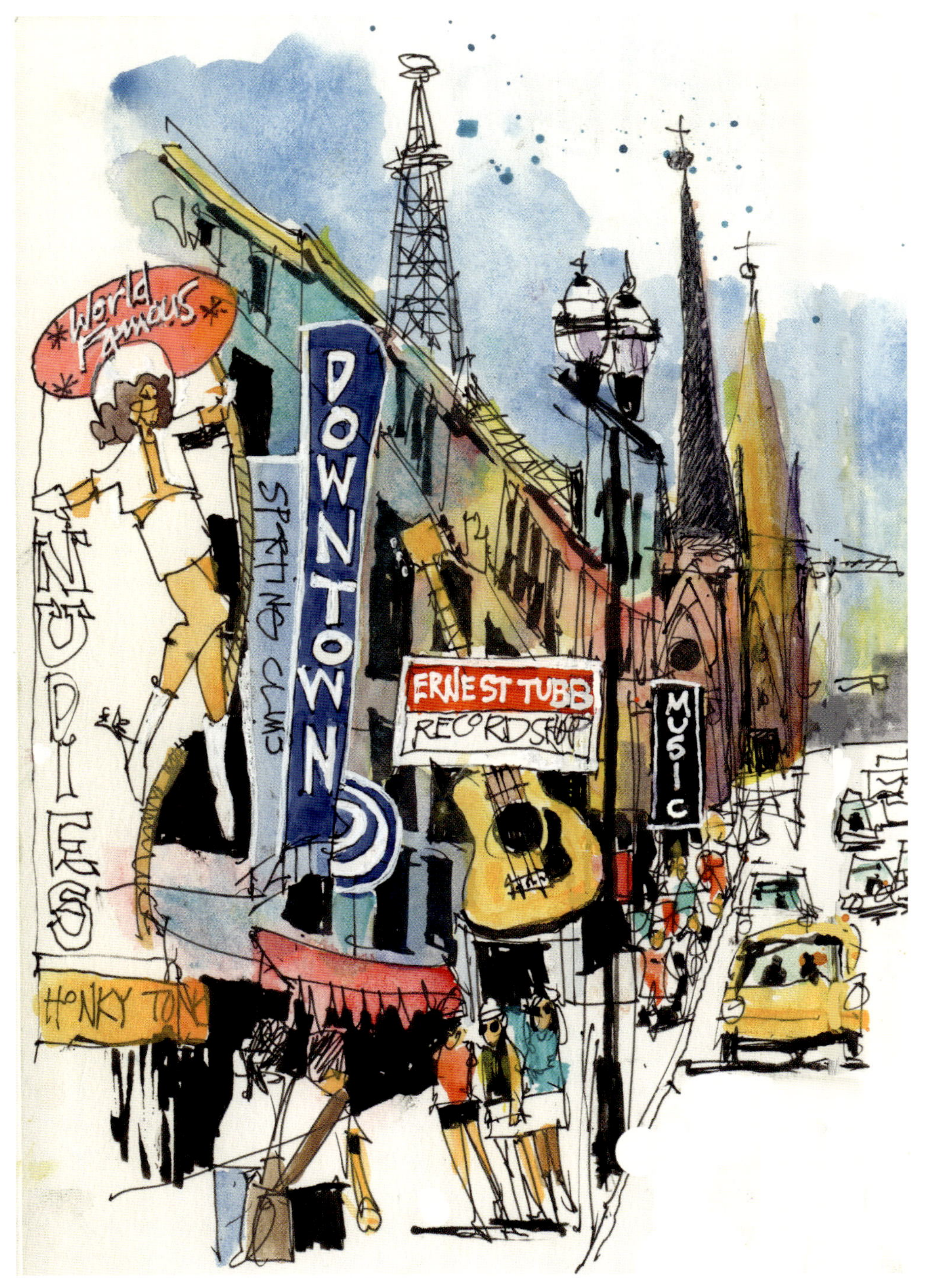
World Famous
NUDIES
HONKY TONK
SPORTING CLUBS
DOWNTOWN
ERNEST TUBB
RECORD SHOP
MUSIC

CHAPTER 1

Early Influences

I WATCHED AN INTERVIEW where John Lennon described sitting in dark theaters as a teenager watching rock and roll movies. At one point he made an insightful decision that changed everything. "You know, you'd go to see the movies where there was Elvis or somebody in it, and they'd all scream when he came on the screen. So I thought, that's a good job!" I experienced a similar revelation the first time I saw a book of Paul Hogarth's deceivingly simple but very evocative drawings made on assignment in Majorca. Something clicked. Over time, seeking out and finding the work and stories of artist travelers showed me that, with practice and luck, actually getting paid to travel, explore new places and draw them might be remotely possible.

Three traveling artists a generation older than me—Paul Hogarth, Ronald Searle and Earl Thollander-- had an outsized influence on my visions. All three had line drawing at the heart of their style. That attracted me first. The work was less like fine art than playfully drawn field sketches or cartoons, and all with a journalistic, storytelling bent. Probably most attractive to me was that their art seemed accessible—it looked like something that, with practice, I could do.

I found Hogarth first. Where most drawing books I could find as a student came off a bit stilted, academic and self-important, Hogarth's books jumped off the shelves. The drawings were informal and fresh. Perspective informed but didn't dictate his approach. This resulted in more dynamic and interesting building and streetscape drawings than were possible with a properly serious architectural approach. Even

Opposite: My on-location sketch of Broadway Street in Nashville shows the strong influence of Paul Hogarth and Ronald Searle with its informal style, strong shapes, loose, lively lines and a bit of humor to depict the stuff of everyday life.

serious subjects seemed to have a sense of fun and a story to tell. And they were marvelous to look at.

For much of the second half of his career, Hogarth was tied to great writers that were his contemporaries, especially Graham Greene and Lawrence Durrell. Their novels were deeply rooted in sense of place, and the settings of their stories were central characters. Hogarth collaborated with the novelists to track down these key settings—towns, buildings, plazas, waterfronts. His drawings of these exotic places were my first glimpse of what a life of travel and drawing could look like. And I liked it very much.

Over time, seeking out and finding the work and stories of artist travelers showed me that, with practice and luck, actually getting paid to travel, explore new places and draw them might be remotely possible.

I first noticed Searle's unmistakable loose, linear drawing style in animated movie credits I saw as a kid in the 1960s—things like Those Magnificent Men in their Flying Machines. But it wasn't until stumbling onto a very worn copy of his Paris Sketchbook and his illustrated reportage for travel magazines that I saw him as another guiding spirit... someone whose energetic lines gave an instantly recognized, quirky personality to the places and the equally quirky characters that lived there. Through his style, he made far-flung, exotic places all part of his own lively and slightly subversive world, and invited us in if we dared.

Thollander was more of a homespun stylist best known for his self-illustrated series of Back Roads travelogues. Again, I found the dynamic line drawings irresistible. And knowing that he drew the vast majority of them on exploratory drives in his pickup truck only added to the appeal for me. In the pre-internet age, I haunted used bookstores searching for anything he'd drawn and written, using whatever cash I had left from the week to snap it up on the spot.

Here I had great fun practicing bodies, postures and facial features by filling a sketchbook page with "Ronald Searle people."

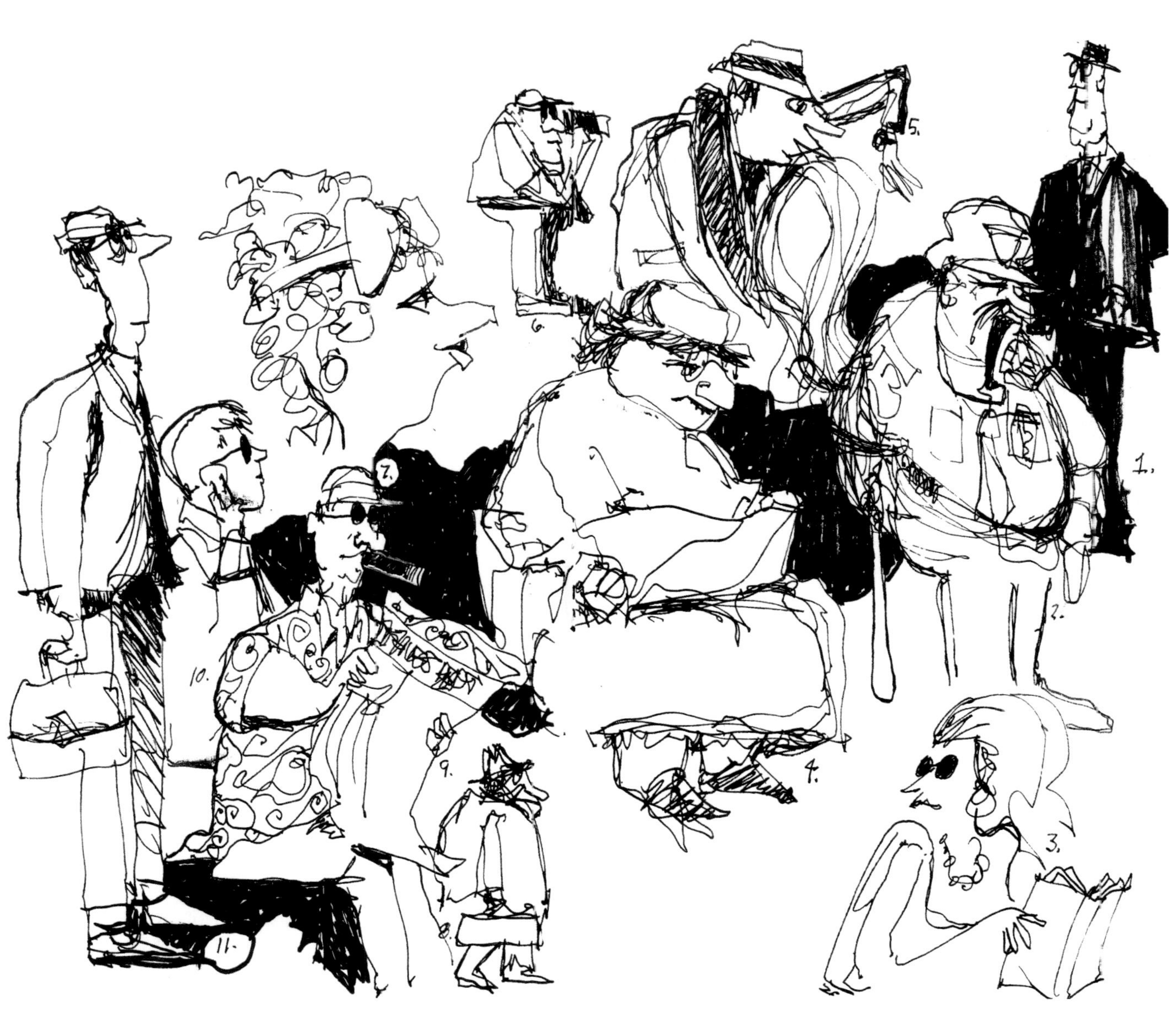

Below: Thollander also had a loose, line-driven style and many of his subjects had a bit of a dynamic lean to them, as my trees do here.

Right: My on-location sketch of Pietrasanta, Italy aims more for creating a dynamic, interesting and eye-engaging scene than on the "correctness" of its perspective.

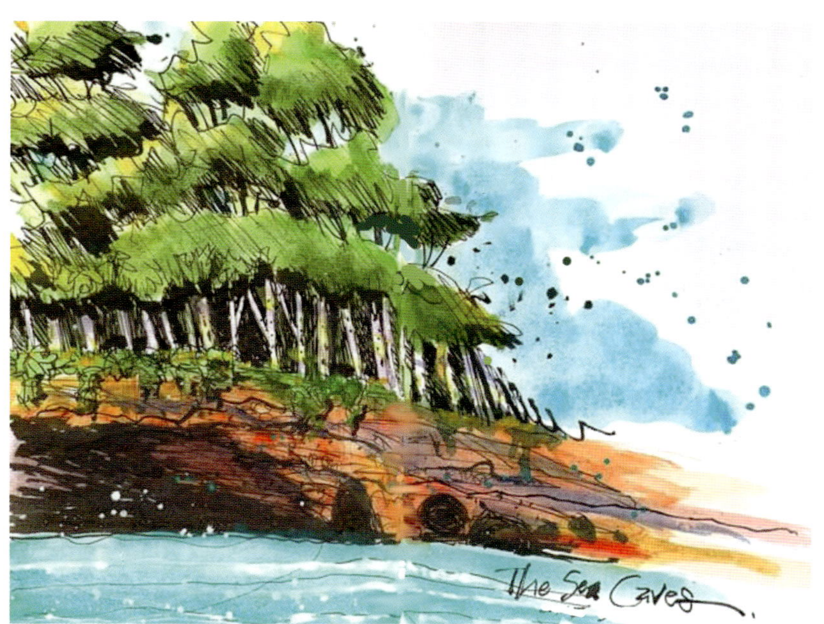

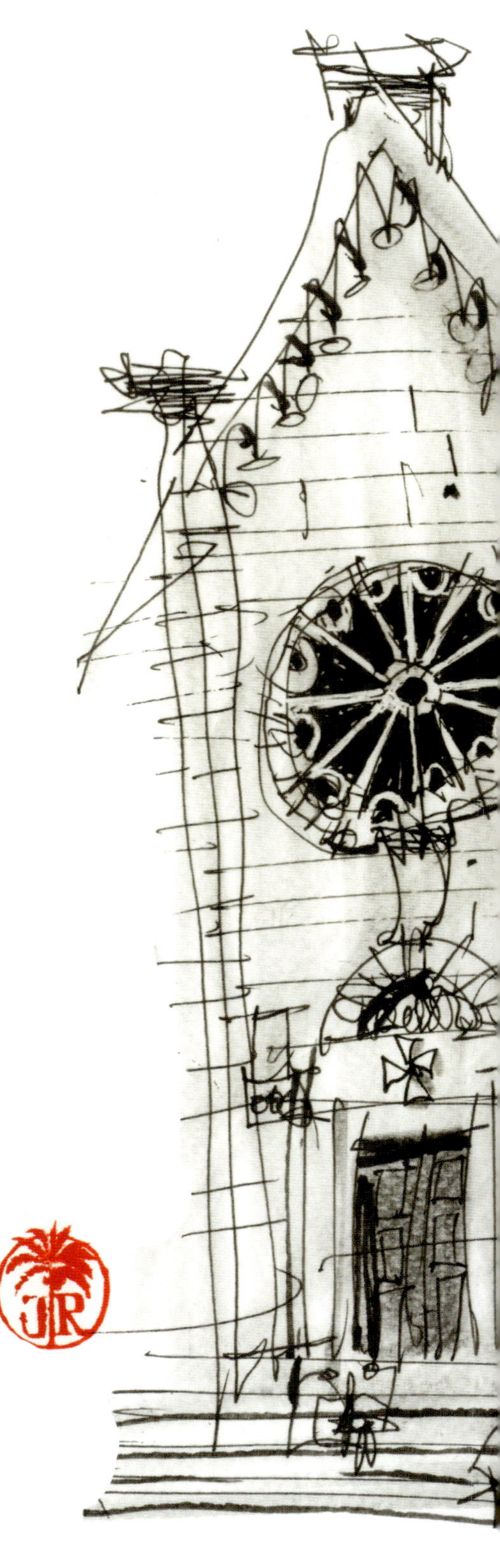

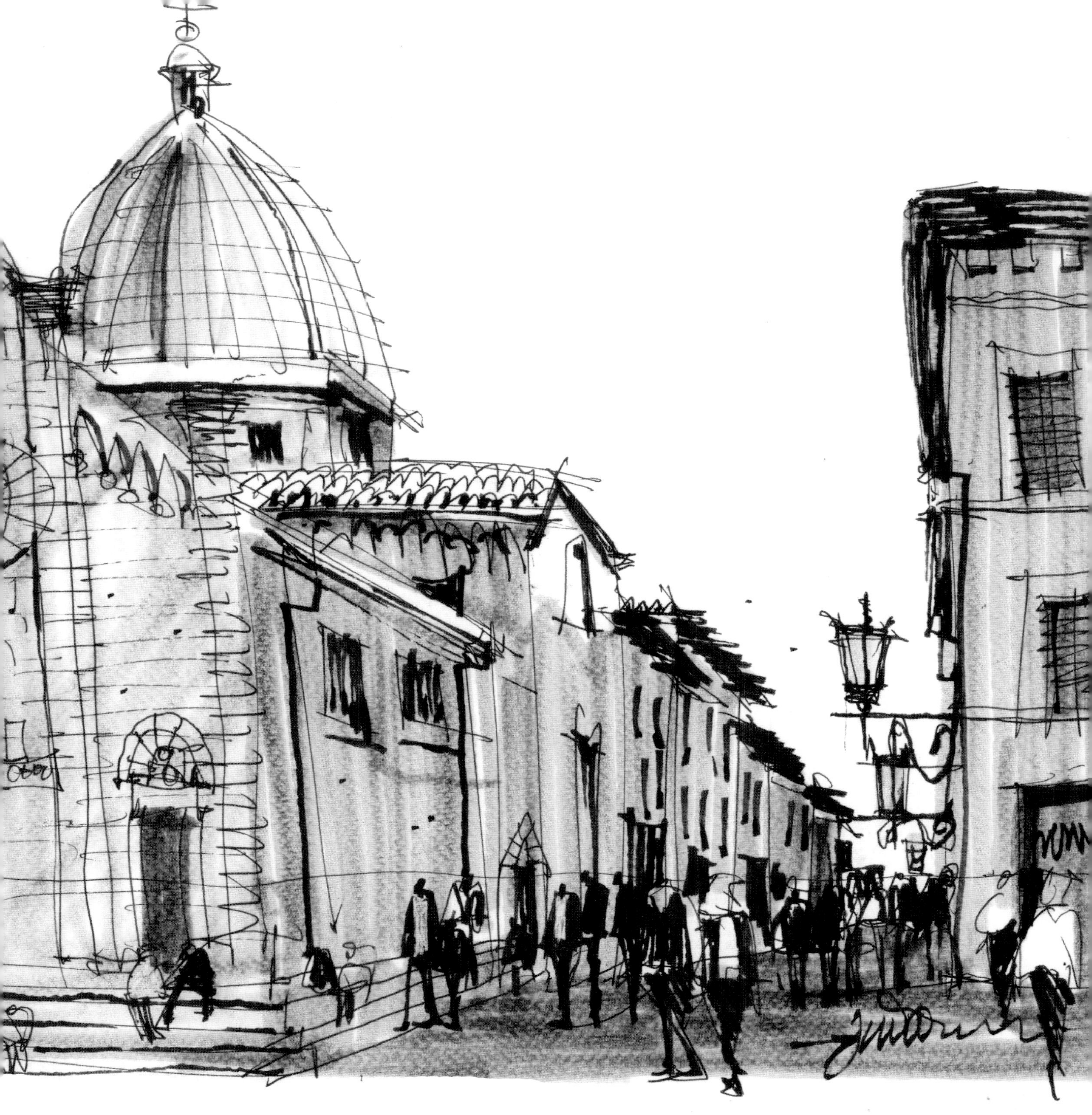

The loose, line-driven styles of these three and the life of travel they drew hit me at a gut level—I'd discovered my native language. But I was also struck by the fact that all three were pretty good writers—their words and drawings complemented each other in ways that pulled me in and made for rich storytelling. They were more than illustrators. They were authors who drew. "Yeah," I thought, "THAT'S a good job!"

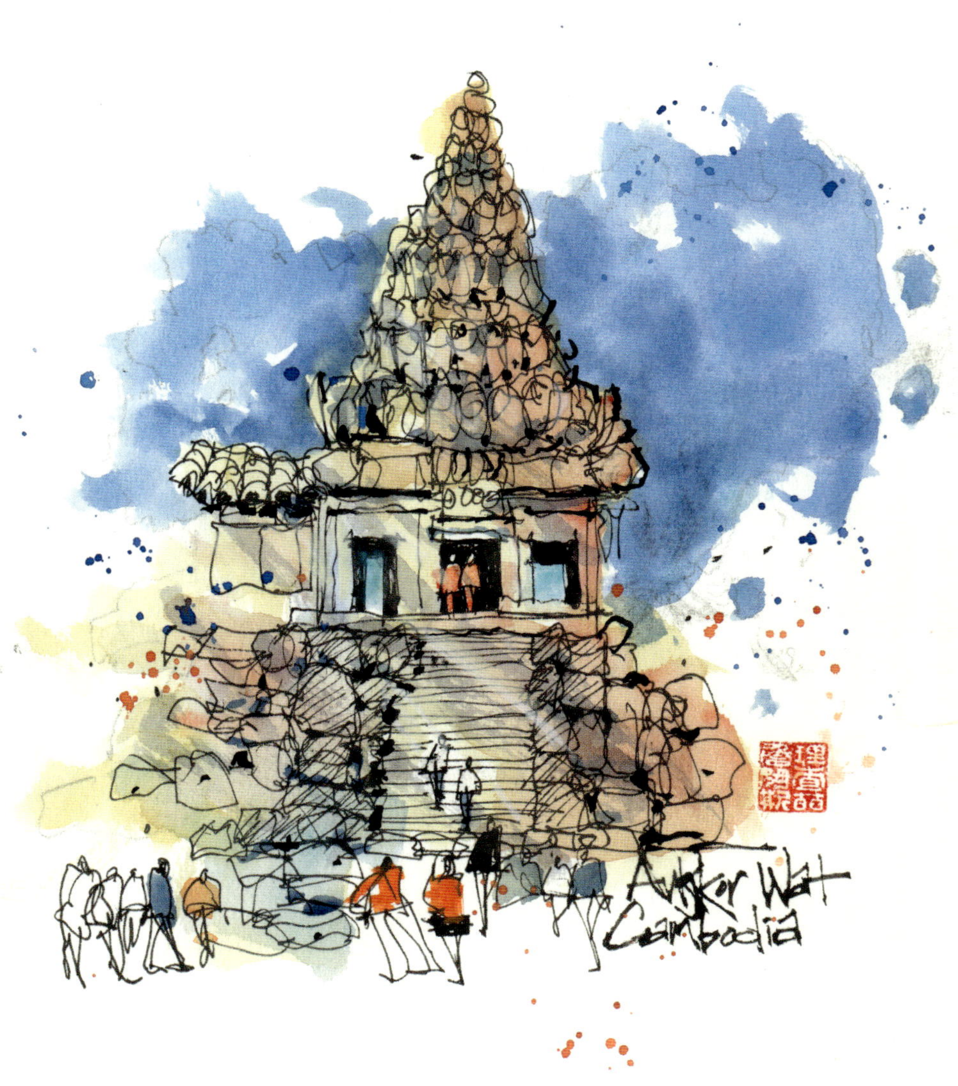

Right: Angkor Wat, Cambodia.

Opposite: Travel is an incomparable teacher, and sketching brings to it heightened awareness, a sense of purpose and a real creative rush. Civita di Bagnoregio, Italy.

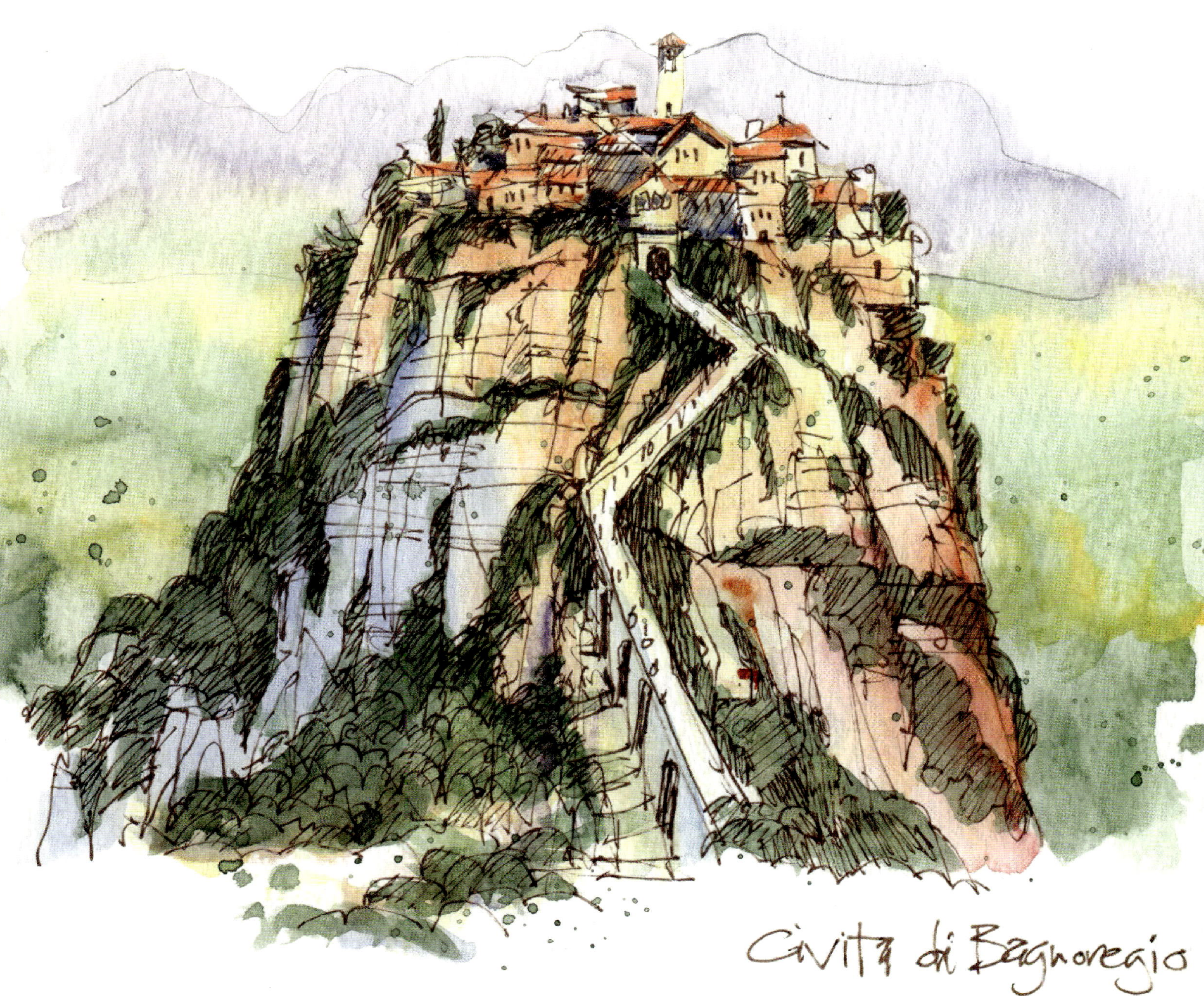
Civita di Bagnoregio

Seeking out these particular mentors I'd never meet and finding the work of many, many others was a decades-long compulsion for me. Travel, on the other hand, came to me through divine providence or dumb luck--probably both. After a few semesters in journalism school, I found myself in LSU's dynamic landscape architecture department, where traveling widely and documenting what we observed were non-negotiable parts of the curriculum. Get a camera and sketchbook, get on the bus or go home.

These trips did exactly what they were designed to do—they exploded my provincial worldview. There was an amazing world out there, there were endless mind-expanding lessons to be learned, and fascinating cultures to experience—all one had to do was find some time, scrape together some funds in any way you could, and have an open mind. A sketchbook was as basic a provision as shoes. The travel addiction that took hold on those trips snowballed into decades of travel around the world, mostly with my longtime professor Max Conrad and a band of road-worthy friends from school days.

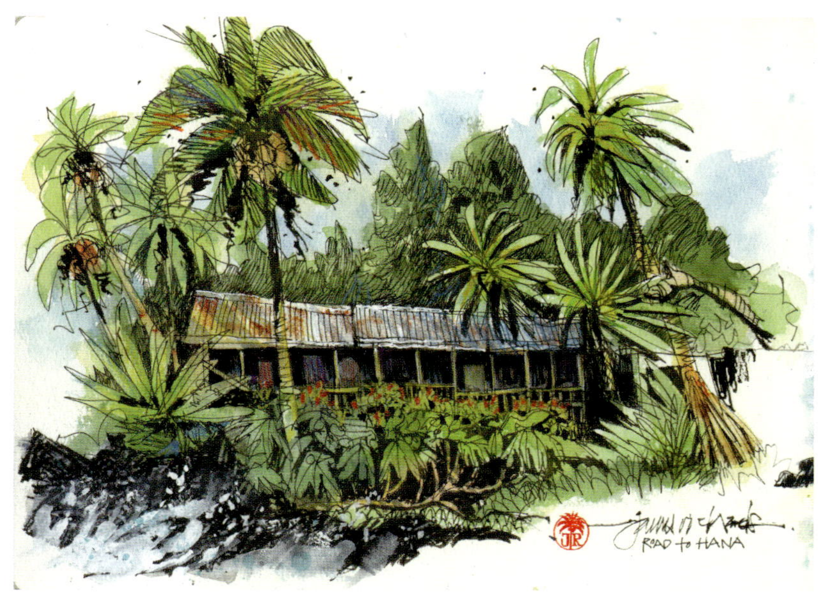

On the road to Hana, Maui, Hawaii.

Long story less long, the experiences, stories and scores of filled sketchbooks from these trips vastly enriched my career in urban design, where I found more seminal drawing mentors, especially Bill Johnson and Gordon Cullen. Years of drawing like a madman and the ability to write about it resulted in magazine articles, offers to write books, and invitations to give sketching workshops to universities, arts groups and travel companies across the globe. The following chapters are a glimpse into that world. The long list of destinations is still growing, and will as long as there are provocative new places to experience, we feel we're making a difference and enjoying the ride.

Museum of the Rockies, Bozeman, Montana.

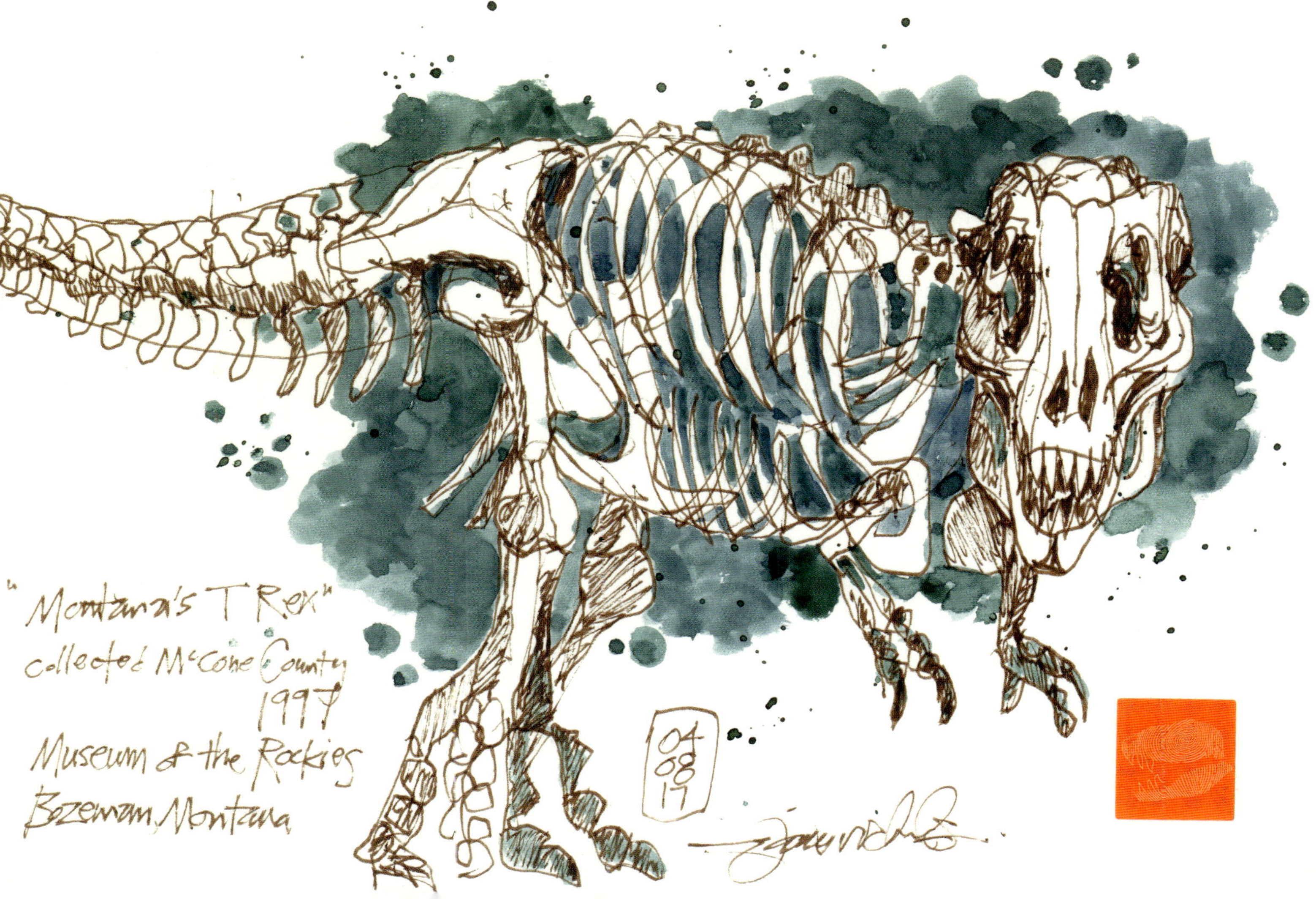

Who are Your Influences?

The Commitments is a 1991 film about a young music promoter in Dublin trying to assemble an R+B band. When musicians arrive and knock for auditions, the door opens and the promoter asks in a no-nonsense voice, "Who are your influences?" The musician's answer (or even partial answer) instantly determines if the door closes in their face or stays open. Brilliant.

So, who are your creative influences? A few of mine are mentioned in this chapter. But for reasons a therapist might be best equipped to explain, the list is too long to capture, all over the place and kind of weird.

My guru du jour is the legendary music producer Rick Rubin, who by his own admission plays no instruments and knows almost nothing about music. But Rick Rubin KNOWS things, and his dance card stays full with a waiting list. So many more: Graphic designer Alan Fletcher. Walt Disney and Jim Henson. Mozart's Flute Concerto No. 1 in G. The Beatles' Sgt. Pepper. Trappist monk Thomas Merton. Pee Wee Herman. Charles and Ray Eames. Ernest Hemingway. Chefs Francis Mallman and Dario Cecchini. Gonzo illustrator Ralph Steadman. MAD Magazine (during the subversive 1960s era). Poet and novelist Jim Harrison. David Byrne. Anthony Bourdain.

I hope your door is still open.

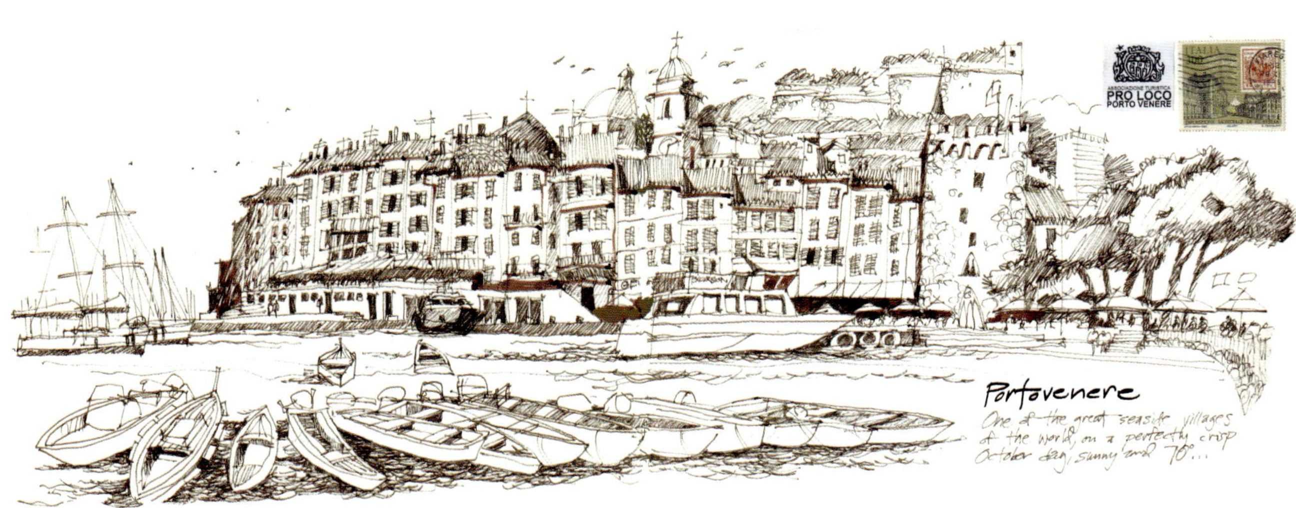

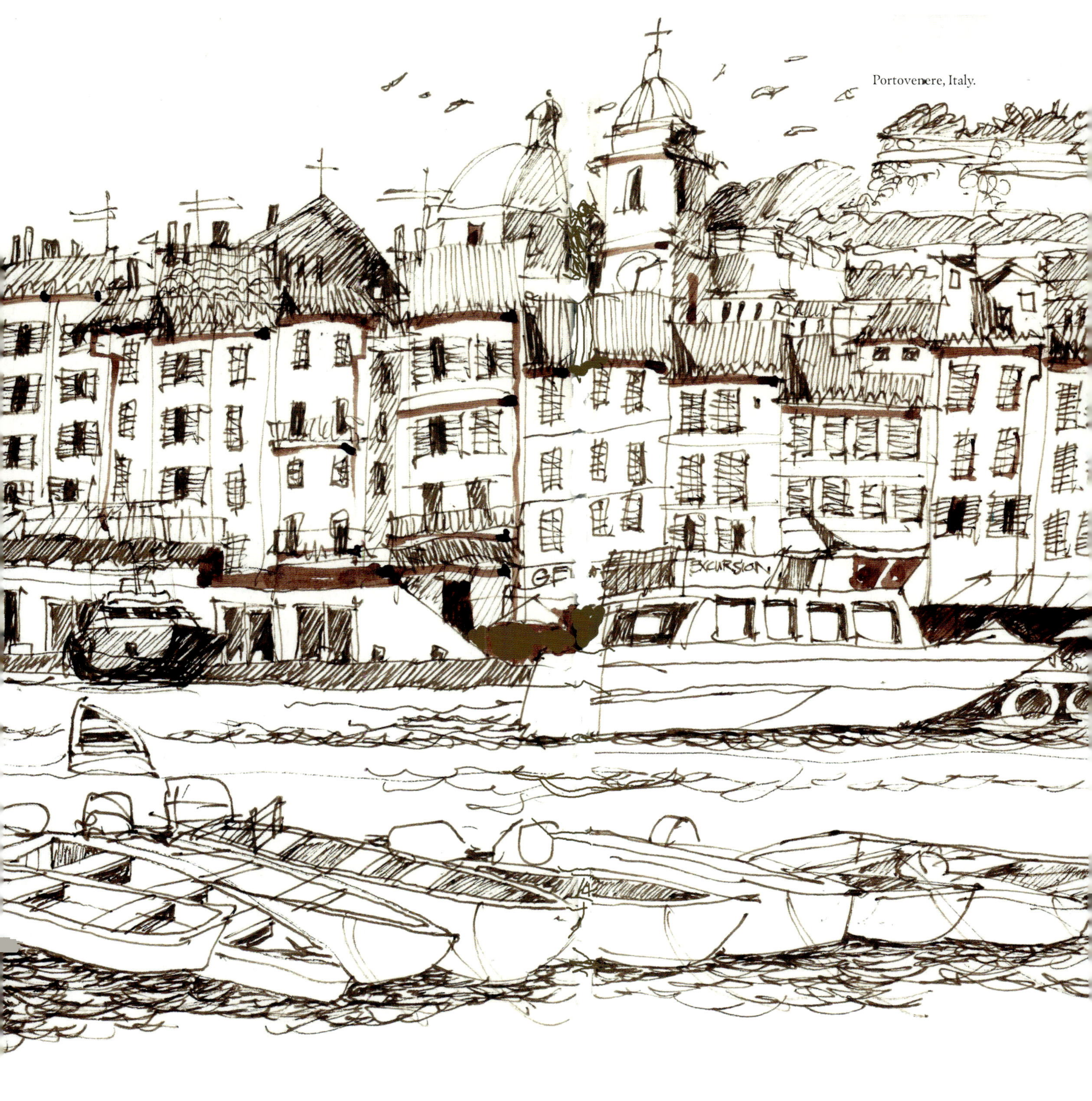

Portovenere, Italy.

The Sketcher's Code

It's not about art.
It's about authenticity.

Avoid the comfort of drawing from photographs. A sketch made in a real-life 3D location by your 3D self will capture how you're personally experiencing a place differently and better than what you can copy from a 2D photo.

There's an authenticity—a sense of being there in the moment and feeling that energy—that people pick up on, and that's hard to achieve any other way. Be genuine about the place, about yourself. If you're doing what you love, and if you're honest about it, people will connect with it.

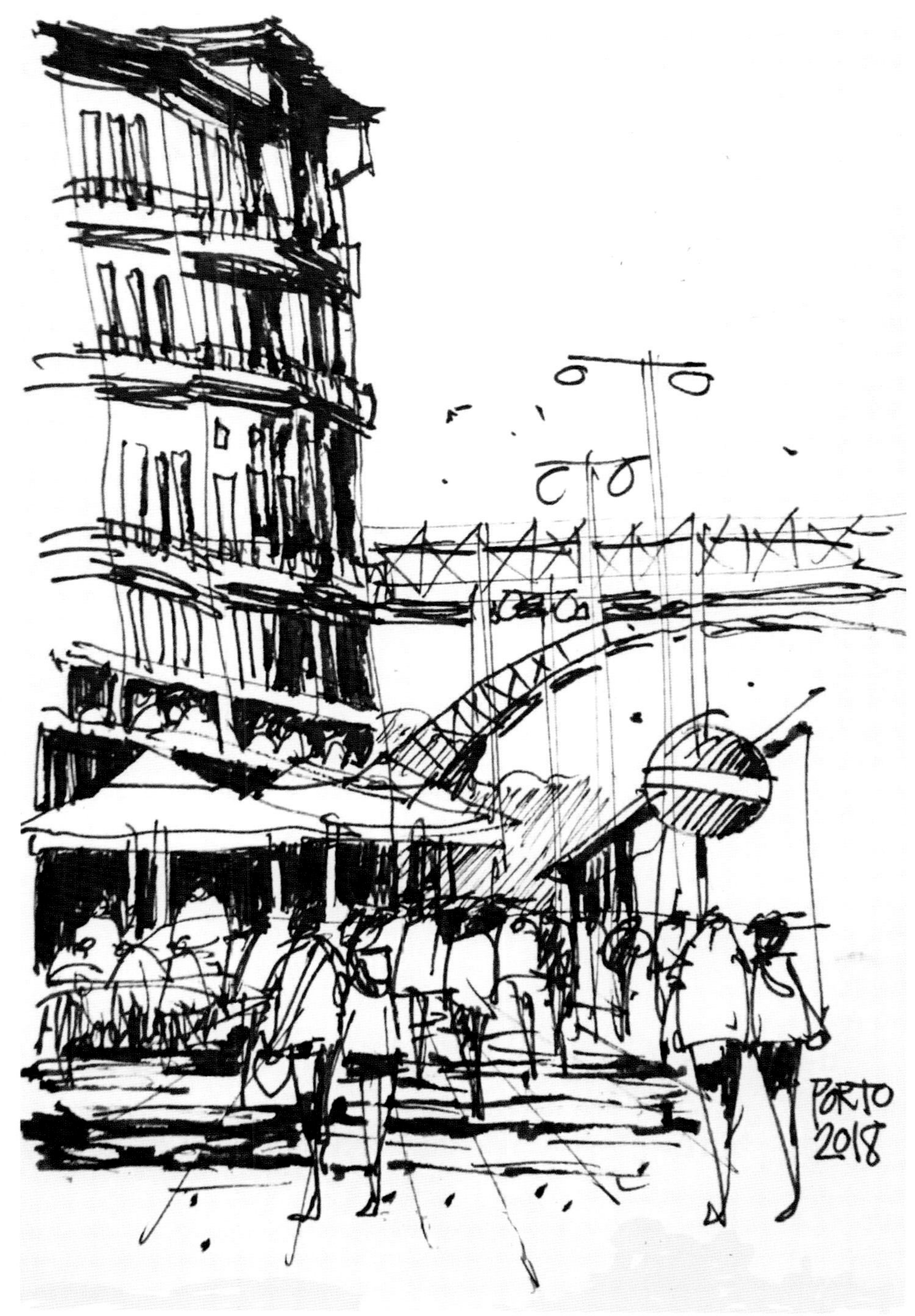
PORTO
2018

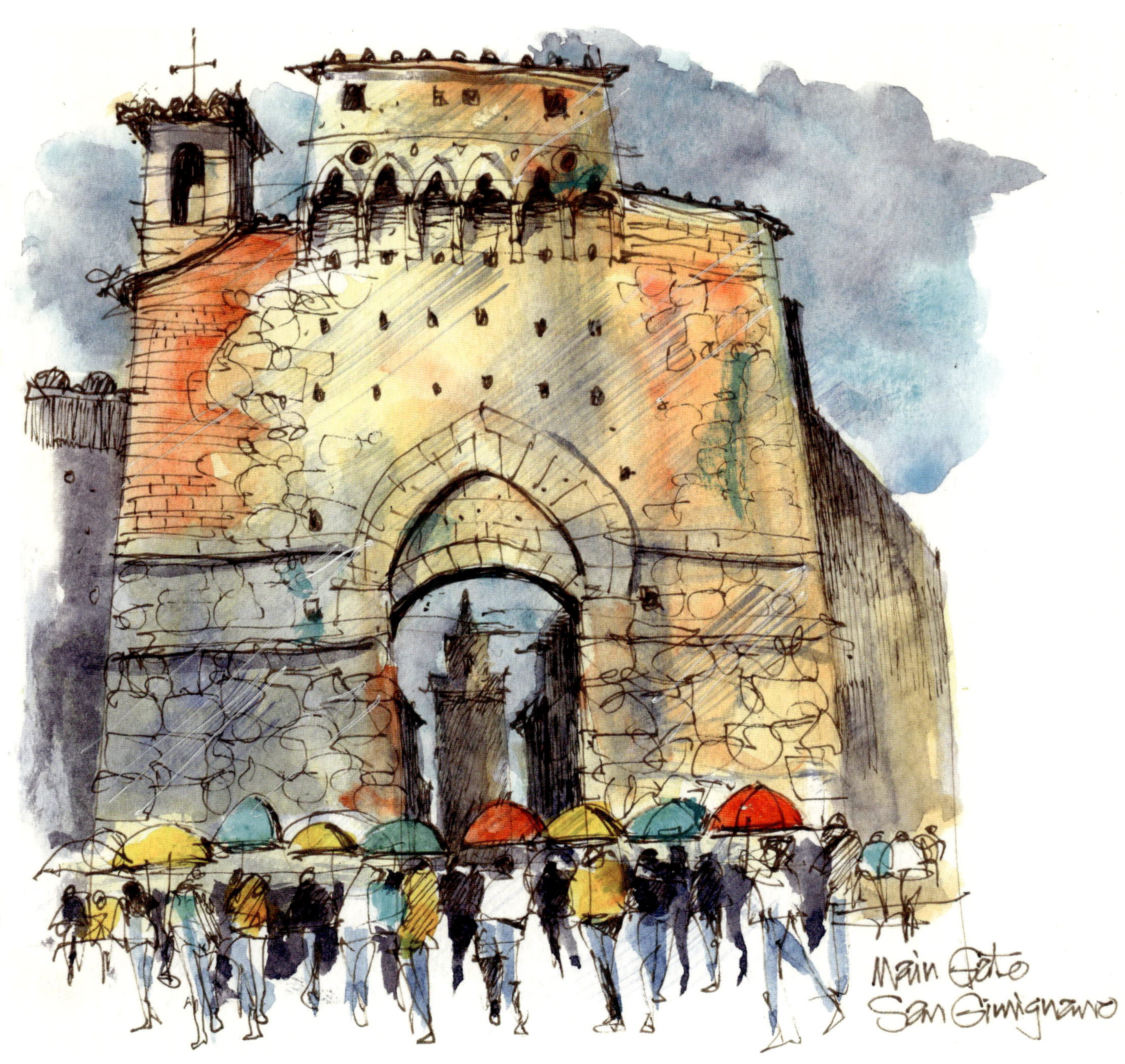
Main Gate
San Gimignano

CHAPTER 2

Tuscany: One Table, One Family, One Community

ONE OF THE GREAT DISAPPOINTMENTS of my adult life was when I received the results of my DNA testing for evidence of ancestral roots, and I showed zero Italian blood. Niete. Nada. Zip. This is especially hard when walking the streets of a city like Florence, where the locals are elegant and confident, and where I want desperately to fit in, but feel so pudgy, so pasty, so—American.

I'm not yet a part of it, but man, Italy's part of me. If you told me I could never return to any number of destinations, I could adjust. If I were told I could never return to Italy, it would be like a light going out: a window into la dolce vita, the sweetness of life, forever closed. So, with the sketching bag overstuffed and The Grown-up navigating logistics, I return as often as I can. And I don't feel like a stranger for very long, because after a Negroni—or maybe two—some good gnocchi with pesto and a couple of sketches down, Italy's got me. Whatever she's seduced me with, I want more.

And honestly, who wouldn't? This land, its cities and culture have given rise to some of the West's greatest achievements in art, architecture, and design. Who would put their catalog up against DaVinci, Michelangelo, Pavarotti, Ferrari? It's synonymous with delicious regional foods, fine Italian wines, the Renaissance, the invention of opera, the Vespa, cappuccino, and a dignified, unpretentious elegance in appearance and behavior that's part of Italian DNA called la bella figura (the beautiful figure). Here, the hill towns, historic villas, and seaside villages complete rather than compete with the natural landscape. It's about

Opposite: A medieval gateway into San Gimignano, the "City of Fine Towers," sketched as light rain started to fall. The Grown-up tried to protect me with a small umbrella, with some success.

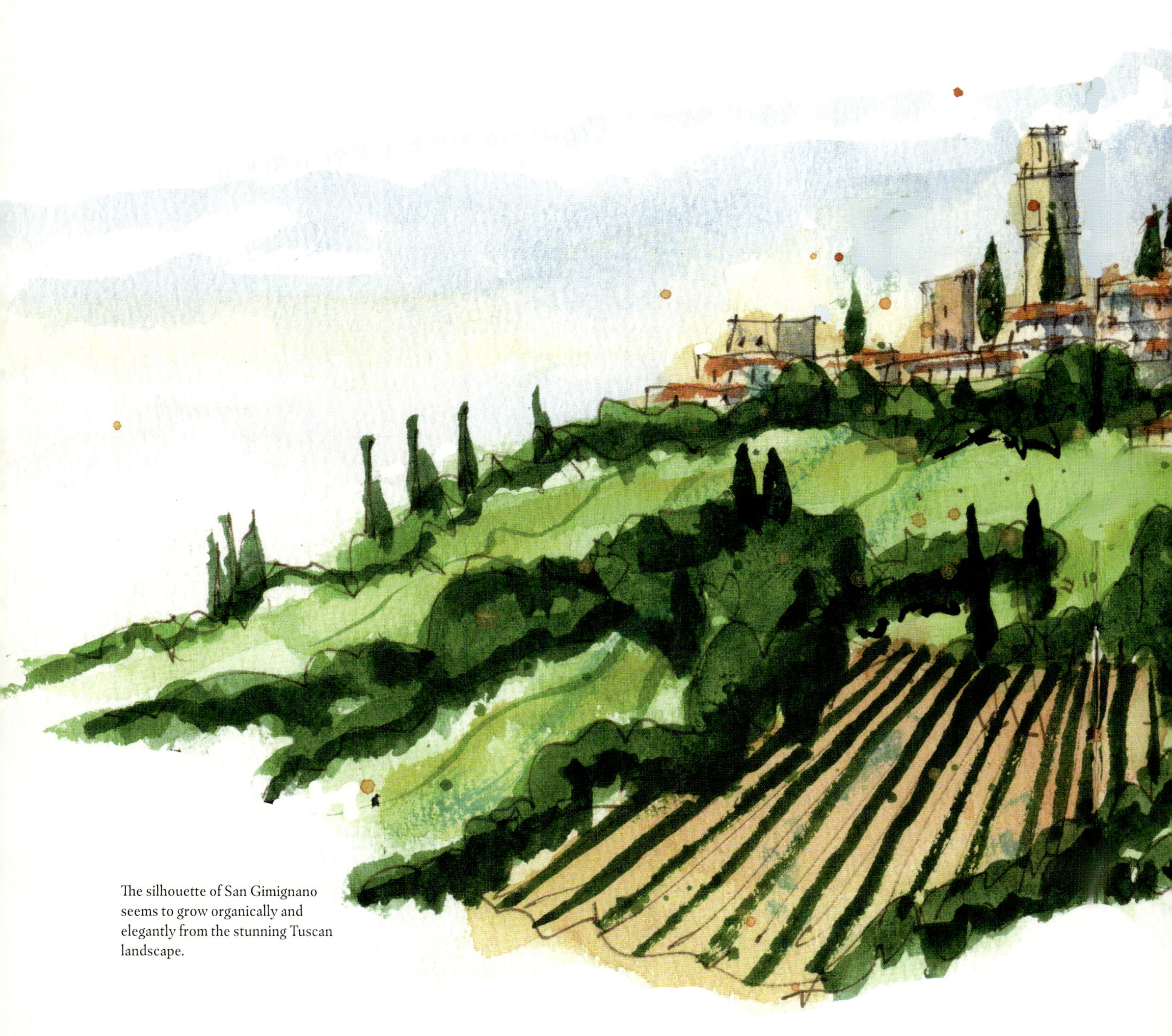

The silhouette of San Gimignano seems to grow organically and elegantly from the stunning Tuscan landscape.

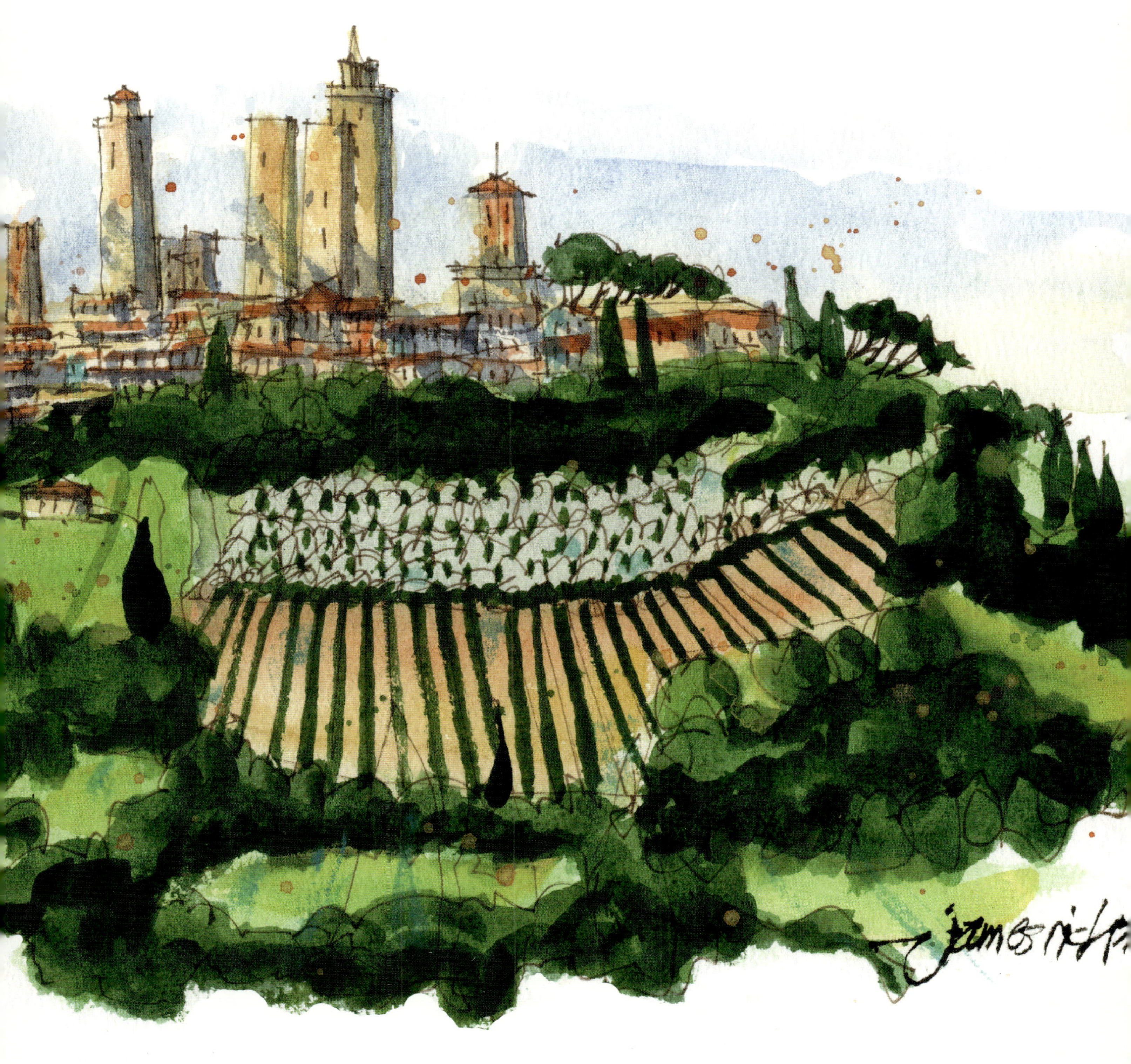

four generations of family at a restaurant table, ancestral connections to the land and its cultivation going back hundreds of years, swimming in the Mediterranean, laundry hanging from clotheslines strung between windows, grandfathers sitting together in chairs on the side of the street, doing nothing in particular, while enjoying watching the young lovers, the boy carrying cannoli, the red Vespa, and the older women walking by with a grace that comes with age. I find it all beautifully intoxicating and seductive.

It's about four generations of family at a restaurant table, ancestral connections to the land and its cultivation going back hundreds of years, swimming in the Mediterranean, laundry hanging from clotheslines strung between windows, grandfathers sitting together in chairs on the side of the street, doing nothing in particular, while watching the young lovers, the boy carrying cannoli, the red Vespa, and the older women walking by with a grace that comes with age. I find it all beautifully intoxicating and seductive.

So how does the American find a way in? Start sketching in a public place and wait. People are intrigued, approach, and a conversation begins, sometimes in the same language, sometimes not. I guess they figure if you're an artist, you're probably harmless, and that's how I've met and become friends with a number of locals and expats. These friends introduce us to their friends—the 86-year-old butcher on the hillside whose handmade salami melts in your mouth, the 91-year-old woman who makes the cheeses we're enjoying with a good vintage from a dear friend's winery. And over a few years, these interactions have grown into an understanding of the interconnected web of local relationships that form a mutually supportive extended family and community. For all its hill towns, piazzas and Aperol spritzes, these local relationships have emerged, for me, as what this place is all about.

Travel entrepreneurs and Tuscan hosts Chef Karolina and Dawid Lenart have become our trusted friends, workshop hosts extraordinaire, and entrée into this world of relationships that tourists don't see. Recently Dawid said, "I want to take you to meet our friend Dario in Panzano. He's a cool guy, you know, he's a butcher there, he has a restaurant." Now, we're down for anything Dawid and Karolina want to do. But this felt familiar. Then I remembered seeing an entire episode of Netflix's award-winning *Chef's Table* devoted to an Italian butcher.

"Wait," I said. "Is he that guy?"

Opposite: The Torre delle Ore clock tower in the heart of Lucca dates to the 14th century.

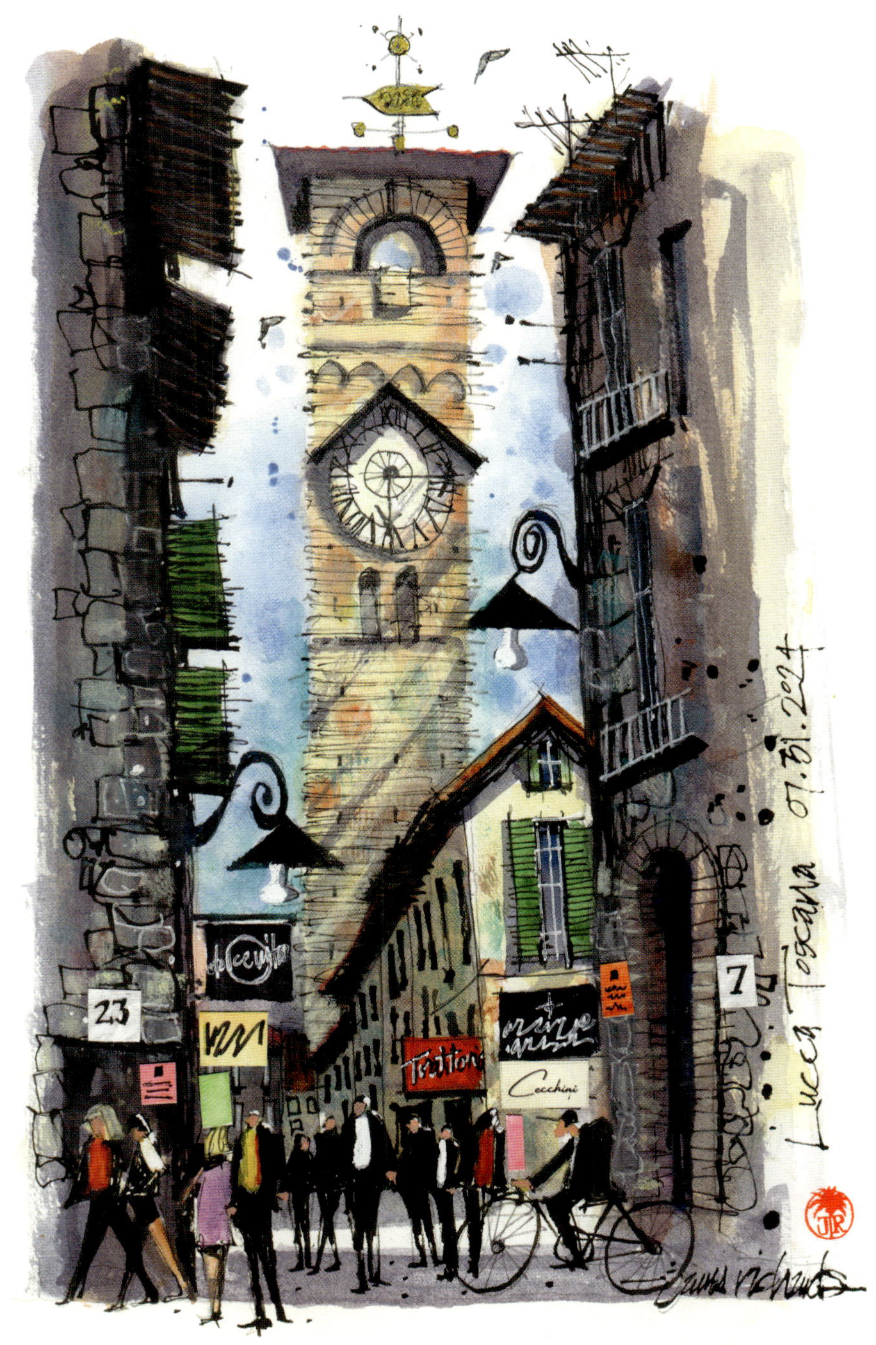
Lucca Toscana
23
7
Cecchini

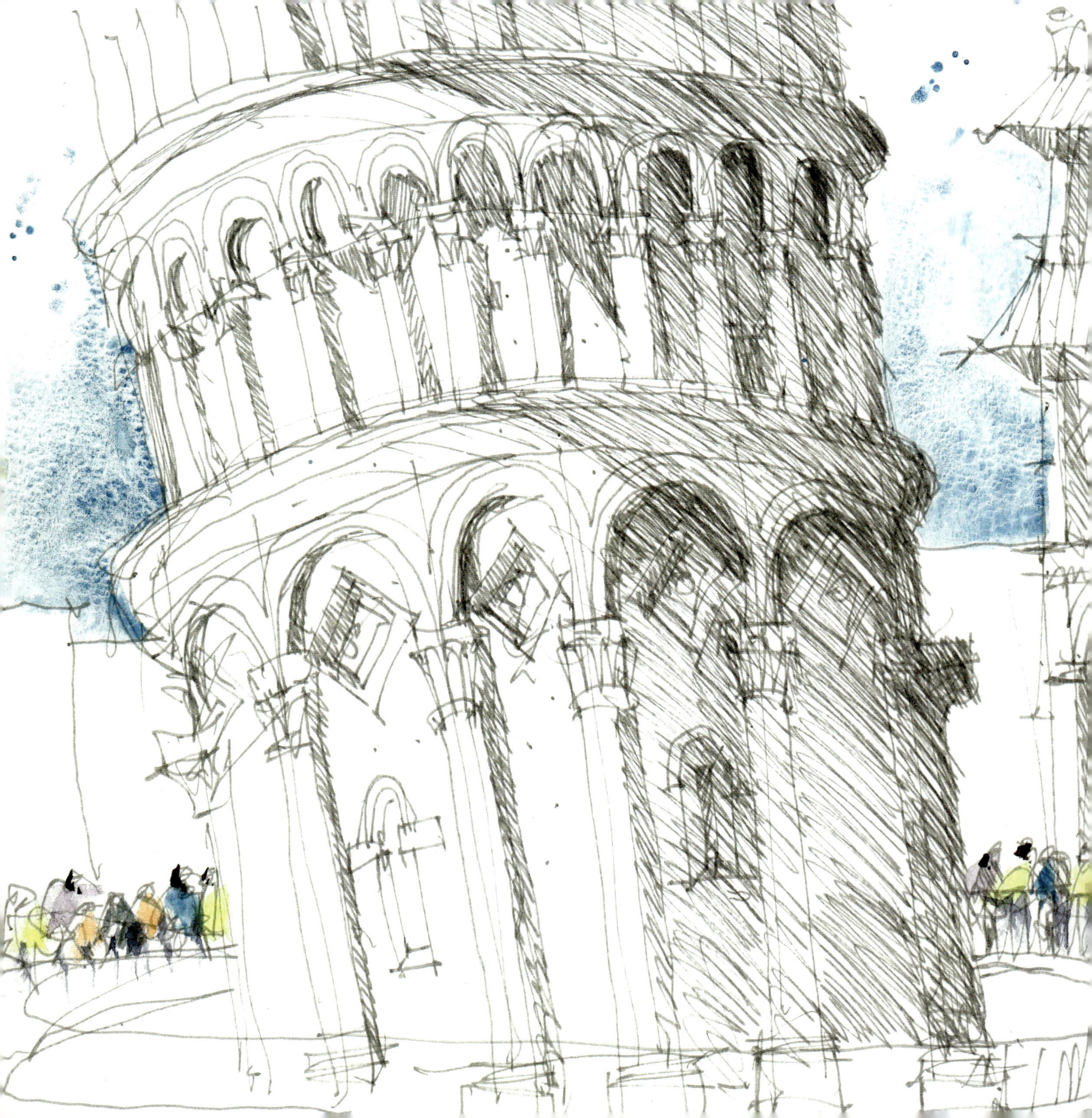

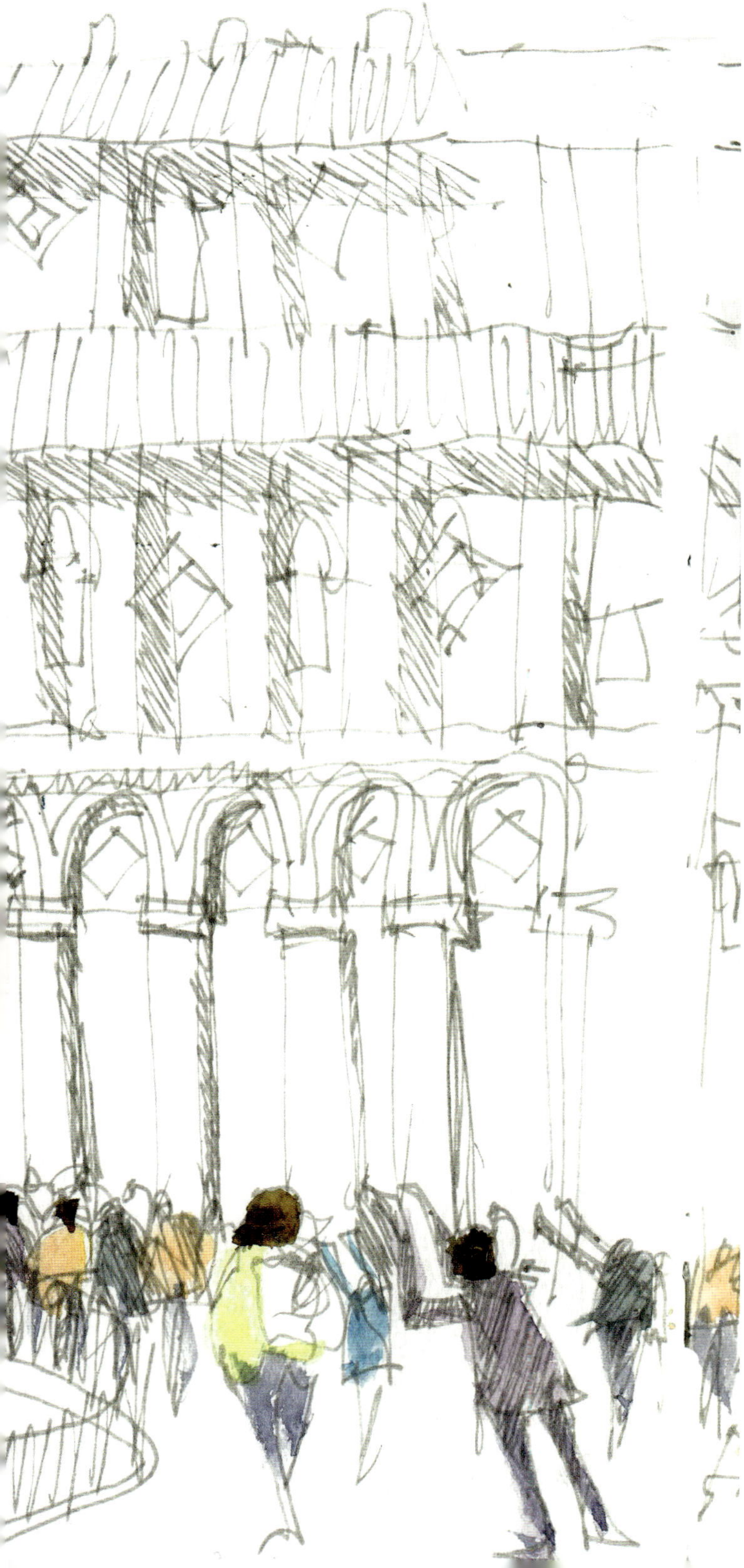

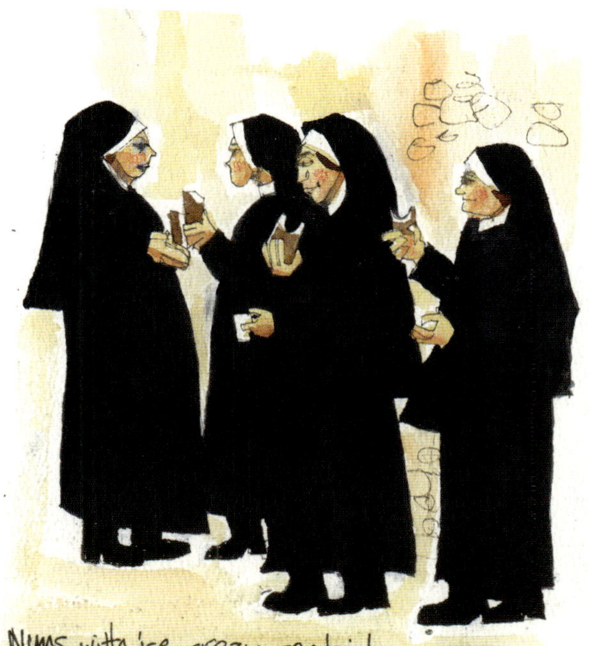

Nuns with ice cream sandwiches near the leaning tower in Pisa...

Left: A close-up sketch of the Leaning Tower of Pisa, revealing some of the exquisite play of light on the white marble, as well as the line of early visitors waiting to climb the 294 steps to the top.

Top: I try to find a story to sketch. A group of nuns isn't a story. A group of nuns eating ice cream sandwiches is a story.

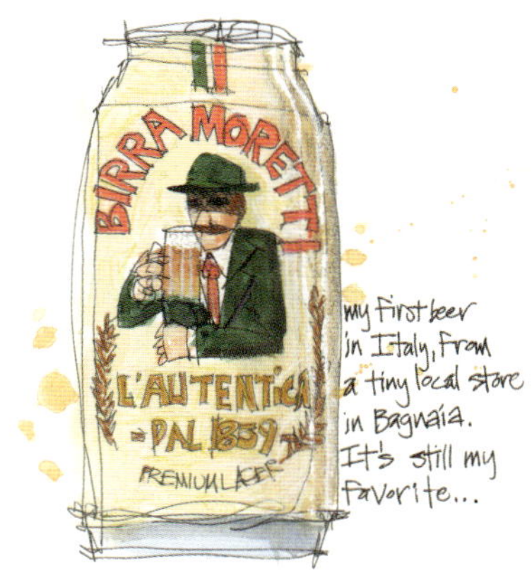

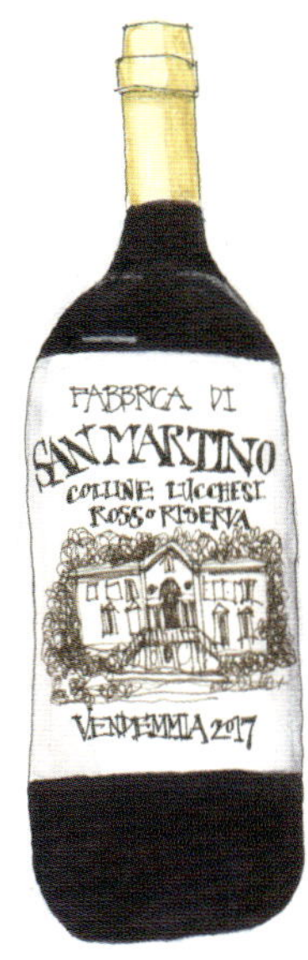

Top: A pale lager with sentimental value for me.

Below: An exquisite red by a winemaker and neighbor in the hills outside Lucca.

"Yes." Dawid fished his phone out of his jeans pocket, scrolled a bit and pulled up a photo. And there was my humble and soft-spoken friend, casually hanging out with one of the most interesting and mission-driven figures in the foodie world.

The road trip took us deep into Chianti, the 65-square mile region within Tuscany of famously gorgeous landscapes of rolling hills, small towns and villages, olive groves, and vineyards that have given us the wines of the same name. And Dario Cecchini.

Dario's story is well-known. Born into the family of eight generations of butchers in Panzano, and with a lifelong love of animals, he was denied his early dream of becoming a veterinarian due to his father's sudden illness and death. With his mother already gone, he sadly left university in Pisa and returned to Panzano to provide for his family in the butcher store owned by his family for over 700 years. Through years of learning the craft and his deep love for the animals and Tuscan traditions, he developed a philosophy and mission to change the world's thinking about the life, dignified death, and ethical butchery rooted in deep respect for the animal. Along the way, he became an internationally renowned chef, the world's most famous butcher, a philosopher who quotes Dante and, yes, a Netflix star.

A sold-out crowd from across the globe shows up at Dario's doorstep in tiny Panzano every day. But Dawid and Karolina had been able to personally introduce us to Dario earlier in the day and mentioned that I was an artist and teacher. I briefly showed Dario a few pages from my sketchbook. From that moment, art became our common language. Dario took me under his wing and walked me to a large, original oil painting that hangs in the butcher shop, and of which he is rightfully very proud. "This," he said enthusiastically in his halting English, "is the first painting of a butcher shop! 400 years old! I have it here. It reminds me!"

Later, as we entered the restaurant with the long line of diners for dinner seating, Dario took my arm, stood in the doorway and pointed again to the painting. His eyes were gleaming. "See? This—this is my road! Every day, I see—my road!" As all the guests took their seats at just a few long, communal tables, Dario came over and stood beside me. He raised his arms toward the room and said, "You see? One seating. One price. One table. One family. One community!"

The evening was remarkable. We made new friends up and down the table. People bonded over the food, but even more so over the man whose dedication, passion, and enthusiasm for his mission was totally infectious. I left inspired. I still am. Thank you, Dawid and Karolina, for sharing another slice of your community with us and for your belief that art makes meaningful connections. Thank you, Dario, for following your road, and for taking us along.

One of Lucca's stone gateways inside the city's well- preserved medieval walls.

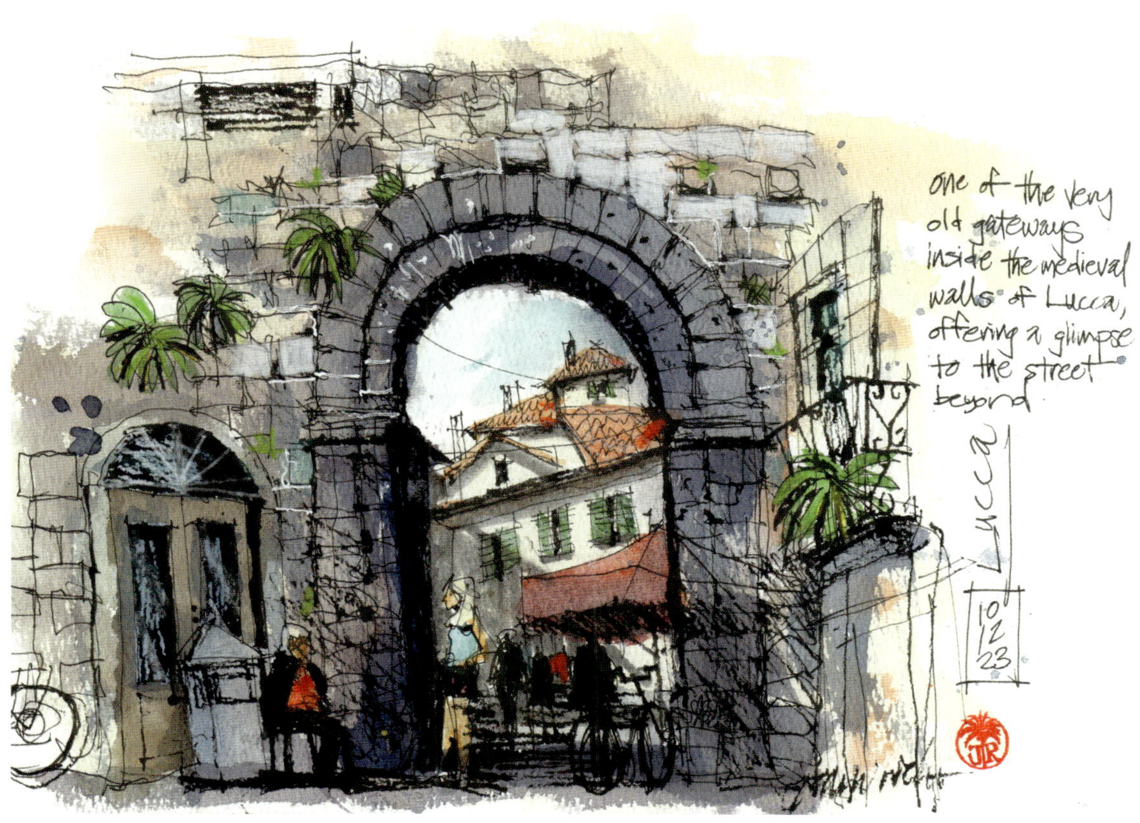

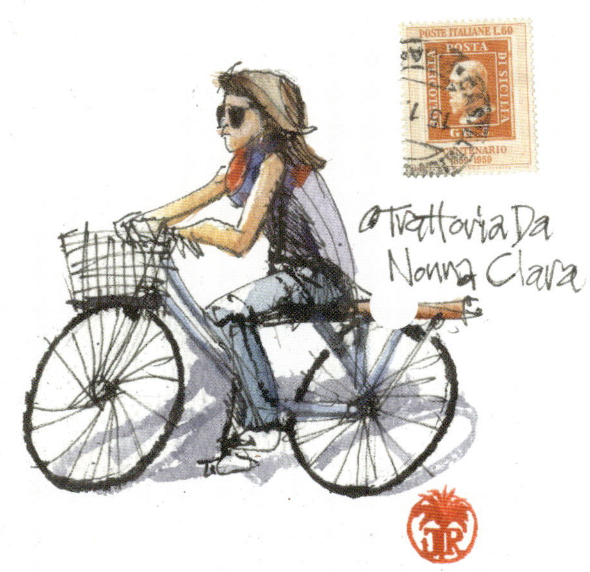

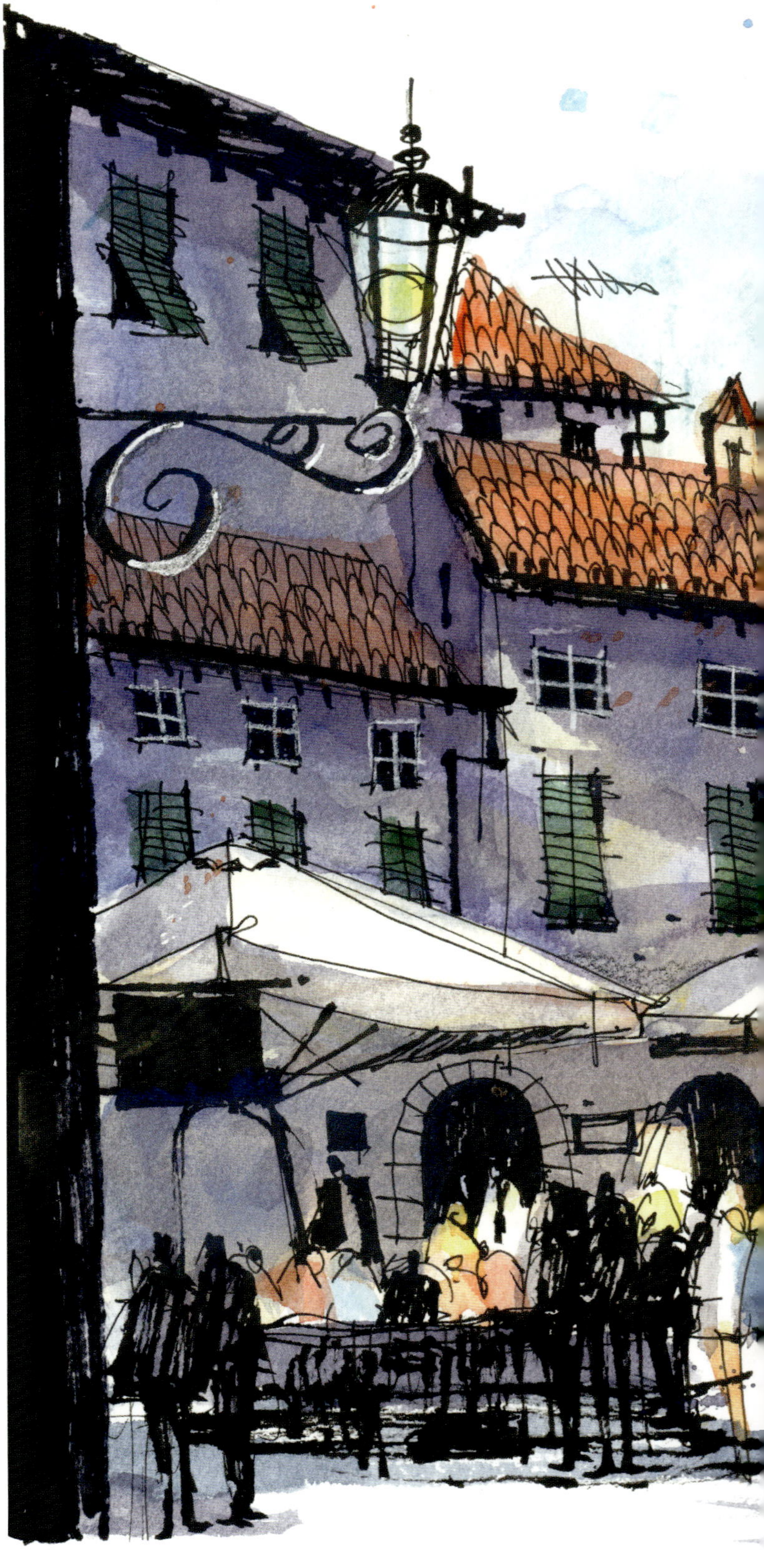

Top: A local woman cycling past our café tables, the picture of *la bella figura*. I didn't quite do justice to her poise, but I keep working at it.

Right: A view into the beautiful oval Piazza dell' Anfiteatro in Lucca, sketched while sitting across the plaza. The ringed shape of the "outdoor living room" follows the footprint of the city's former second-century Roman amphitheater, parts of which are still visible from the street that follows the backside of the buildings.

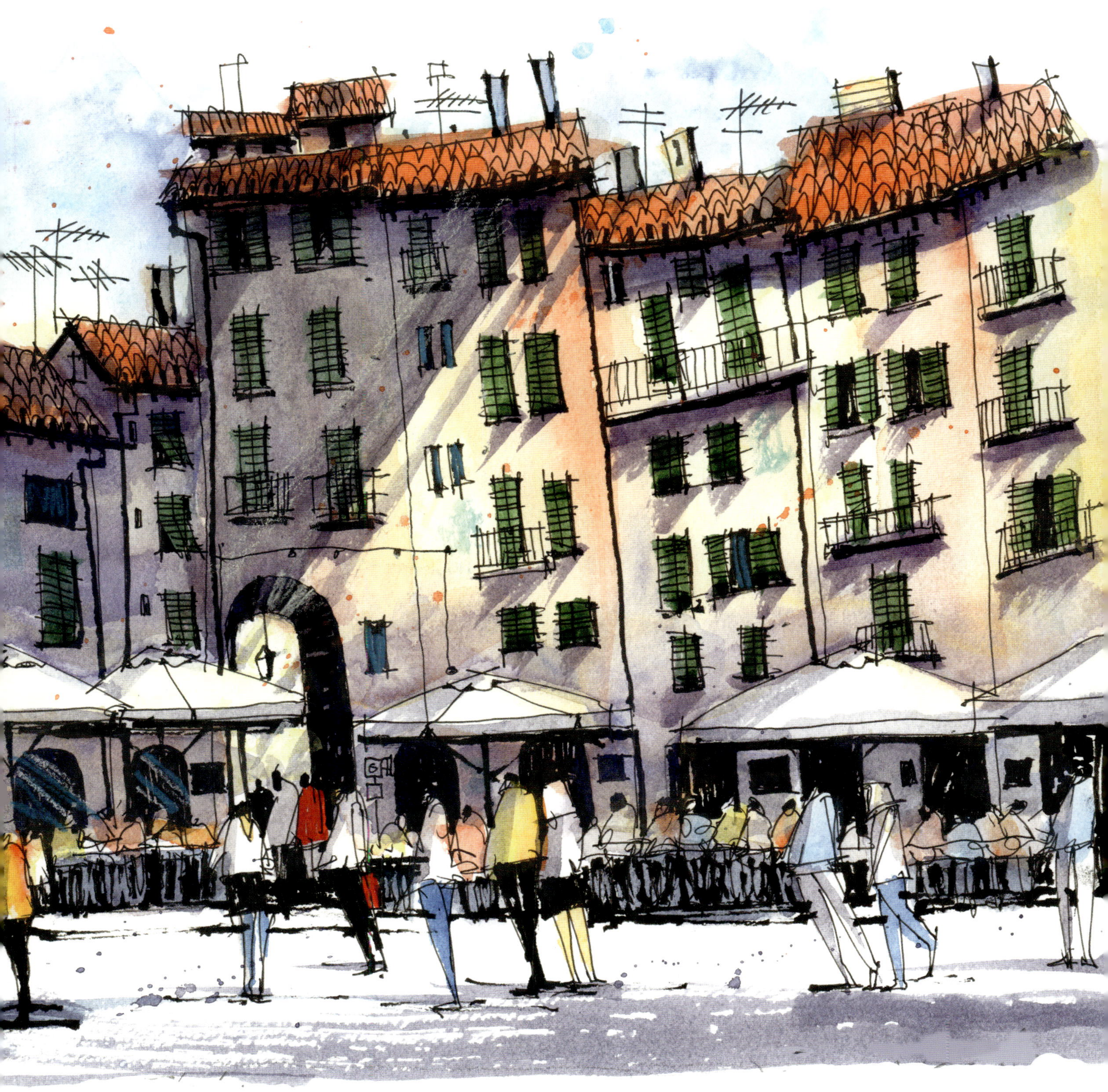

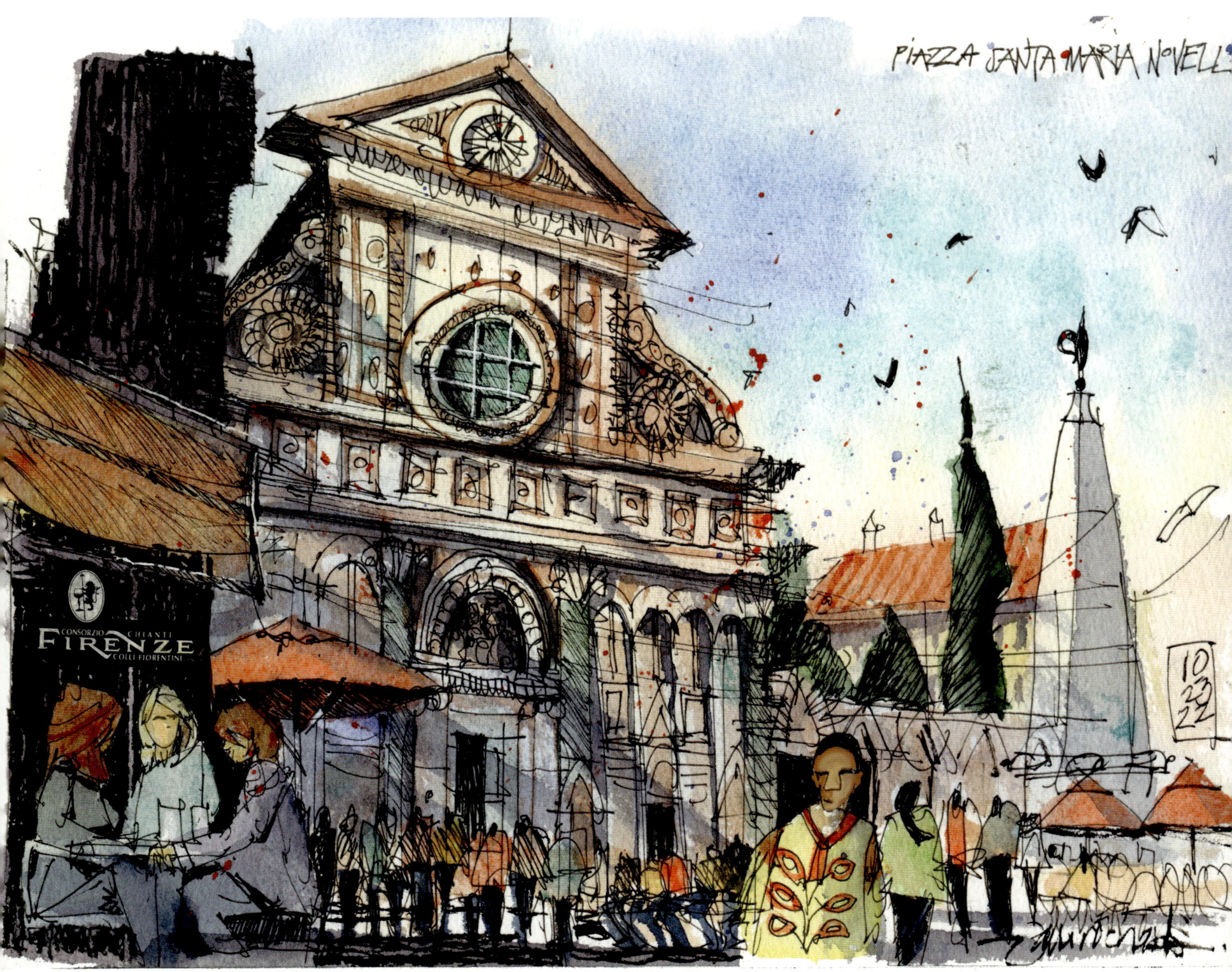

Piazza Santa Maria Novella in Florence.

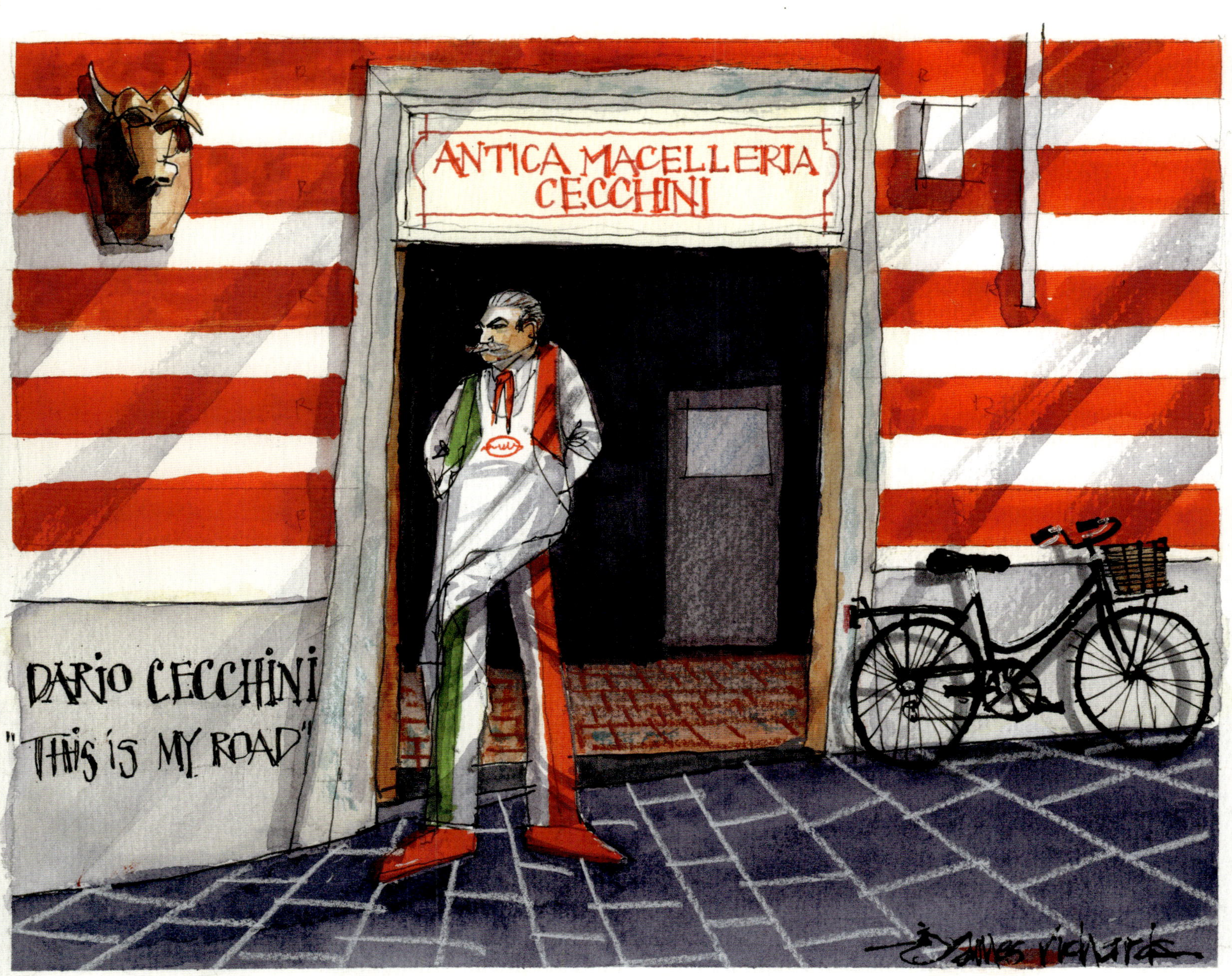

Dario Cecchini in front of his restaurant and butcher shop in the small village of Panzano, Italy.

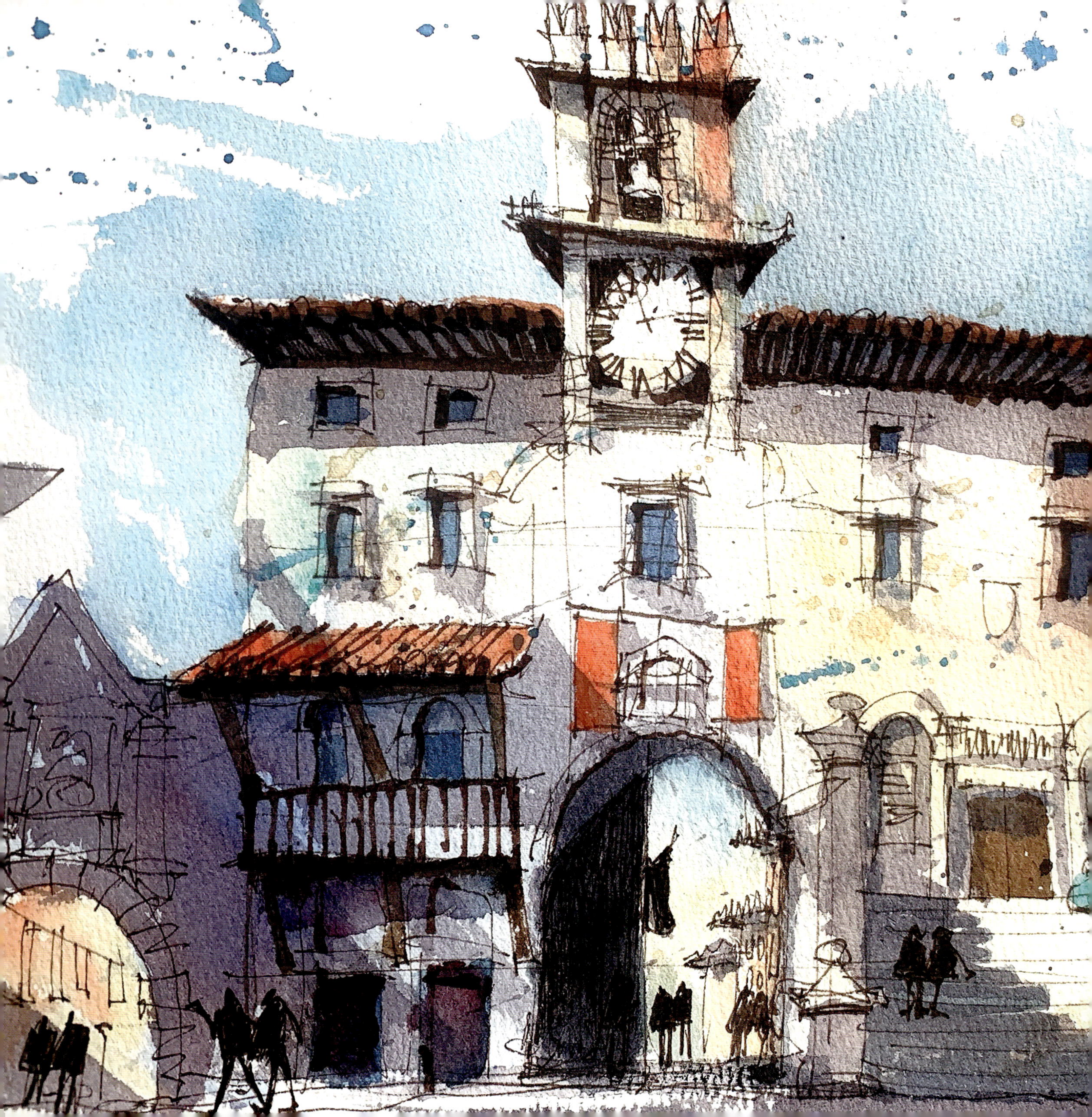

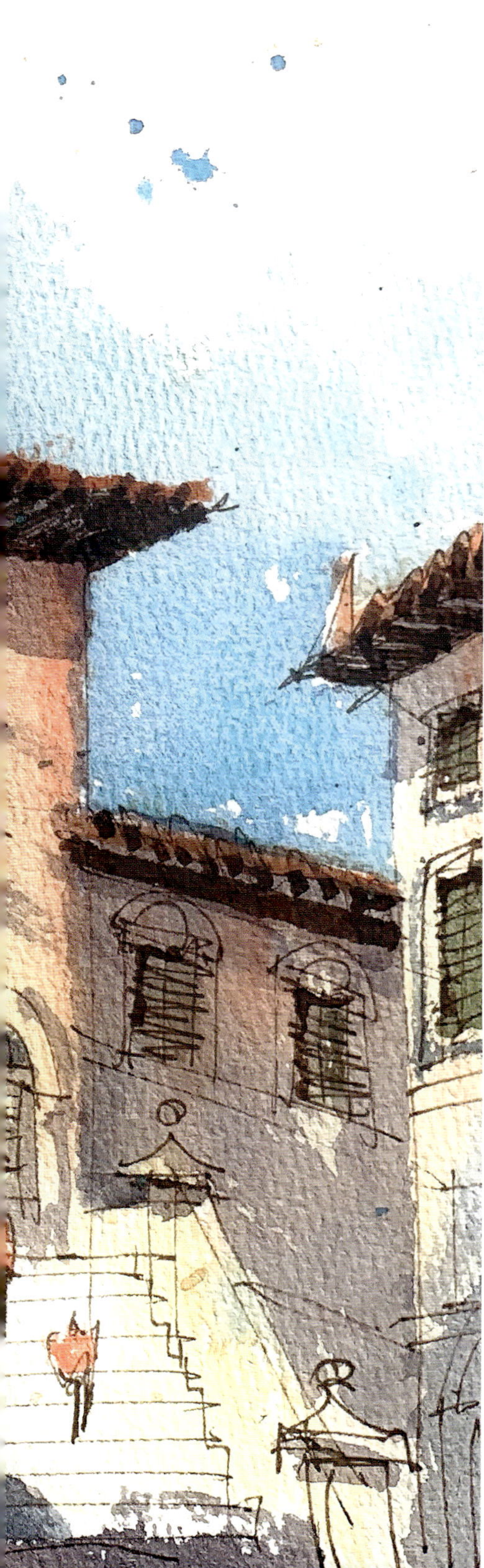

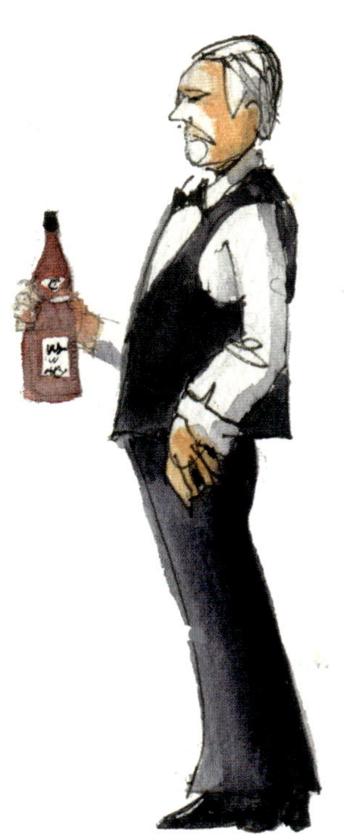

Left: The Town Hall of Cortona faces the lively Piazza della Republica, one of the town's storied gathering places for its social scene, festivals, evening strolls, and even kid's soccer games. Several Americans have told me they have fond memories of sitting on the grand steps in the evenings and watching life in the piazza when they were study abroad students here.

The Sweetness of Doing Nothing

One of the many thoughtful lessons Italians have to offer the fast-paced, relentlessly driven culture of my country is an idea they call *Il dolce far niente*—the sweetness of doing nothing. It's not laziness or avoiding the priority of the moment. It's a conscious decision to take time to temporarily unplug oneself from life's pressures to enjoy the pleasure of some delicious, idle moments. We're not talking about a vacation or a long weekend. It's a purposeful, elegant, and often daily practice of intentionally pausing to enjoy the small pleasures of life. I aspire to be one of those old men on the street corner relaxing in a chair, conversing, watching life parade by while enjoying a glass of wine. This is a lesson in understanding the culture that I teach in my travel sketching workshops, especially in Italy, right alongside things like composition, color, and perspective. Don't have time? Try it. Then try it again. Doing nothing takes practice.

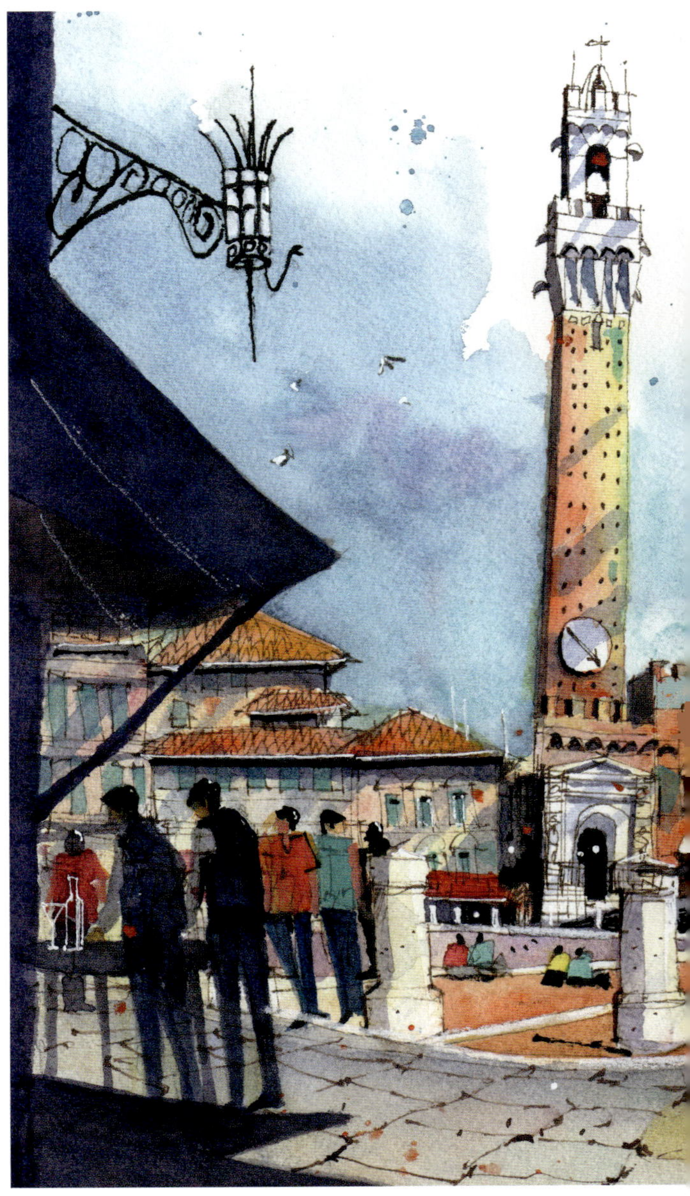

Piazza del Campo, Siena, Italy.

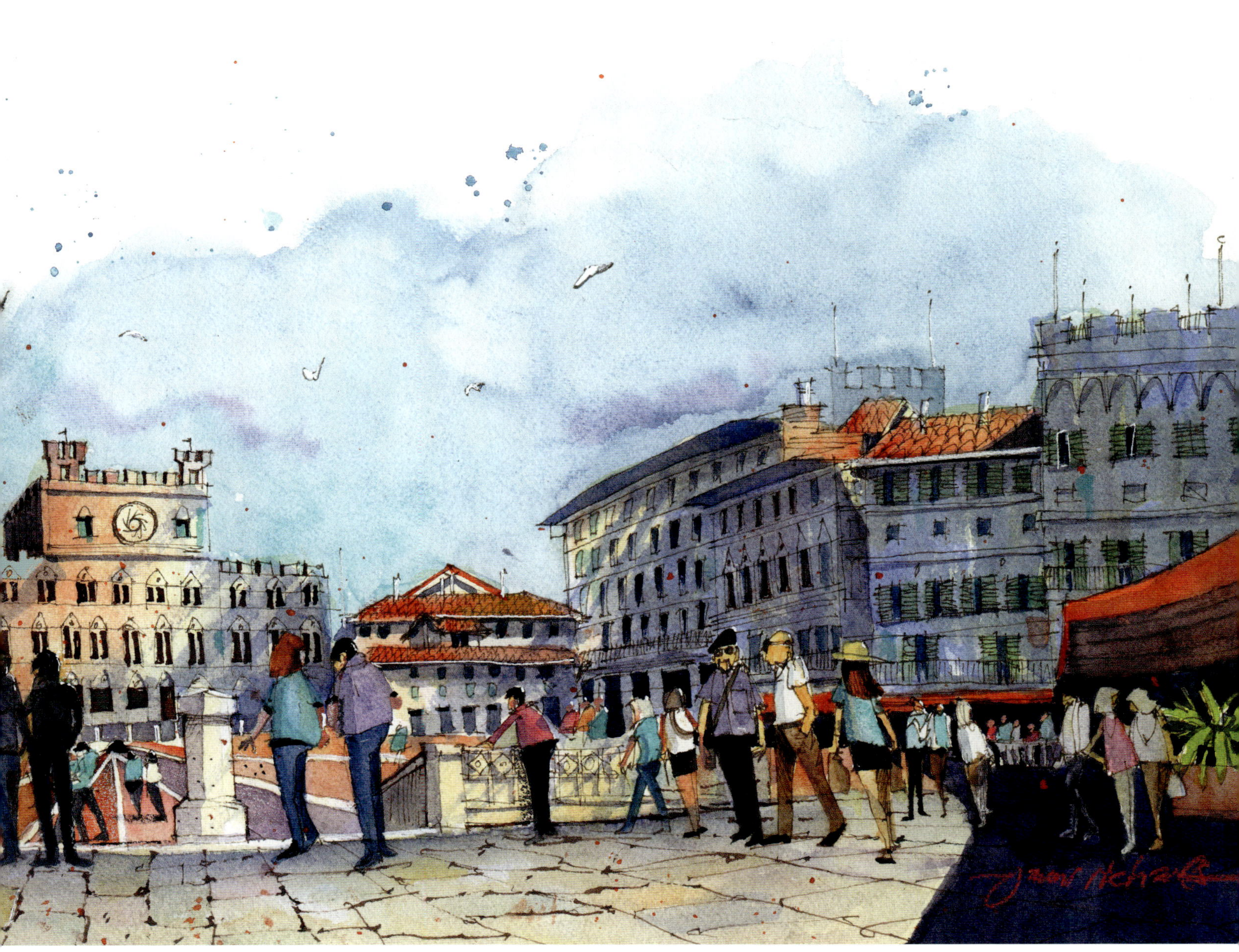

The Sketcher's Code

Don't worry about style.

Every successful band I ever heard of started out doing covers. So why do so many of my sketching students say with overblown indignation, "I refuse to do it like anyone else! I have to find my own voice!" Can I offer some advice? Get over yourself. Emulate. Copy. Learn the basic chords, then follow your instincts with knowledge, confidence, and speed. Yeah, speed. Give it a try. Speed shoves you out of your own head. It short circuits insecurity so that instinct can kick in. That's when your own style emerges.

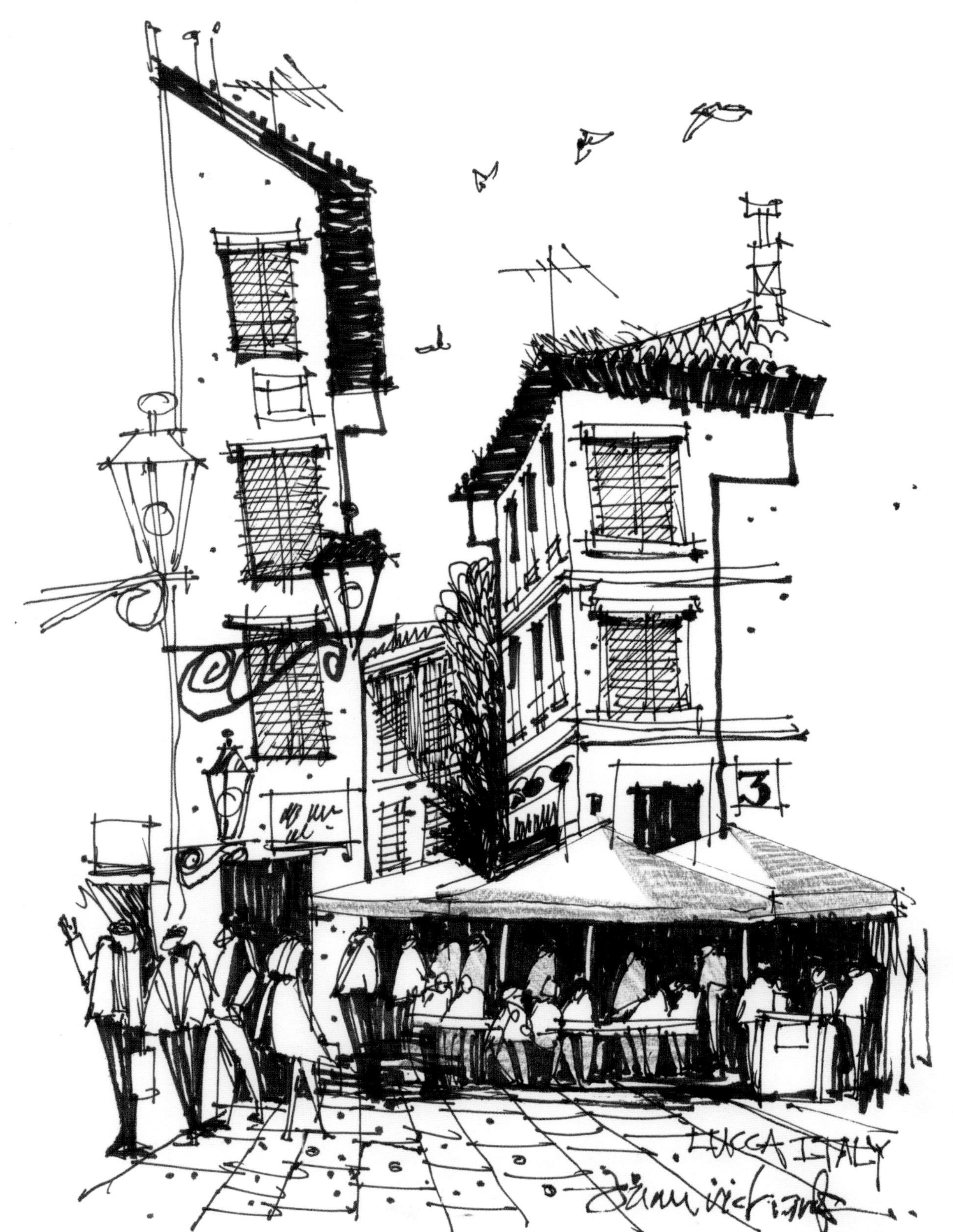
3
LUCCA ITALY

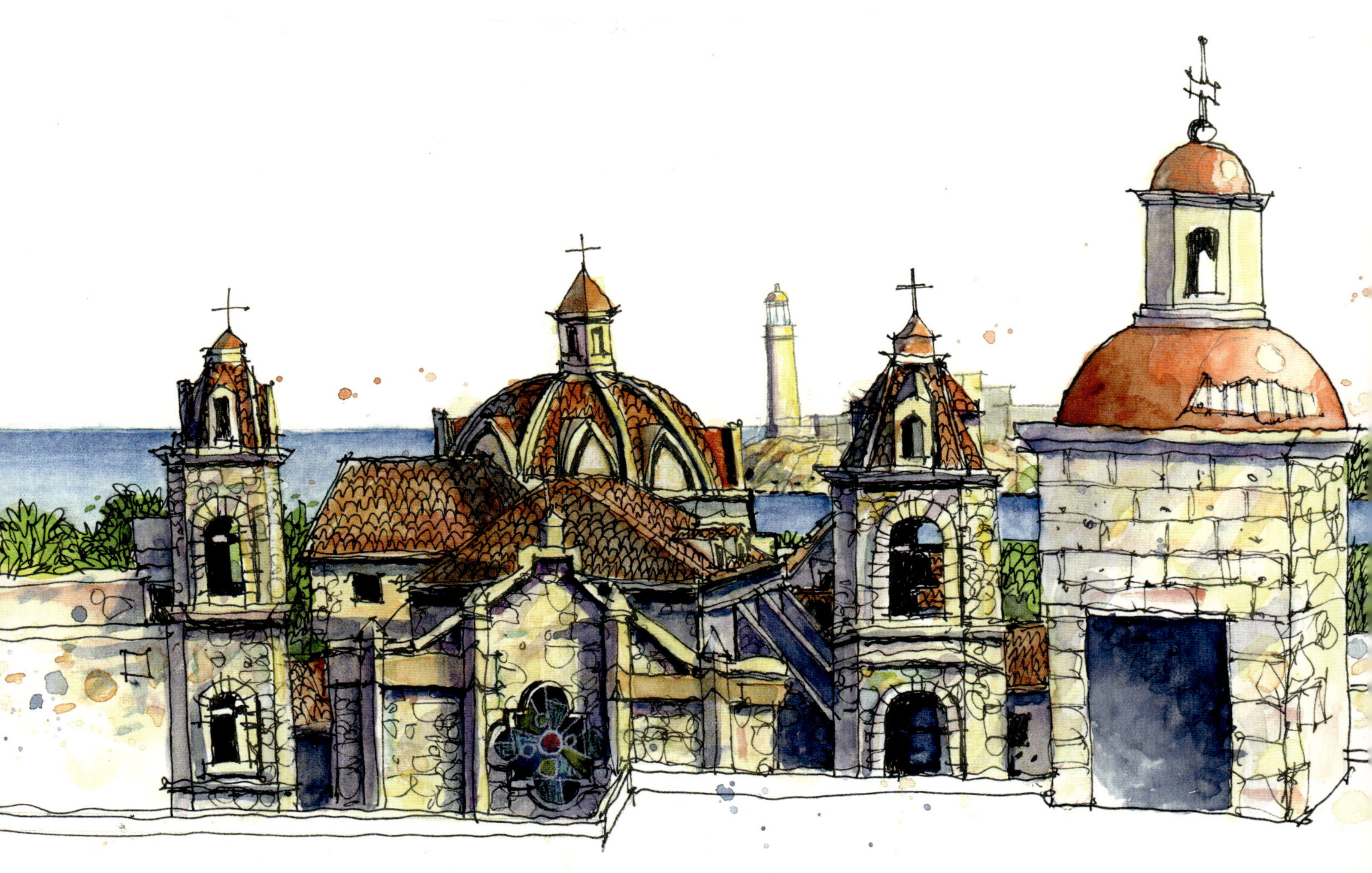

CHAPTER 3

Cuba: Hemingway's Muse

My fascination with Hemingway and Cuba started as separate but parallel paths. Hemingway struck me early on as the consummate outdoorsman and adventurer, fond of trophy fishing, boxing, bullfighting, African safaris, and hard drinking; and with his worldwide celebrity, he helped shape the idea of male virility in his time. But here's the thing: he was, above all else, an artist. His spare, powerful writing style and stories rooted in his own life experience transport us into the worlds he created the way great cinema, music, or paintings can. His study and appreciation of art in Paris' museums taught him lessons about how to see and feel and how to translate those into a form that could communicate his interior world to others—not a bad definition of art.

Cuba grabbed my imagination when, as a young urban designer, I poured over books filled with photographs of Old Havana's once beautiful architecture, now the victim of decades of institutional neglect since the city's takeover by Castro's revolutionaries in 1959. In his 1962 book *My Brother, Ernest Hemingway,* Leicester Hemingway called Havana, "... one of the loveliest, wickedest, most mysterious and enchanting cities in the world." Now, with the exception of a few areas that have undergone renovation, what's left is a time capsule of this once elegant city in a state of relentless, continuing decay. Even in this state, the photos revealed a visually stunning place—unlike any I'd explored. Add to the mix that, for almost my entire lifetime, Cuba had been off limits to Americans. Forbidden fruit. That alone is enough reason to go.

Opposite: View to the sea from the rooftop terrace of Hotel Ambos Mundos

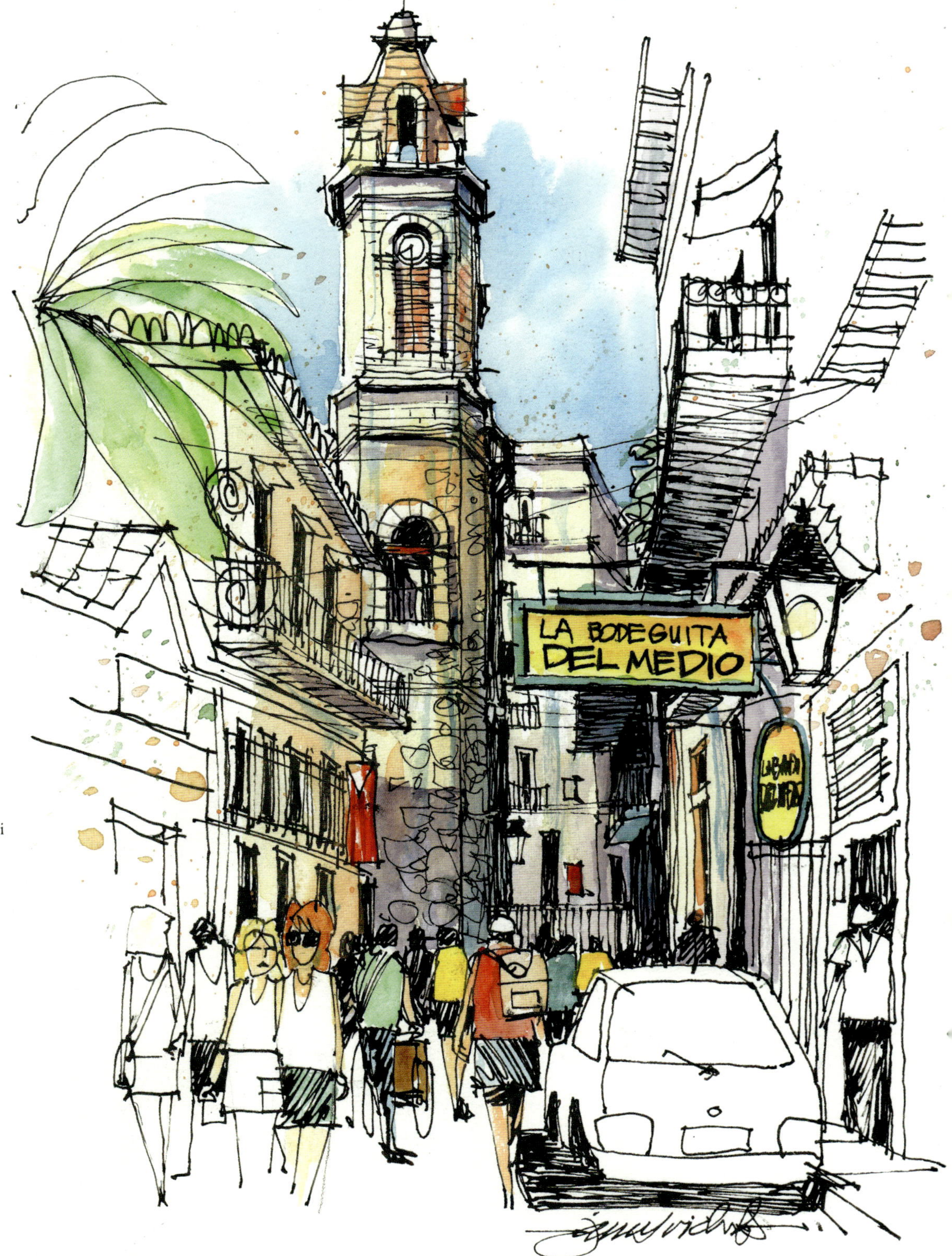

A framed inscription in La Bodeguita del Medio reads, "My mojito in La Bodeguita, my daiquiri in El Floridita" and has a signature that says "Ernest Hemingway." It also claims to be the birthplace of the mojito. Neither is likely true, but it's fun to believe that they are and to enjoy the live music downstairs, the 1940s ambience, and one of those mojitos. The Bodeguita is just a few doors down from the 18th century Havana Cathedral (Catedral de San Cristóbal), both providing their respective services for the community and both exceptional subjects for travel sketching.

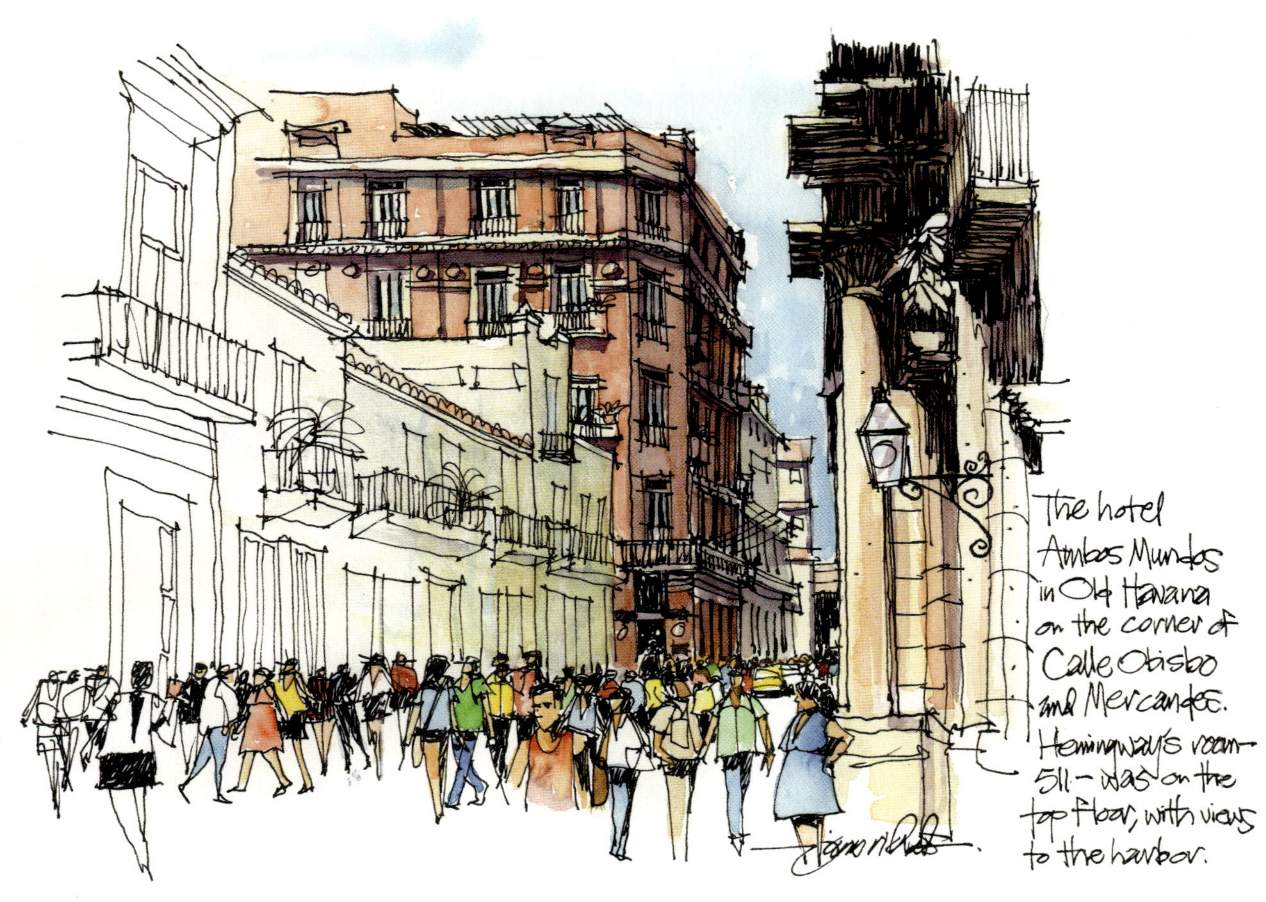

The Hotel Ambos Mundos, where Hemingway lived and wrote for seven years, is in the heart of Old Havana. His room, 511, is simply furnished as he might have left it and serves as a small museum with views across the city and out to the harbor.

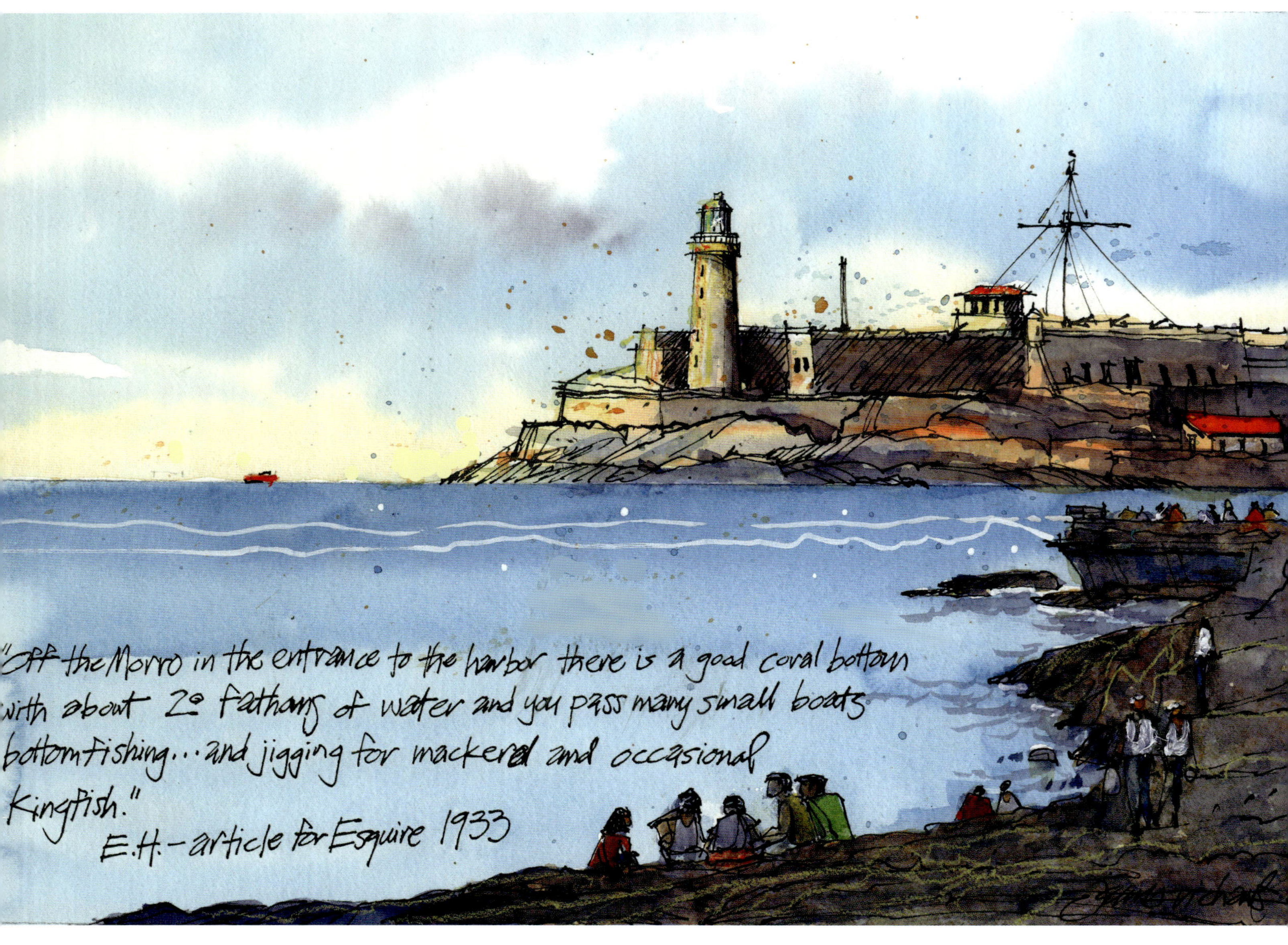

The Morro fortifications and lighthouse at the entrance to the city's harbor are a landmark in Havana, visible from much of the city. The quote on the drawing is from a 1933 Hemingway article for Esquire magazine, "Marlin Off the Morro—A Cuban Letter."

These parallel streams came together when a friend emailed that there may be an opportunity to shoehorn Patti and myself into an excursion of Hemingway scholars from Arkansas State University (ASU) into Cuba as part of a "cultural exchange." This was a richer prospect than I could have hoped for, and I was willing to move heaven and earth to get us onto that plane. It became the first of three excursions there.

A focus on Hemingway's Cuba was an excellent starting point for exploring the place and the people. Hemingway lived and worked there on and off for 30 years, longer than in any other place. He started making regular visits to Cuba in the early 1930s to fish for blue marlin in the Gulf Stream and to escape the growing number of uninvited visitors and gawking tourists in Key West. He eventually moved into the Hotel Ambos Mundos in Havana. He lived and worked there for seven years, until the purchase of Finca Vigia (Lookout Farm) in 1940, a rambling 15-acre estate 12 miles outside Havana found by his then-wife, war correspondent Martha Gellhorn. Hemingway left Cuba for the last time in 1960 amid a wave of executions by the Castro regime.

When we arrived, my impressions started with the water. Surrounded by the Caribbean, the Gulf of Mexico and the Atlantic, the sea is Havana's reason for being. Shoreline activity and views to the big water are plentiful, tying the island to the rest of the world while reminding us that living on a Caribbean island is a game of chance against inevitable hurricanes.

Then there's the light. We're in the topics, so sun-washed walls and crisp shadows are the daytime norm. The architecture in the central city ranges from ornate Spanish Colonial to Modernist boxes, and reflects the colors, textures, and patina of a faded elegance. It's softened by a profusion of palms, flowering trees, and other tropical vegetation in parks and along streets that voluntarily rises between buildings like weeds through broken concrete.

There are the vintage American cars, a few restored beautifully, but most are rusted hulks held together with duct tape and baling wire, as well as old boxy compacts from Cuba's Soviet era. There's sophisticated public art on the streets. There are rusted iron balcony railings with long, radial spikes to deter intruders, a maze of crisscrossing overhead utility lines, and streetlamps ranging from historic and ornate to worn out, butt-ugly relics of 1950s public works.

The people that fill the streets, sidewalks, parks, and plazas are a rich gumbo of races and cultures. Some of the men are dressed in white *guayaberas,* but most are in worn tank tops or t-shirts and pants cut off at the knees to deal with the damnable heat and humidity. Many women are in loose-fitting dresses. They gather along El Malecon, the broad, curving boulevard along the seawall, in the cool of the evening to watch the sun set over the Straits of Florida.

I sought out Hemingway haunts, especially watering holes like the Bodeguita del Medio and the Floridita. I found the Floridita most accommodating, and, based on vintage photos, very much unchanged from Hemingway's time. I conducted my research responsibly, sitting at the corner of the bar where Hemingway held court, having several Papa Doble daiquiris (a recipe refined by Hemingway himself with one of the bartenders) and sketching the atmosphere of the room. Most memorable was realizing that, while urinating in the men's room, I was peeing in the same fixture on the same tile floor and experiencing the same relief that Papa himself did in this room thousands of times. Now THAT brings history to life.

...I was peeing in the same fixture on the same tile floor and experiencing the same relief that Papa himself did in this room thousands of times. Now THAT brings history to life.

We made a short ride east to Cojimar, the fishing village where Hemingway docked his fishing boat Pilar, played cards, and told stories with local fishermen in the La Terraza bar. I ordered a Bucanero beer and stood at the corner window next to the house band to sketch the view to the big water. This is the same window view mentioned in the powerful closing passage of *The Old Man and the Sea*. The band took a break and the guitarist approached me. He'd been watching. He asked to see my sketch. He smiled as he looked it over and approved of what I'd drawn so far. He told me that his uncle in Havana had been an architect and that the man loved to sketch the buildings, streets of the city, and the landscape surrounding it. The boy loved watching his uncle's magic and wanted some of the magic for himself. In a few short years, he found his

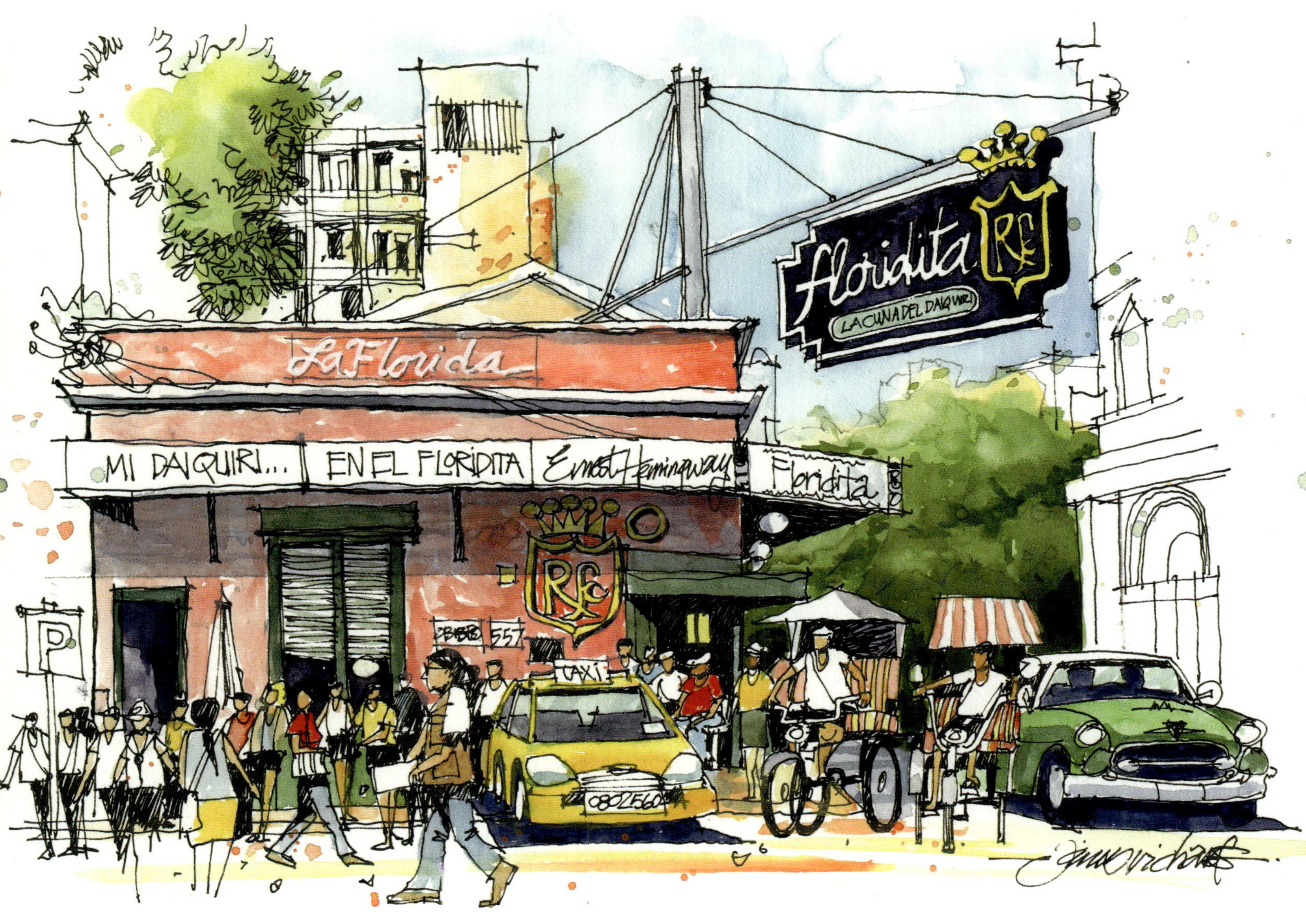

The Floridita bar in Havana, where Hemingway held court with visiting writers, film stars, and local characters. Here he "invented" his namesake Papa Doble daiquiri—double rum, no sugar.

own creative voice through music, but my sketching had released a flood of memories. It was a good feeling to share a genuine appreciation for his uncle's passion and for each other's creative journey. I'm sure that from the corner of the room, Papa Hemingway was watching and smiling.

I captured what I saw in a series of sketches gathered during planned tour stops and unauthorized exploratory walks. On the final day of touring, the director of the Hemingway Center, who happened to be sitting next to me on the bus as I fleshed out a drawing, asked if I'd be interested in having an exhibition of the drawings at his university. I was. It was a grand affair, but most memorable to me because, in a stroke of negotiating genius, I traded two of my paintings for $1000 worth of premium cigars to a renowned law professor emeritus turned cigar company

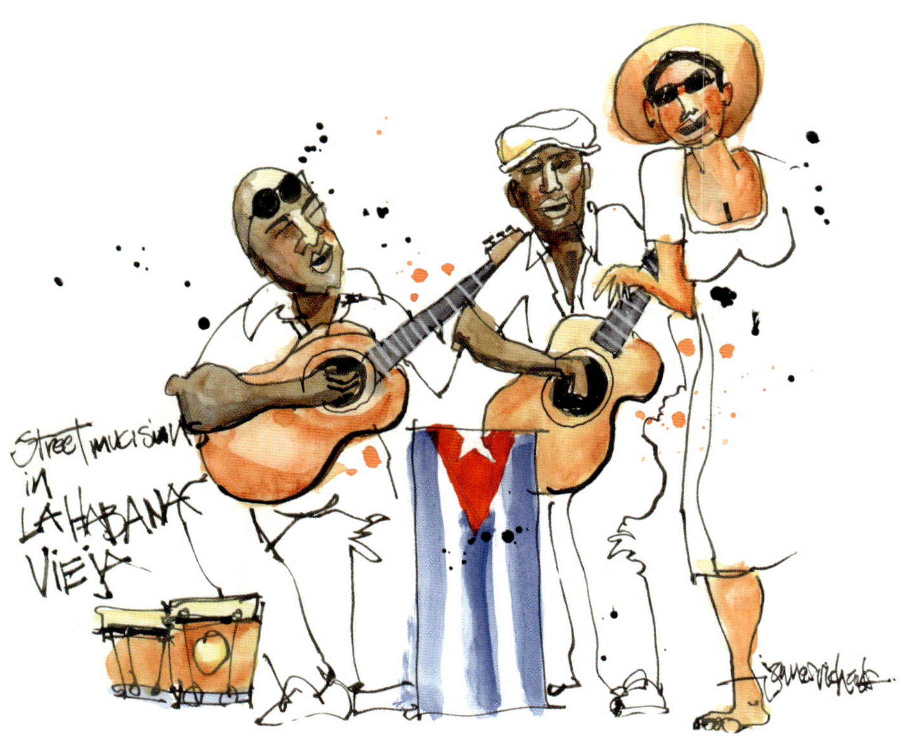

Street musicians near the Plaza de Armas in La Habana Viejo (old Havana). Cuban music stirs the soul; I can never get enough of it.

La Terraza tavern in Cojimar, where Hemingway talked baseball, traded fishing stories, and played cards with local fishermen.

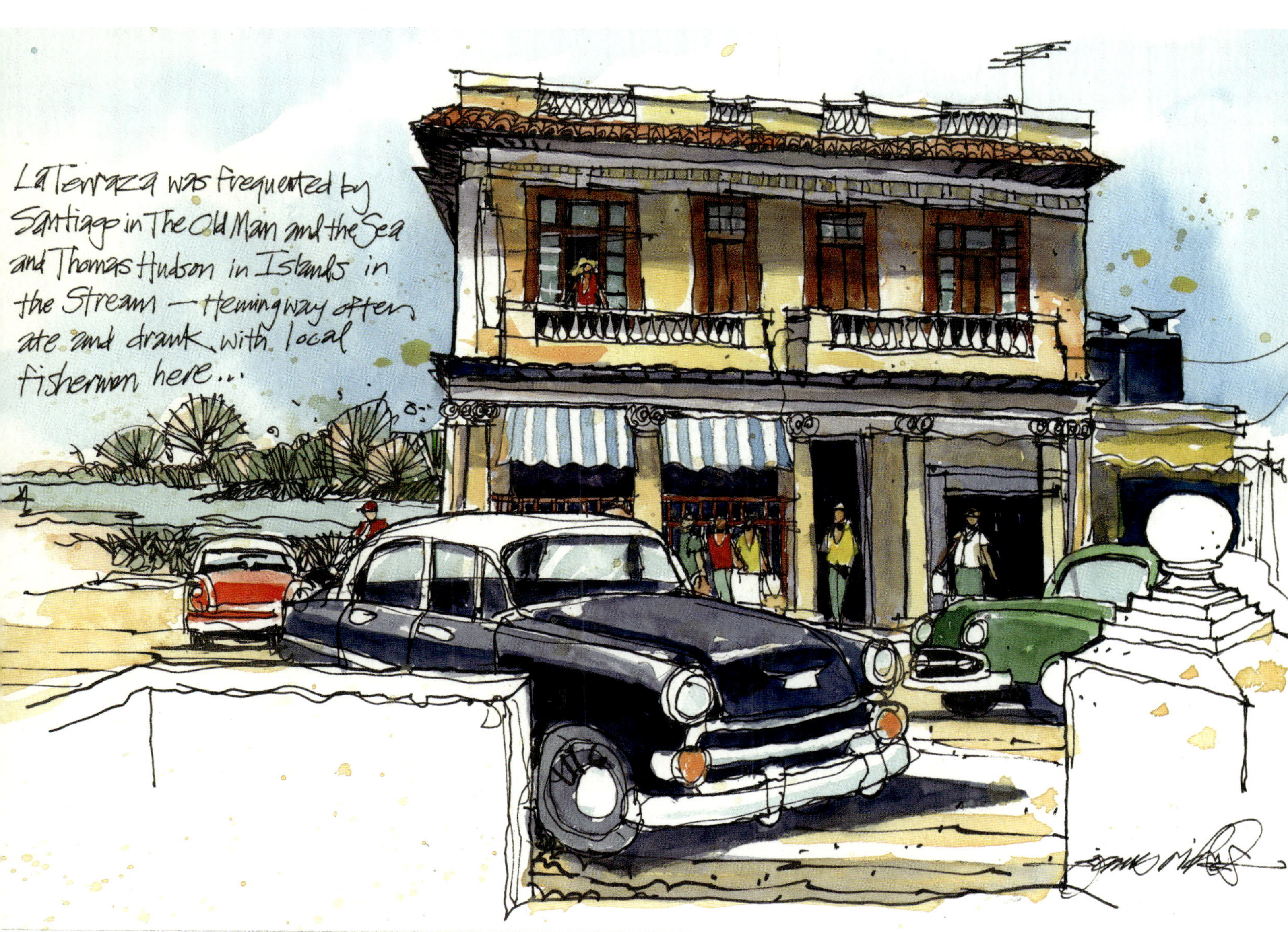

owner as we told each other exaggerated stories in the parking lot. The Grown-up was not pleased. As the adult responsible for all things related to money, she'd already sold the paintings during the reception in the exhibition hall. All told, Patti forgave me, the law professor and his wife still enjoy their paintings, and the cigar stash lasted for two years. Good trade.

The ASU exhibition led to an invitation to lead a group of American artists on a week-long sketchbook discovery tour of Havana and western Cuba and, incredulously, an exhibition of my watercolor drawings at Hemingway's Finca Vigia. Somehow, I'd become the first American ever invited to have an exhibition at the Nobel Prize-winning author's estate, arranged over several months by our miracle-working guide and fixer, Mayra Crespo, a Cuban native, and her longtime friend Ada Rosa Alfonso, then the director of the Museo Hemingway at Finca Vigia.

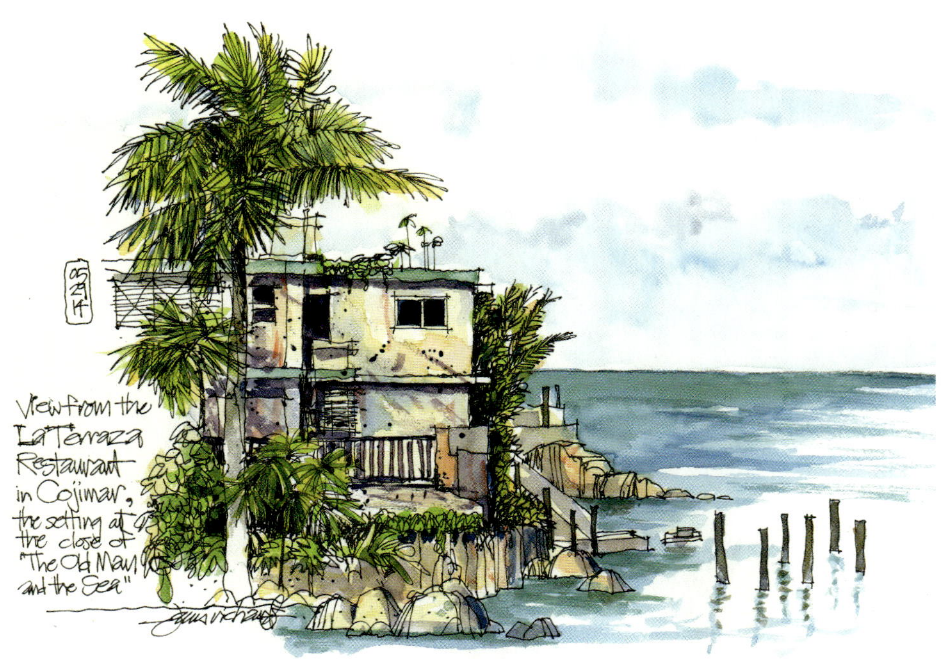

I made this sketch looking out the same window of the La Terraza tavern that Hemingway's characters did in the closing of his Nobel Prize-winning novel, *The Old Man and the Sea*.

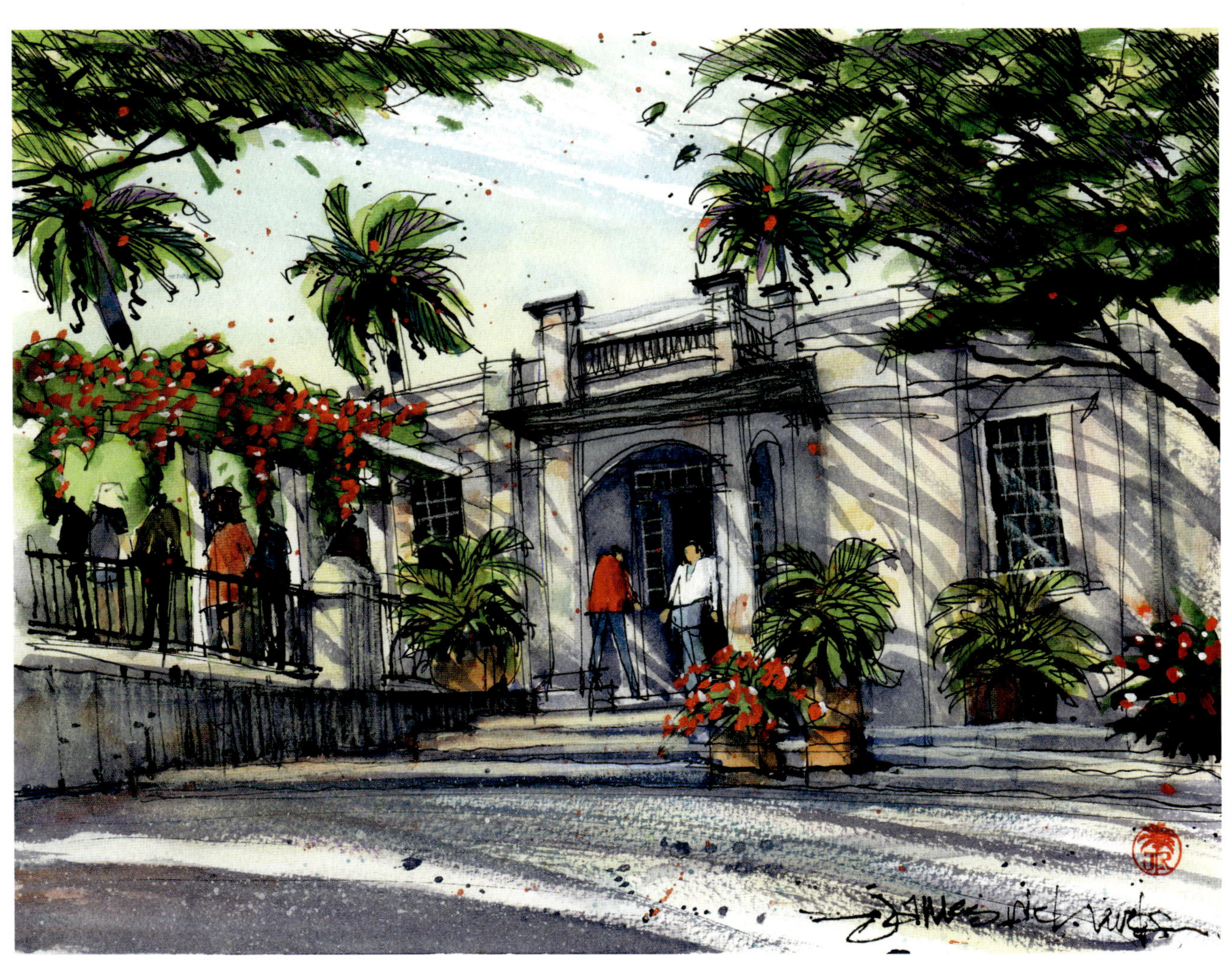

The entrance to the main house at Finca Vigia, Hemingway's 15-acre estate 12 miles outside Havana.

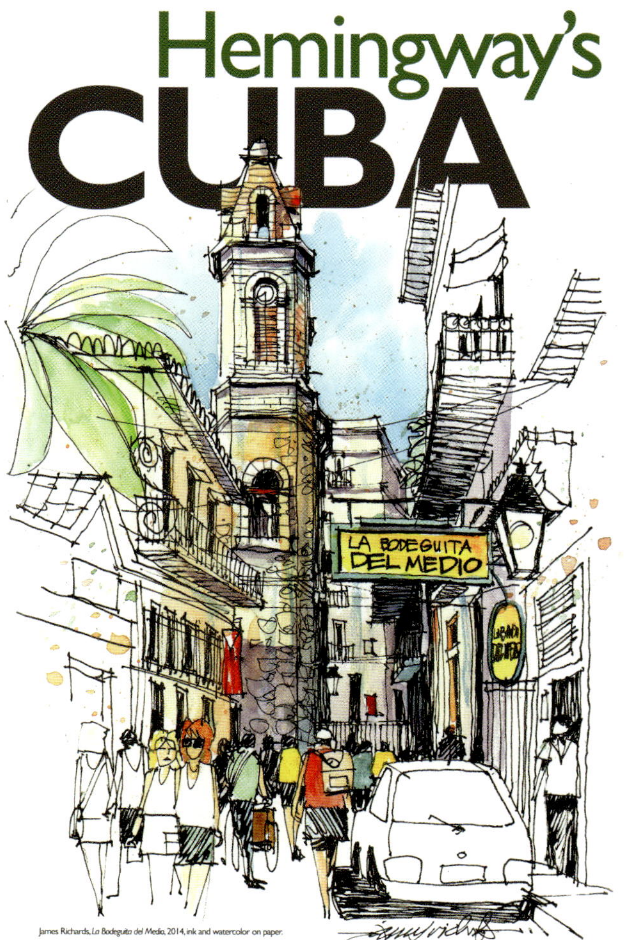

Bocetos de Viaje/Travel Sketches by **James Richards**

Del 4 al 22 de Junio, 2015

Museo Ernest Hemingway. Finca Vigía. San Francisco de Paula. Cuba.

La vida y la escritura de Hemingway siempre han sido un atractivo para los aventureros de espíritu, en parte porque el espíritu de Hemingway sigue siendo una presencia palpable allí. El propósito de Hemingway, fue siempre el de encontrar lugares propicios para su escritura como Paris, Key West, por mencionar algunos. Sin embargo, fue en Cuba, donde vivió y trabajó más que en ningún otro lugar. Estas acuarelas son una exploración de esa fusión entre 'lugar y creatividad'. Estas obras ofrecen una visión de los entornos que alimentaron la imaginación de Hemingway y por consiguiente la creación de algunas de sus mejores obras literarias.

Hemingway's writing and life have long beckoned the adventurous in spirit. Likewise, Cuba is a place of fascination for intrepid travelers, in part because Hemingway's spirit remains a palpable presence there. Hemingway was drawn to places conducive to his writing—Paris and Key West, among others—but he lived and worked in Cuba longer than in any other setting. These watercolor sketches are an exploration of the intersection of place and creativity, and offer an eyewitness's look at many of the largely unchanged settings that fueled Hemingway's imagination and some of his best writing.

"You could tell them you live in Cuba because…you work as well there in those cool early mornings as you ever have worked anywhere in the world."

--Ernest Hemingway, "The Great Blue River"

Poster Design by Ryan M. Brown

The poster for my 2015 solo art exhibition, "Hemingway's Cuba," held at Finca Vigia, the author's home outside Havana.

The exhibition reception still feels surreal. My watercolor drawings stood on tall wooden easels in the first-floor room of Hemingway's four-story writing tower, built as a gift by his fourth wife but rarely used. A steady stream of guests—dignitaries from Cuba's tourism authority, invitees from Havana, locals from the surrounding towns, our own artists, and Cuba's national media—filed through the smallish space, taking time to look over each image, and often calling me over to ask a question or to tell me a personal story about the subject of the drawing. The Cubans in attendance seemed delighted. Even uniformed security, holding a no- nonsense, straight-ahead stare, allowed me to pin a "Sketch CUBA" button on their uniforms (which quickly disappeared when I walked away).

We finished the affair with toasts, drinks, and more stories on the large, pergola-covered terrace dripping with bougainvillea in bloom—the same terrace I knew from photos of Hemingway holding court there with friends.

In the course of my three visits, I fell in love with Cuba, as Hemingway did: with the landscape, with Havana's architecture and street life, with the addictive music, with the beautiful mountains and tobacco plantations in the west, mangos, cigars, and Havana Club rum. Recognizing the crushing poverty and direly limited opportunities, I admired the exuberant spirit of the local people, especially the artists. These soulful qualities of the place predate the revolution. Hell, they long predate Batista. To me, that's the real Cuba. That Cuba will be there long after the revolution fades.

I was happy that my work had been well-received by locals who knew and loved this place. No surprise, really, if you're taking the time to truly observe and draw the place they love. It speaks to respect for the place they've spent their lives, and a mutual appreciation for some of the things that make it special, which can lead to a mutual respect for each other. The sketches are the cultural bridge. As always, it's about much more than the pictures.

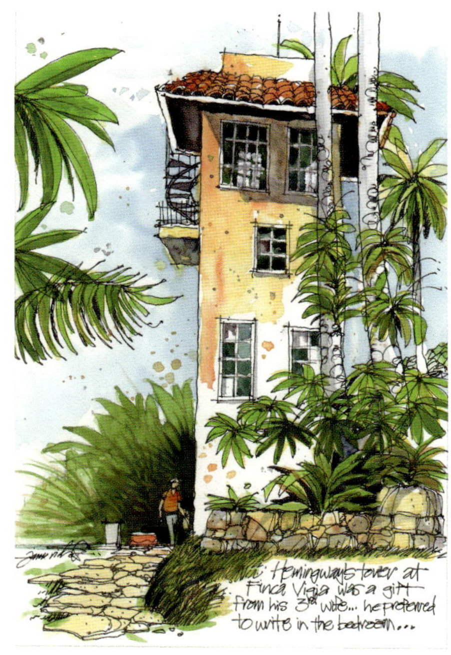

This tower was built by Hemingway's fourth wife, Mary Welsh, as a writing retreat with a view to the gulf several miles away. He preferred to write standing at the typewriter on his bedroom bookcase; the tower was enjoyed by the cats. The ground floor of the tower was where my solo exhibition was held.

Papa Doble

(Hemingway's Double Daiquiri, Circa 1947)

- 3 ¾ oz. white rum
- 2 oz. fresh lime juice
- 1 oz. fresh grapefruit juice
- 6 drops maraschino liqueur
- No sugar

Shake well with ice. Pour into a large, chilled goblet. Hemingway's improvements to the classic daiquiri recipe, perfected with Floridita bartender and owner Constantino Ribalaigua, included no sugar and double rum (hence Papa Doble). The Floridita and the Papa Doble made memorable appearances in Hemingway's novel *Islands in the Stream*, including an epic daiquiri binge by the book's protagonist, painter Thomas Hudson. Hemingway's personal record was 17 in one sitting.

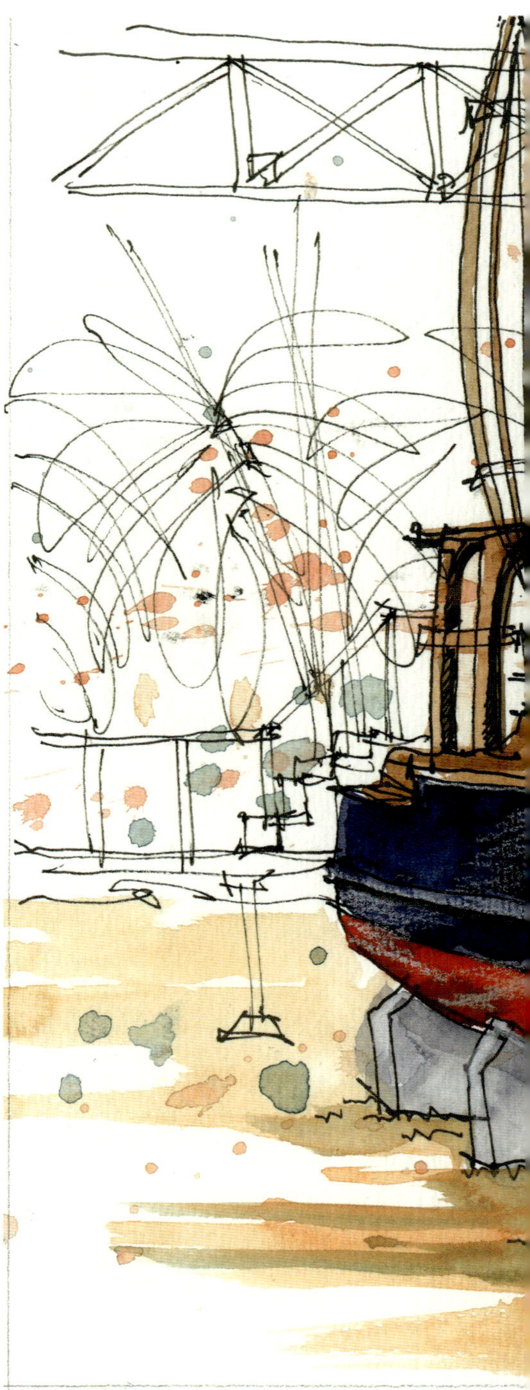

Hemingway's prized fishing boat, *Pilar,* is fully restored and sits in dry dock at Finca Vigia.

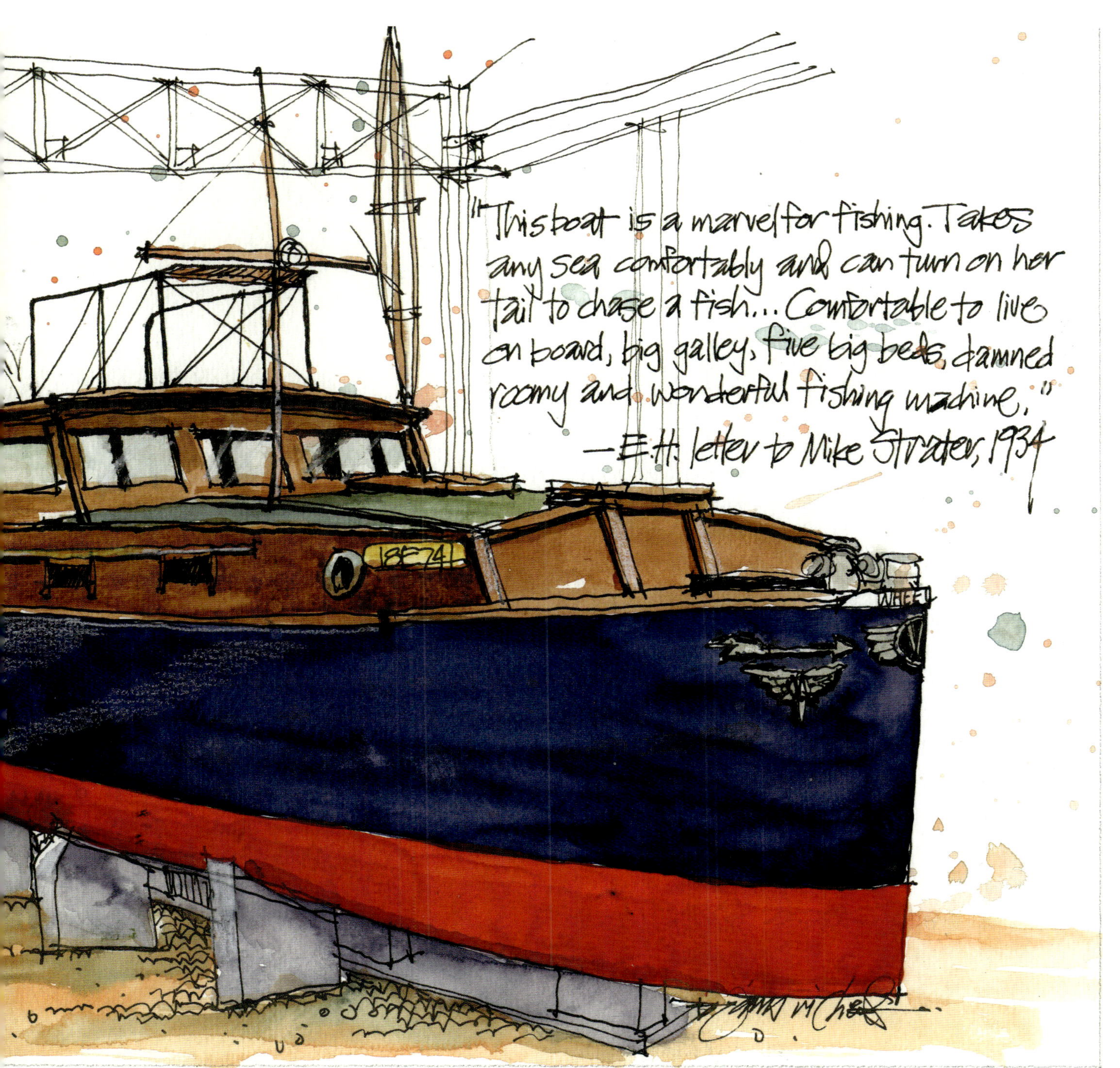
"This boat is a marvel for fishing. Takes any sea comfortably and can turn on her tail to chase a fish... Comfortable to live on board, big galley, five big beds, damned roomy and wonderful fishing machine."
—E.H. letter to Mike Strater, 1934
18E741

The Sketcher's Code

Have an idea

Or walk around and make small thumbnail sketches of the area until you find one. You'll know it when you see it. That's what my friend reportage artist Veronica Lawlor told me was "The Decisive Moment." See if you can articulate the idea in one sentence. Jot it down. Draw the parts of the scene that contribute to the idea. Ignore or downplay the parts that don't. Sometimes that's easy, sometimes it's not. But an idea can become a guide for choosing what and how much of a scene to draw. And it can become a yardstick to measure how true your sketch is to your idea. The idea elevates your sketch from a good or bad likeness of what's in front of you to communicating a story and point of view.

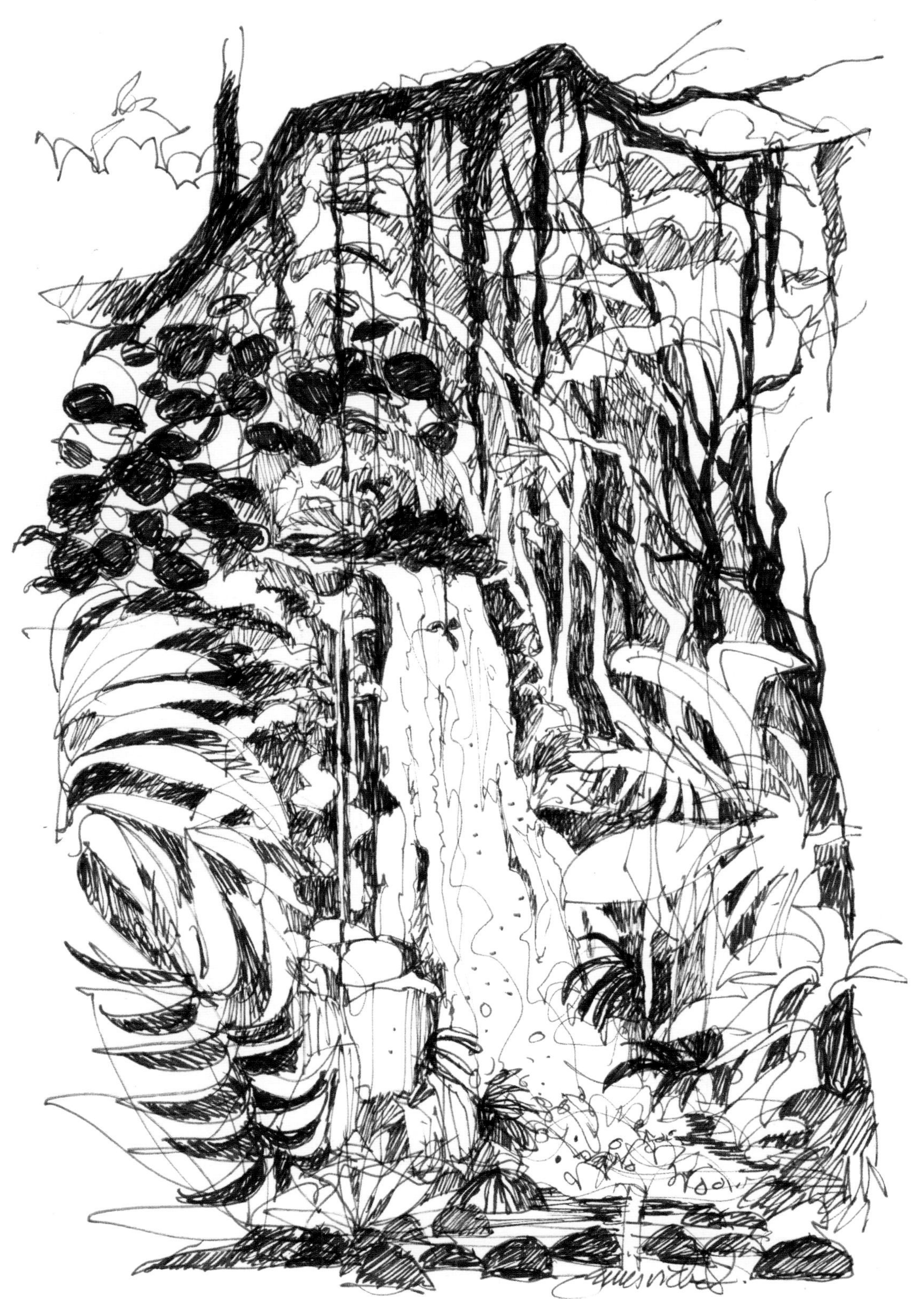

Costa Rica.

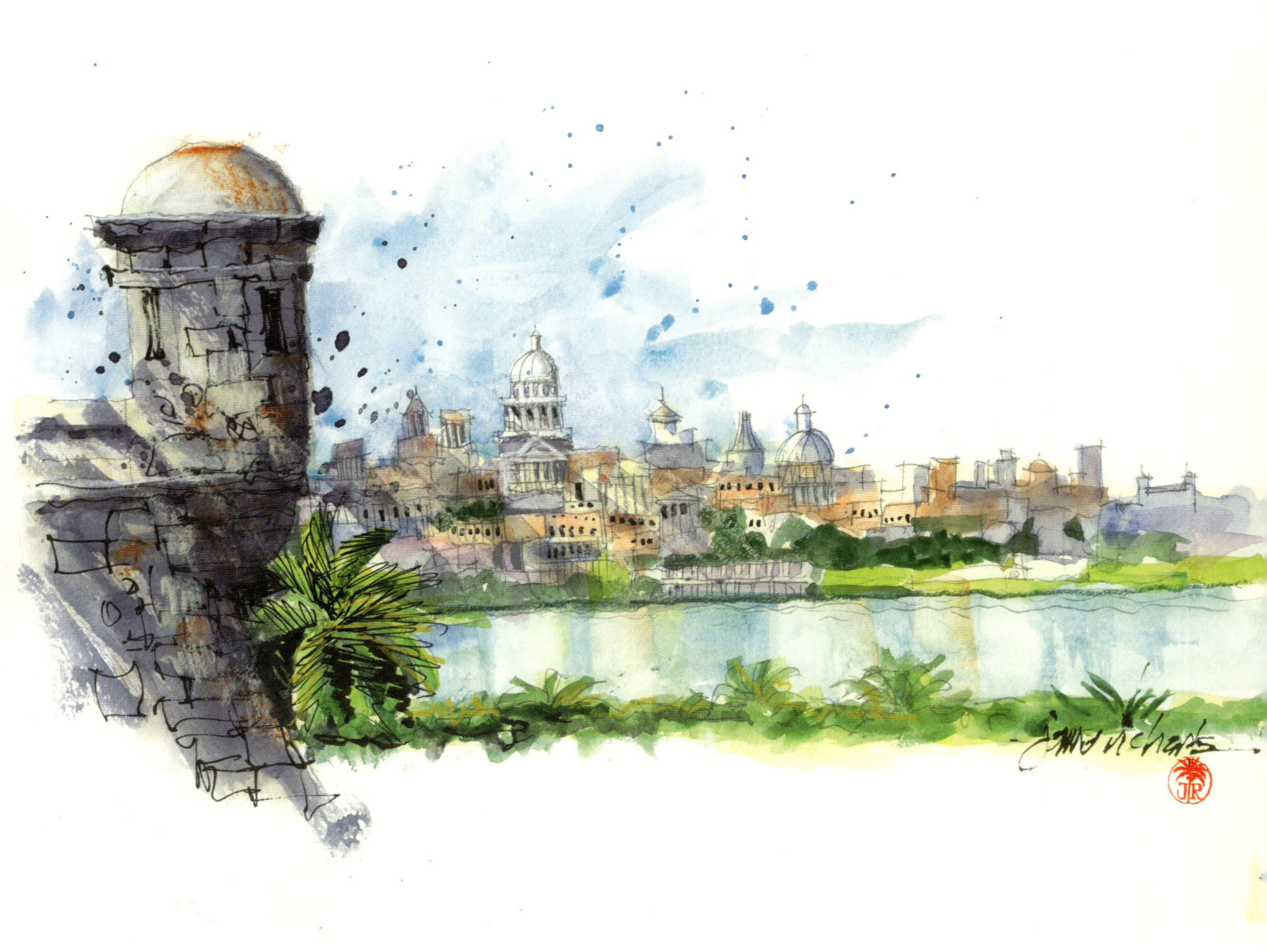

CHAPTER 4

Cuba: Busted in Havana

STANDING IN THE CUSTOMS interrogation room of Havana's Jose Marti International Airport, I knew three things to be true:

1. My large, tightly packed box of 13 framed paintings, fresh from my three-week solo exhibition "Hemingway's Cuba," had been confiscated.

2. My payment for a bribe of unspecified amount requested by our gate agent clearly hadn't been enough.

3. The customs agents who had followed me into the room were not happy.

The room was bare except for a desk, the uniformed woman behind it, and a single empty chair. There might have been the single bare lightbulb hanging from the ceiling like in the movies, or I may just reimagine it that way. The expression and body language of the agent behind the desk conveyed clearly that whatever trouble I was in was serious. The gravity of the situation hit me. My romantic notion of being an artist traveler in the footsteps of my drawing heroes never included jail time in Cuba.

The agent behind the desk spoke sternly in the distinctly Cuban dialect of Spanish that was beyond the very limited grasp of the language I had from school days. I responded with my well-practiced phrase, "Lo

Opposite: The Havana skyline seen from the San Carlos del la Cabaña fortress.

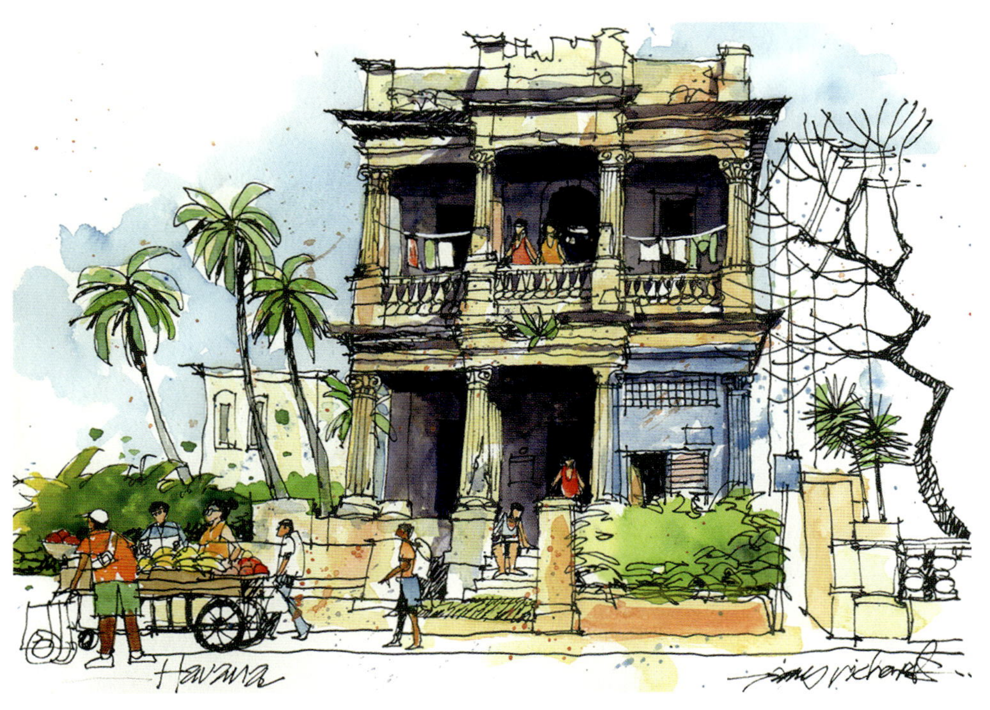

A once elegant mansion in Havana
that now houses several families.

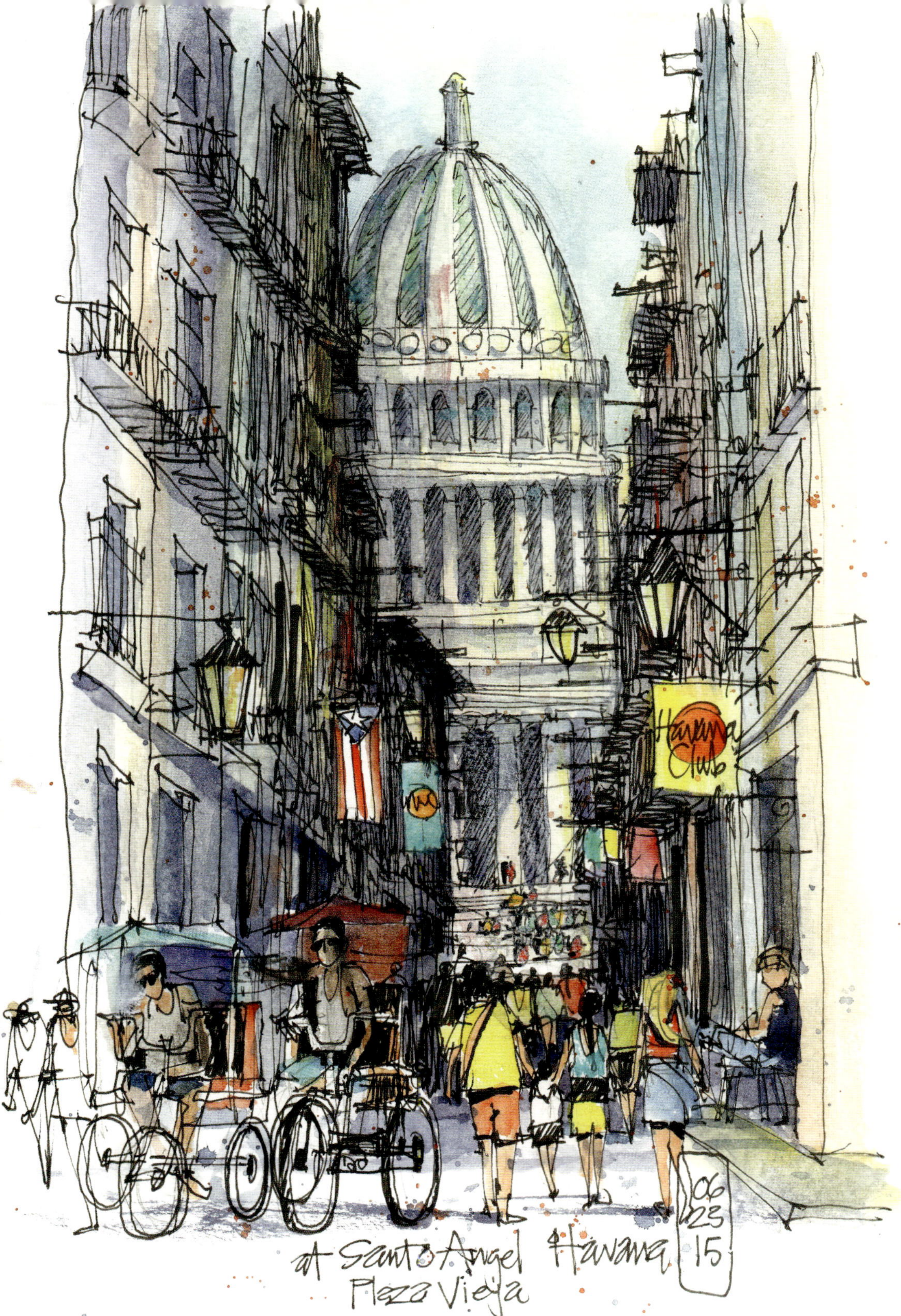

The view and sketch of Capitolio Nacional, Cuba's national capitol, from a café table in Plaza Viejo.

siento, pero yo hablo Español un poquito solamente," which translates something like, "I'm sorry, but I speak Spanish a little only." We volleyed this exchange back and forth, the customs agent growing louder and more insistent each time. Clearly the situation was sliding downhill.

My romantic notion of being an artist traveler in the footsteps of my drawing heroes never included jail time in Cuba.

A second agent and then a third shot questions at me, each more agitated than the one before. One put her nose uncomfortably close to mine and yelled her questions very slowly—in Spanish, of course—so that this hapless gringo might grasp a clue. Still, no breakthrough. Finally, a fourth agent stepped through the door, crossed her arms, and leaned back against the doorframe. She narrowed her eyes, glared with cool disdain and said curtly, "What?"

"Oh, thank God!" I said. "I've just completed an art exhibition at Hemingway's home. That box is my art and somehow, it's ended up..."

She interrupted, "You did not declare this box."

"I did! I completed every form requested I..."

"You did NOT declare the box."

"Look, I filled out every form, I checked it at the gate, the guy said it was all good!"

"This— 'guy.' Did you tip him?"

Shit. Here it is, I thought. How I answer will determine the story from this point forward. Growing up in South Louisiana and having worked in the border region of South Texas, I was familiar with wink and nod transactions. We all know what's going on here.

I grinned at the agent and said, "Of course!"

As I'd hoped, my interrogators laughed, but it was the kind of laughter that, in the classic standoffs in old Westerns, precedes a sudden melee of gunfire with ugly results. Instead, the glare returned.

"Señor, tell me what is in the box."

"I already told you, it's art."

She came closer and leaned in. "Señor, it will go much better for you if you tell me what is in the box."

Shit. "It's ART!"

She glanced outside the door and, with a nod of the head, signaled another agent waiting outside. A tall, uniformed man entered. They exchanged a couple of words. He put my box on the desk and pulled a long folding knife from the front pocket of his pants. I visibly cringed as he cut open the top and two sides of the box, where only the edges of the stacked frames were visible. He reached for the top frame. "Por favor!" I said. He hesitated long enough for me to reach past him for the box myself. I slowly slid out the top frame, set it on the desk, and pulled back its brown paper wrapping to reveal the painting.

I heard a gasp. Then, "Aye! Que bonita! Mira, mira!" The other agents gathered around, staring at the painting, then looking at each other. The

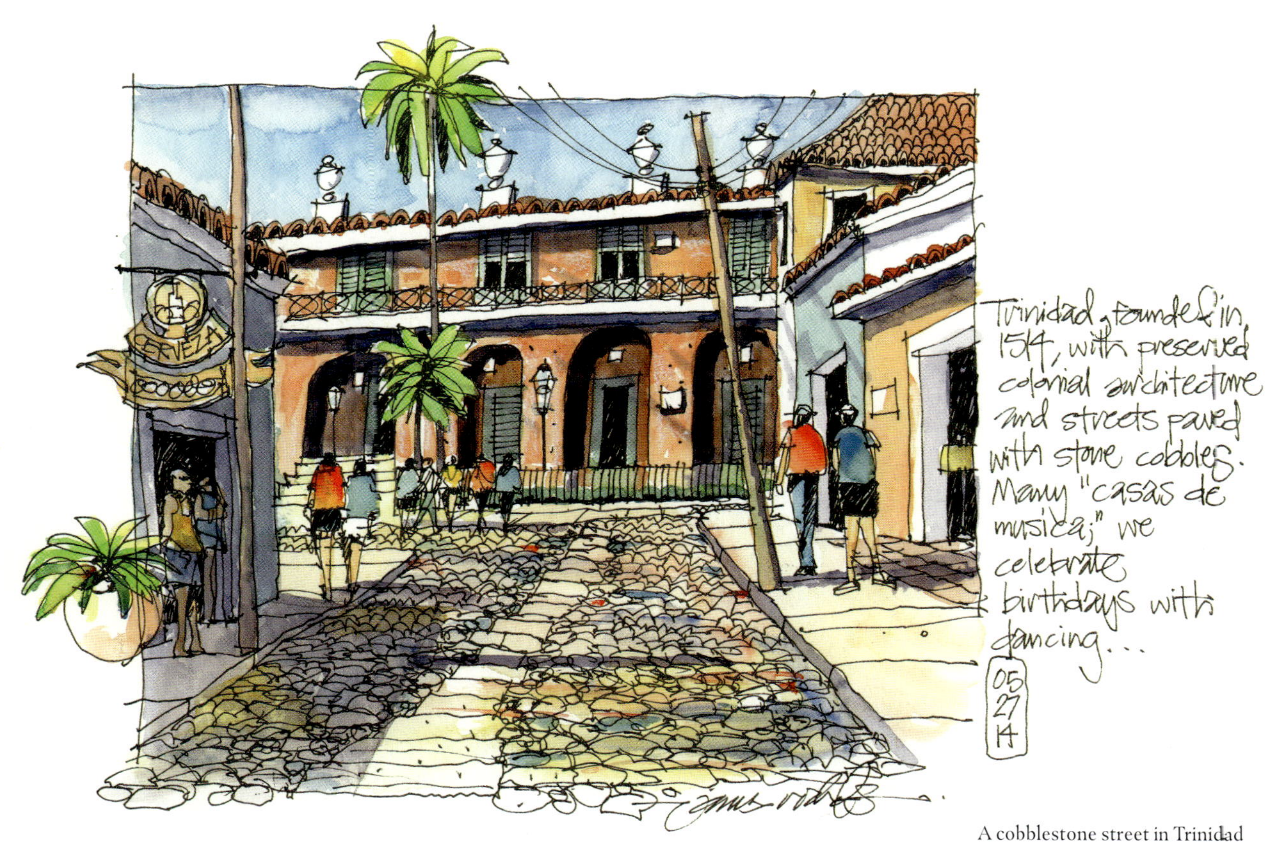

A cobblestone street in Trinidad in Central Cuba, a well-preserved colonial town founded in 1514.

man with the knife studied the painting, then looked at me. He said, in slow, broken English, "My—my uncle—he worked in this tavern. My brother—he has a car—like this one."

"Yes!" I said.

The agent behind the desk pointed at the other paintings in the box. "Mas, mas!" She wanted more. I removed a second painting, then a third. The group removed the paper from the frames and chattered excitedly.

The agent at the door abruptly halted show-and-tell. "Okay, stop!" she said in English. Raising her voice, she said, "How do I know these are your paintings? How do I know you're not stealing this art from my country?"

Okay, fair question. I asked to approach the doorway. She signaled permission with a sideways jerk of her head. I looked out the door and there, sitting a few tables from the door, was Patti. Our eyes locked.

"Bring me the sketchbooks," I said.

After some hurried rummaging through my carry-on, she pulled my current sketchbook and brought it to the door. The agent took it, turned it over in her hands for a brief look, then took it to the desk. The tall man opened the book to the last page. It was a sketch of El Malecon, the broad esplanade, boulevard, and seawall that curves along downtown Havana's shoreline. I'd made an ink drawing of the panoramic view the day before from our hotel balcony.

"El Malecon!" he said. After studying the sketch, he pointed out recognizable buildings in the drawing to the others, naming each, and they exchanged questions and comments in Spanish. Then he pointed to the date in the corner of the sketch and looked at me. "Yesterday," he said in English. "Yes, yesterday," I said. He flipped the page to the next sketch. Again, he pointed to the date in the corner. "Day—before," he said. "Yes," I said. "Day before yesterday."

With the others gathered around to watch, he flipped through the pages, pausing and pointing to parts of each drawing. They chatted away excitedly. Okay, this is good, I thought. I tried to respond their questions as best I could. In relatively short order, and against all odds, the sketchbook was calming the situation.

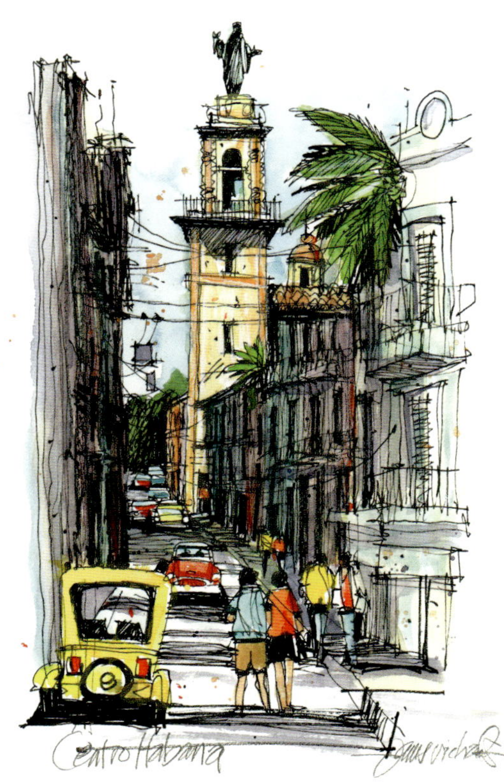

A street view sketch focused on the bell tower of Iglesia de Nuestra Senora del Carmen church, a landmark in the Centro Habana borough of Havana.

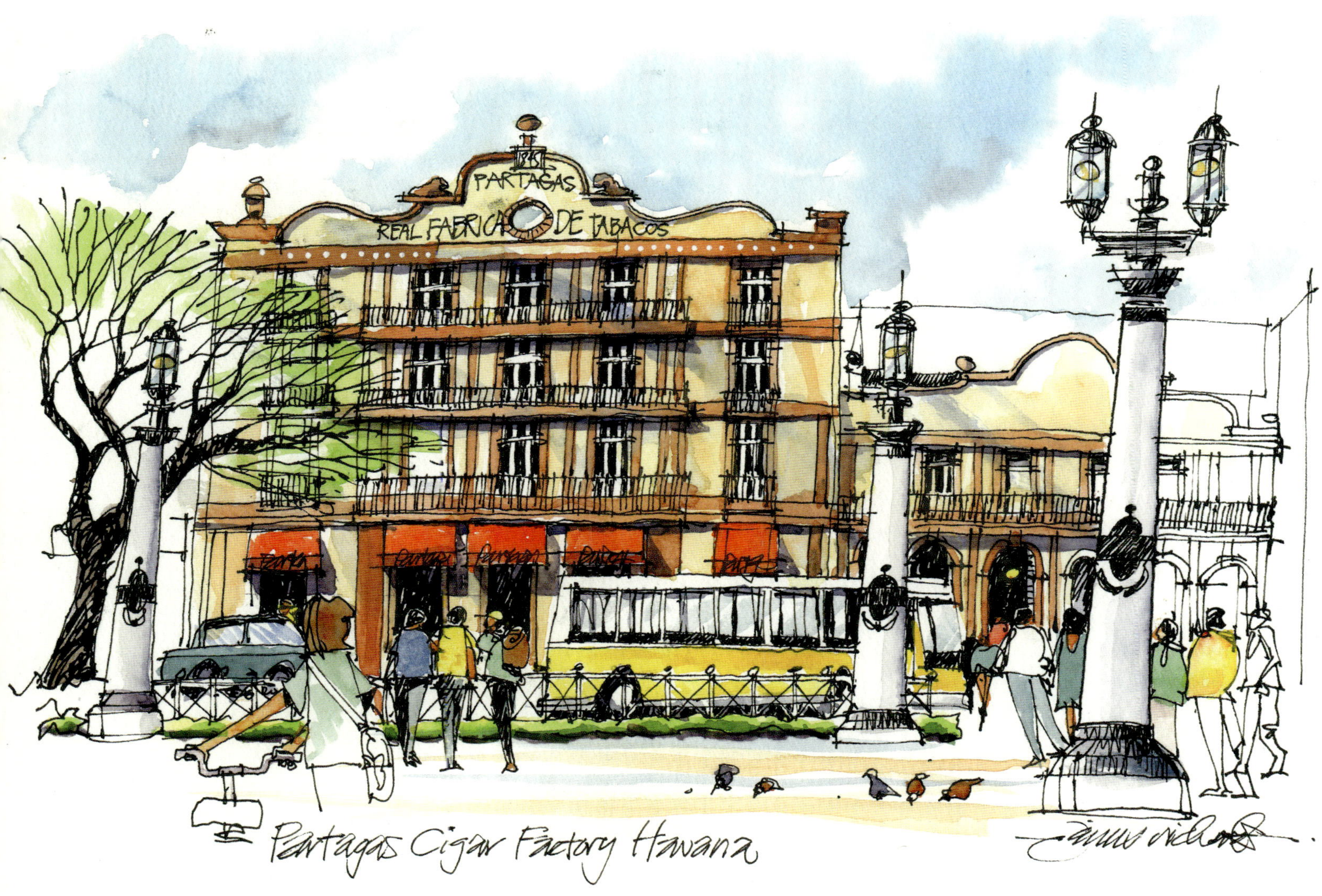

Cigar aficionados around the world recognize the name Partagás. This ornate building behind the Capitolio is the original factory location of the Real Fábrica de Tabacos Partagás, one of the oldest and best-known cigar businesses in Cuba and throughout the world.

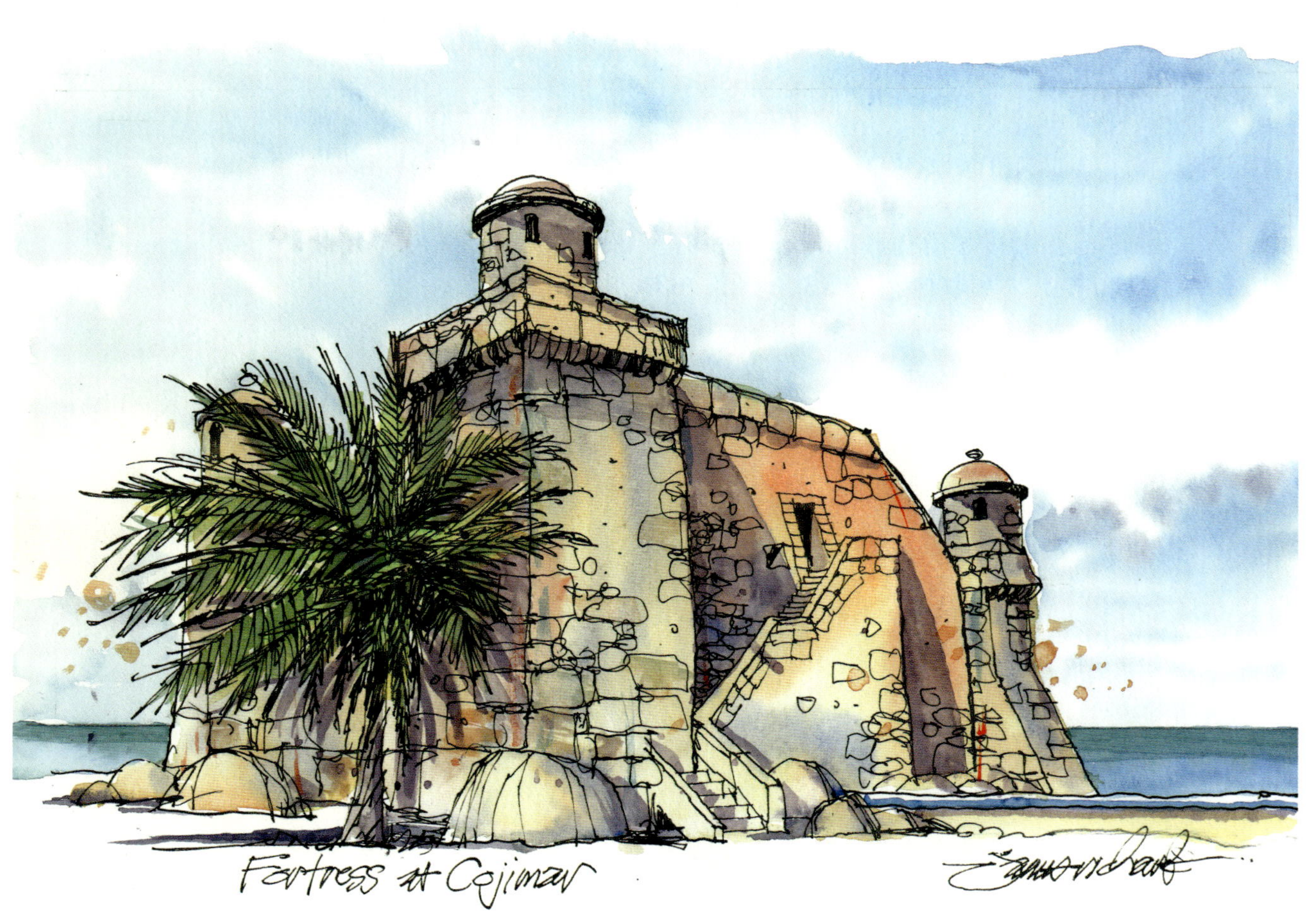

A small Spanish fortress at the fishing village of Cojimar, a stone's throw from where Hemingway kept his fishing boat *Pilar.* It was built in 1649 to protect the coast from the English and pirates, which the Spanish at that time would have said were interchangeable terms.

A few minutes later, the agent behind the desk approached me. She spoke in Spanish. Her tone was calm, but the meaning of her words was still beyond me. Frustrated and still a little nervous, I glanced back to the door, where a small group of concerned American students had gathered around Patti.

"Anyone speak Spanish?" Two girls approached.

"Could you translate for me?" The agent repeated her message. One of the girls turned to me.

"She says, the next time you come to her country, be sure you come to this office first, because she wants to see more of your art."

The agent nodded. Wow. I've seen this time and again: the ability of humble sketchbook drawings to transcend differences in language, culture, even ideology. I'd seen a sketch of someone's city capture their attention, open a conversation, and begin to lower the cultural walls between us. Mutual appreciation and respect slowly start to emerge. And it's clear, in that moment, that this isn't about the drawings. There's a larger story happening here.

I smiled and nodded at the agent and said, "I'll be back."

El Malecon, Havana

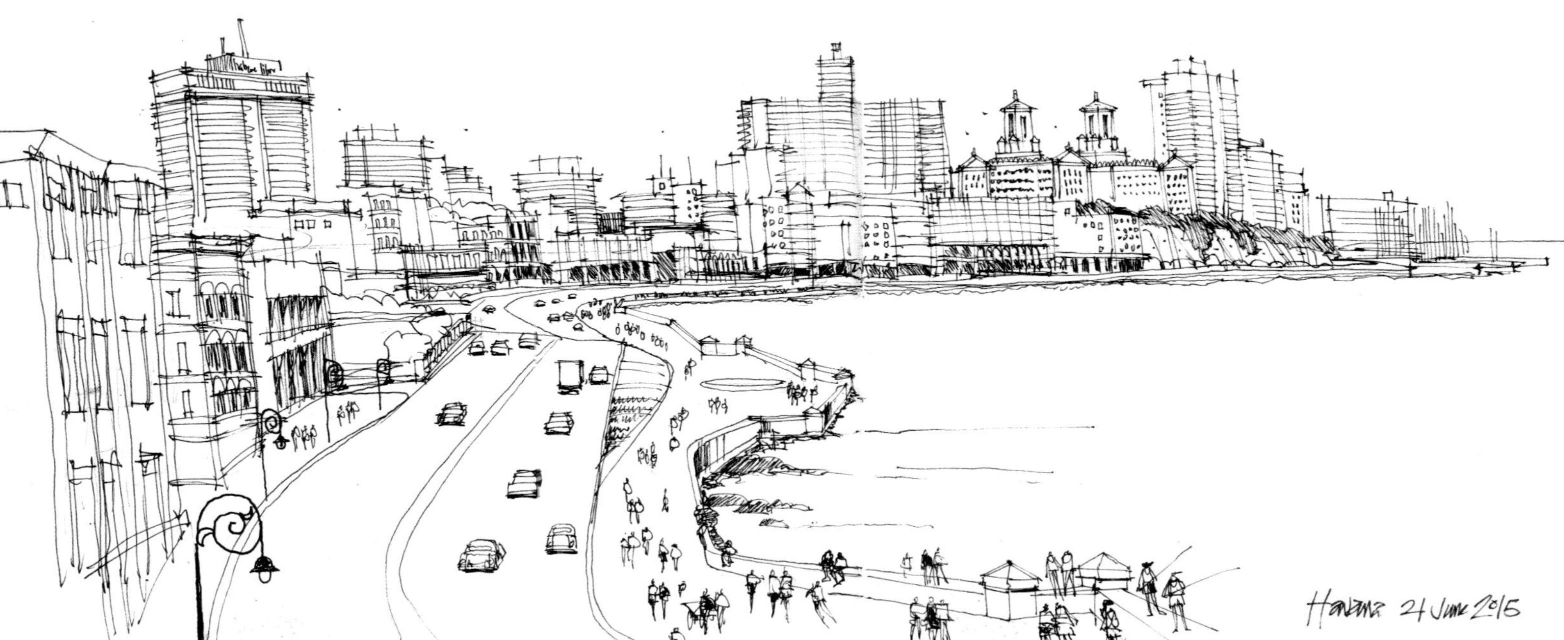

When is the drawing finished?

Great question, and I think it's a universal issue across the entire spectrum of creative endeavor. I have to admit, after decades of drawing professionally, it's one I still struggle with. As I'm trying to bring a drawing in for a landing, I can often hear a little angel on one shoulder and a little devil on the other, carrying on an increasingly loud and annoying conversation:

Angel (in Mrs. Doubtfire voice): "This drawing is beautiful! It's finished. Walk away."

Devil (in harsh Disney villain voice): "No! Don't walk away! Keep drawing! Keep putting more black on it! That's what it needs!" Angel: "No, no, no. It's very nice. Well done. Walk away."

Devil: "NO! DON'T BE STUPID! KEEP DRAWING!"

And a melee ensues in my mind. If the devil wins, I'll add a few more strokes, or a bit of black. And a bit more black. Or I'll try to rework a watercolor wash, just a bit. And just like that, I'm screwed. Send this one to the Island of Overworked Art.

Less isn't always more, but it's a good going in position when you start a drawing. Try to say what you want to say with the fewest lines and tones possible. Ask what's essential. Go for a spare elegance. I try to keep in mind a maxim attributed to Antoine de Saint- Exupéry, the author of *The Little Prince* : "Perfection isn't achieved when there's nothing more to add, but when there's nothing left to take away." Sounds a little heavy for leaning against a lamppost sketching, but it's a pretty good adage for most things, actually.

Especially when you start to hear that devil whispering.

The Hotel Nacional de Cuba, opened in 1933, has one of the most storied histories in the industry, including a military siege, an epic mob summit dramatized in *The Godfather Part 2*, its casino and celebrity heyday years in the 1950s, and its decline and hard times post-Revolution. Our workshop group of sketch artists stayed there in 2015 and found it a fascinating trip back in time. The hotel wears its history and palpable authenticity proudly, like an elegant if faded tuxedo. I found it an experience well worth repeating.

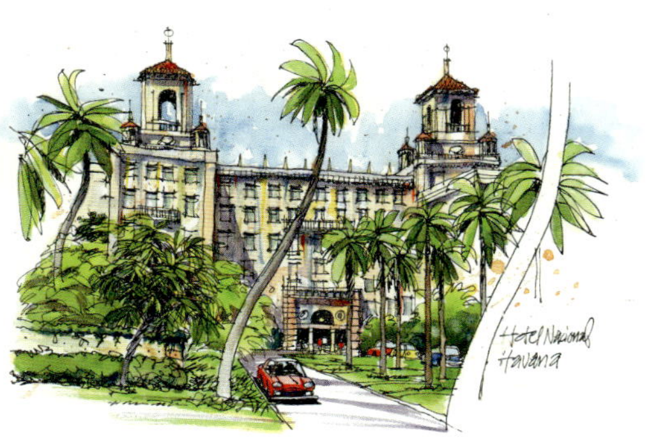

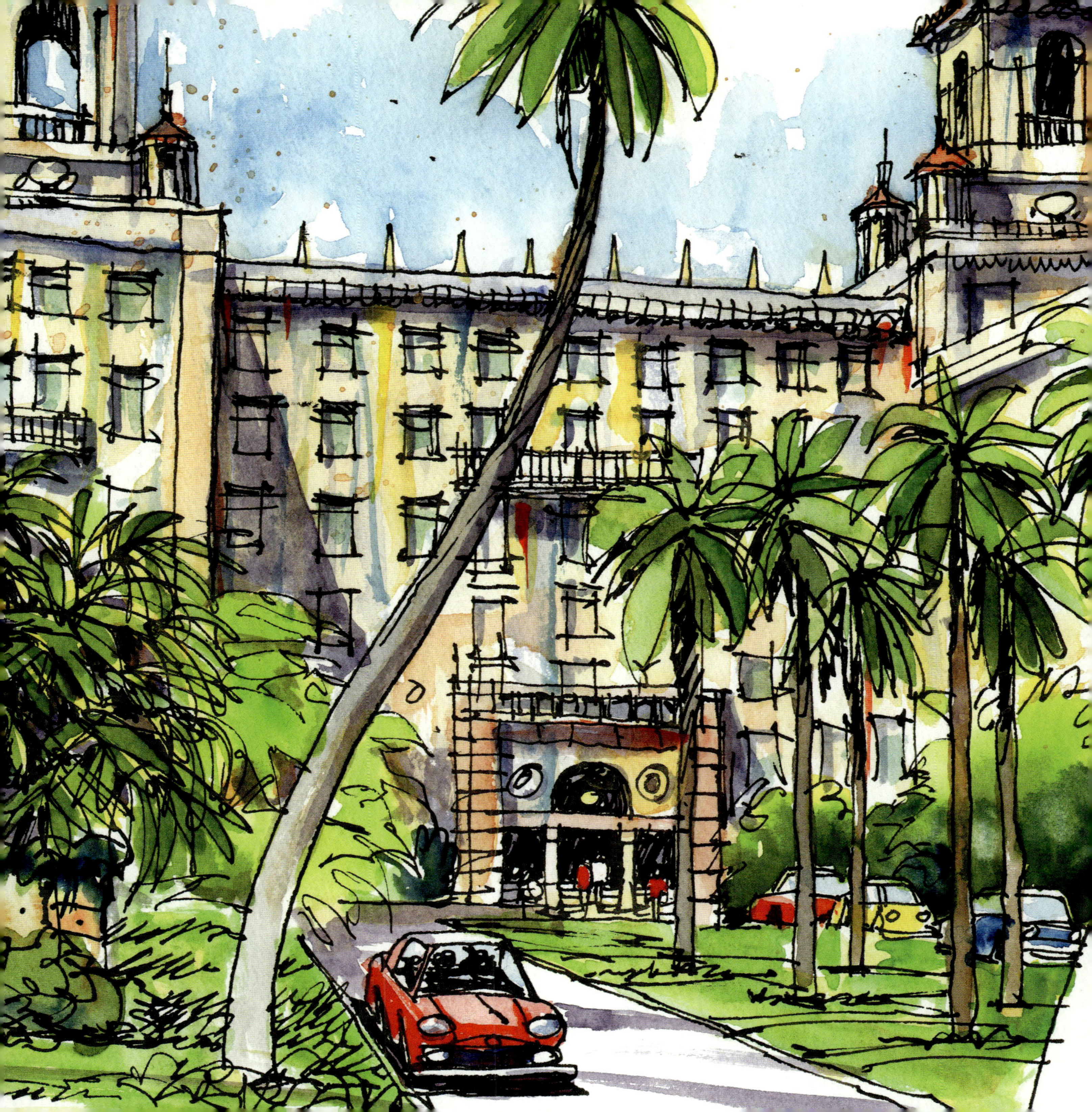

The Sketcher's Code

Notice everything.

A traveling artist should observe and take in the world like a writer.Notice everything. Take visual notes in the form of small thumbnail sketches with a few thoughts jotted down. Look for the big picture as well as the details, sounds, smells, snippets of conversation, and energy.Especially energy. What's the vibe? Paying attention and editing your work down to what you think is important can give your work a sense of authenticity that goes beyond a pretty picture, to transport the viewer into your world.

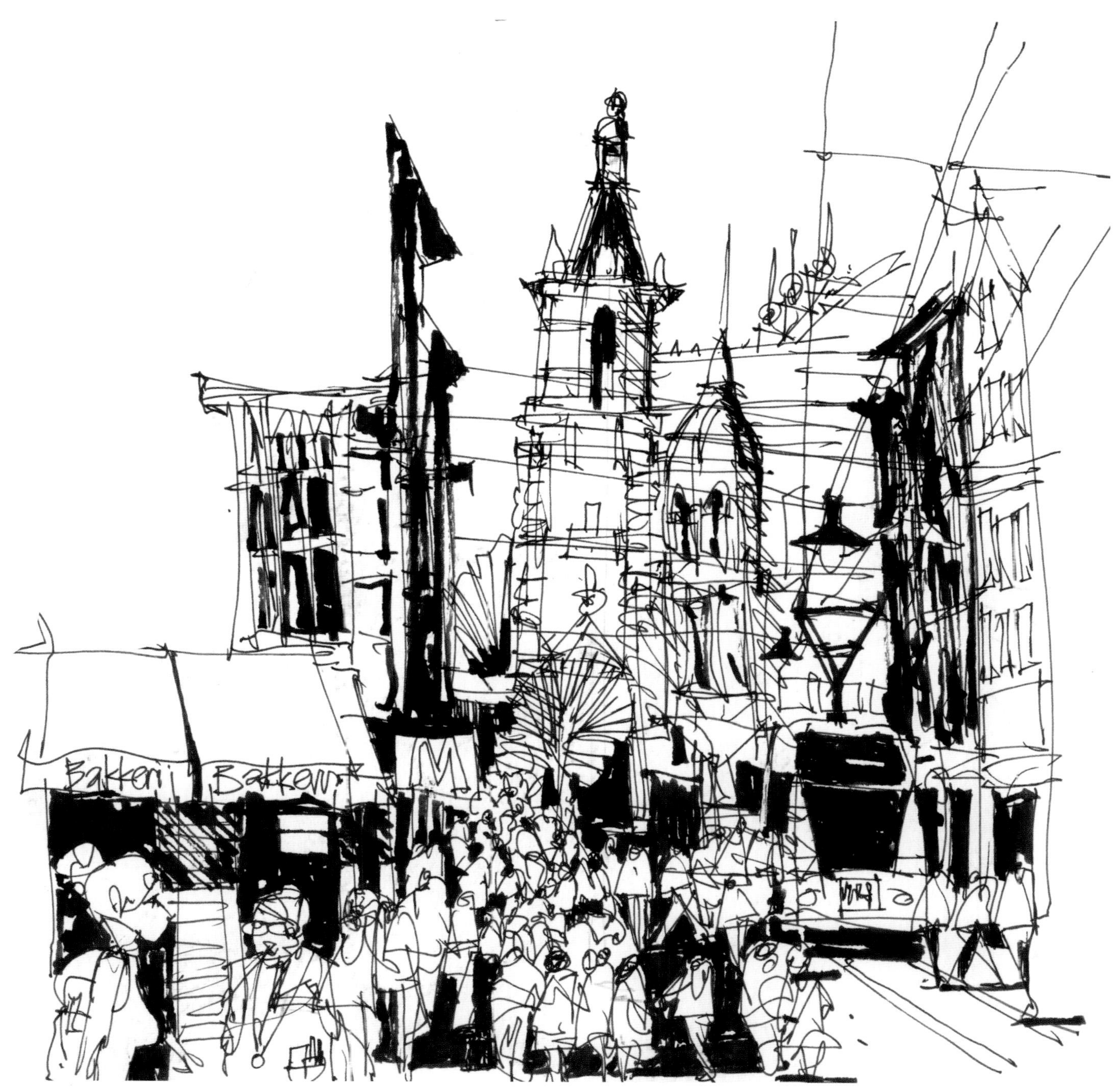

Amsterdam street.

• NATIONAL GEOGRAPHIC •
LINDBLAD EXPEDITIONS

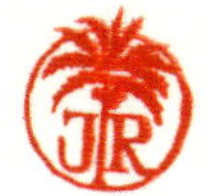

WHALES OF

MAGDALENA BAY

FEB 3 – 12, 2023

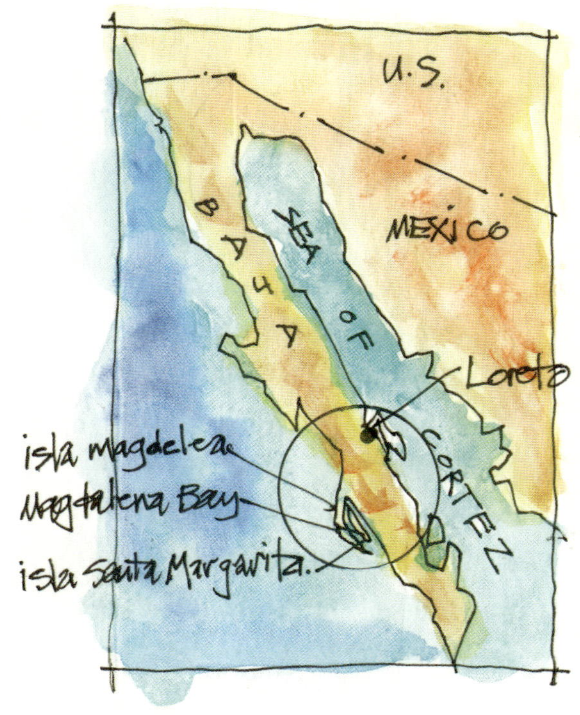

CHAPTER 5

Baja California: The Whales of Magdelena Bay

WE CALL IT "changing the backdrop." When the days and weeks start to look and feel the same and inspiration hits a wall, it's time to move—to put my body and my mind in a different place, literally. Sketching whales off Baja California will do that. The whole immersive "intrepid explorer" mystique surrounding a *National Geographic* excursion and sketching from an inflatable Zodiac speedboat with saltwater spray in your face can shake you out of the rut quickly.

This one was The Grown-up's idea. She loves travel as much as I do, and if she could add whale watching to every trip itinerary, she would. Basically, her pitch was, "You've got a birthday coming up. Trips are more fun than material things. Here's a *National Geographic* brochure on gray whale watching off Mexico. I think we should go for your birthday—you'll like it."

Okay, fair enough. Truth is, I have a soft spot for material things, but the *National Geographic* (NATGEO) angle made this a no-brainer. It promised a different kind of adventure: a small expedition ship with landing craft to access shorelines, staff naturalists and experts, and partnerships with local fishermen who are on intimate terms with the area and its waters. In addition to grays, we'd be searching for blue whales, the biggest damn life form ever to live on the planet.

It also provided a handy rationalization for me buying, well, more material things. I figured I'd need a different sketchbook that would allow drawing and notes more along the line of a scientific field journal than a collection of travel paintings—smaller, softcover, sturdy paper

Opposite: I wanted this sketchbook to more closely resemble the field notes of a scientist or explorer than one of my typical trip journals.

that could survive rain and wake splashes. I could justify a lot of new pens, right? Do we need a better camera? Maps and a guidebook, for sure. Maybe a new bag? One of the dirty secrets of travel sketchers is that many, if not most of us, have a bag fetish. I'm guilty as sin. The search for the perfect solution for carrying all your stuff is relentless and expensive. I have maybe 10 very nice bags gathering dust in the closet and a couple more that are my current favorites—until I find the next one. This was going to be a great birthday.

The whole, immersive "intrepid explorer" mystique surrounding a *National Geographic* excursion and sketching from an inflatable Zodiac speedboat with saltwater spray in your face can shake you out of the rut quickly.

Our itinerary took us from Tampa to Houston, across mainland Mexico and the Sea of Cortez to Loreto on the Baja peninsula. From there a NATGEO bus took us and our fellow travelers through the mountain passes and across the desert plain to San Carlos on Magdalena Bay, where we boarded the *National Geographic Seabird.* Seabird is no luxury cruise ship. It's a working boat with 31 cabins, a shallow draft to allow it to explore the close-in bays where whales spawn, and the inflatable Zodiac speedboats favored by Navy Seals. For our first excursion, however, we were picked up by the local fishermen who doubled as licensed whale watching guides in their six-passenger, heavy fiberglass panga fishing boats. Each had a NATGEO naturalist on board and an outboard motor that could carry it across the water like a bat out of hell.

We headed south and spotted spouting in Bahia Almehas bay. The Grown-up and I had seen pair of grays and a single pregnant humpback in the past. This was different— very different. A little background is appropriate.

The gray whale migration from the Bering Sea, along the Pacific coastlines of Canada, the U.S., and Mexico to Magdalena Bay is about 1500 miles. But this southern bay offers warm waters, is relatively protected, and has no real predators to speak of— ideal for mating and birthing. From January to March, the southern neck of the bay resembles what our naturalists call a raunchy singles bar, with horny whales showing off, courting, and copulating. The males seem particularly fond of exposing their impressive manhood in the most public of ways, and

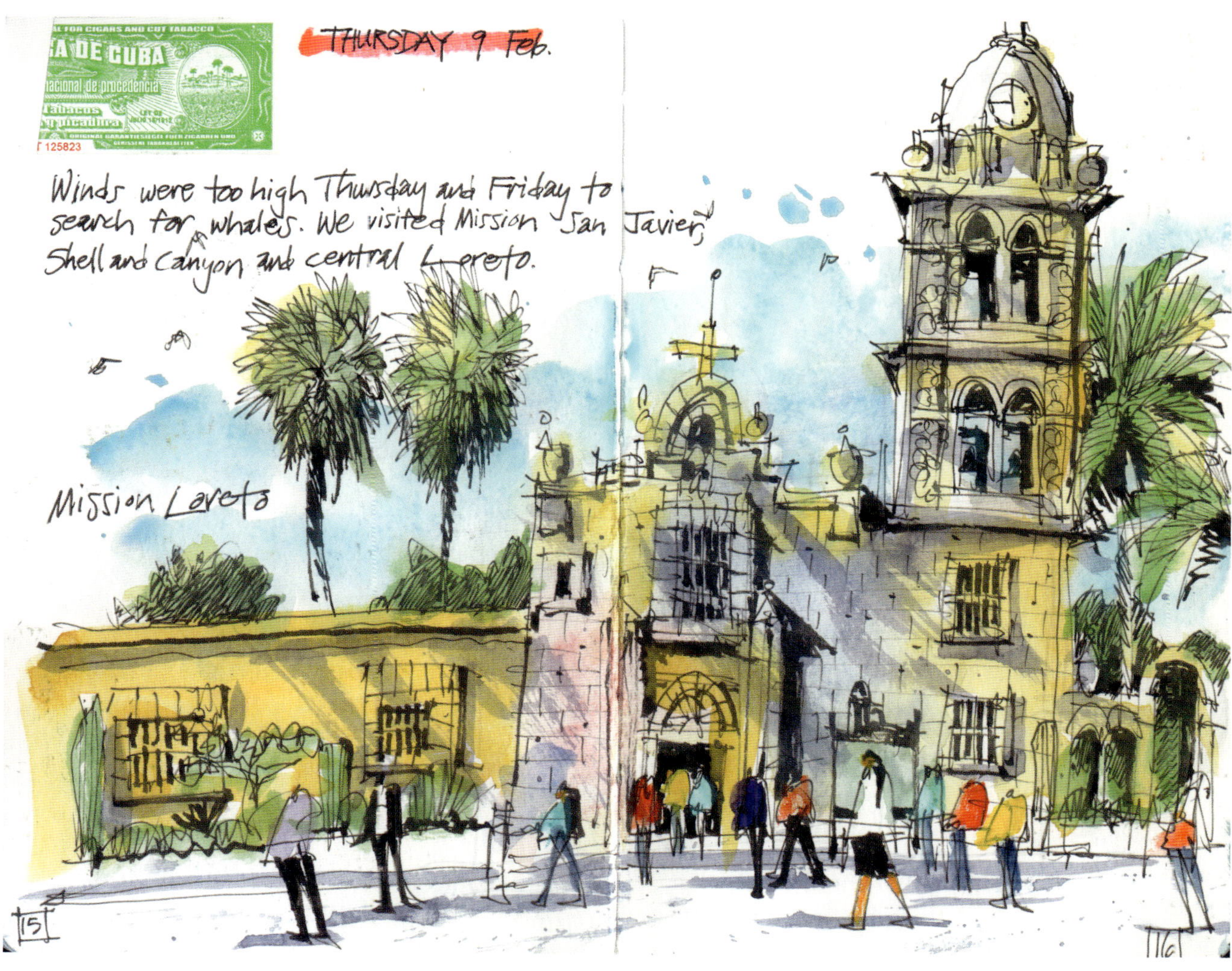

after witnessing this, who can blame them? If all this isn't enough to coax the pods down from Alaska, what would?

Trying to draw in choppy seas forced me to abandon any hope of elegant sketches and to embrace the simple shapes, wonky lines, and sense of immediacy that I was able to capture while rocking on the waves. The sounds of blowholes spouting completely surrounded us.

A mission church in the town of Loreto, where we landed and caught our bus across the Baja peninsula to Magdelena Bay.

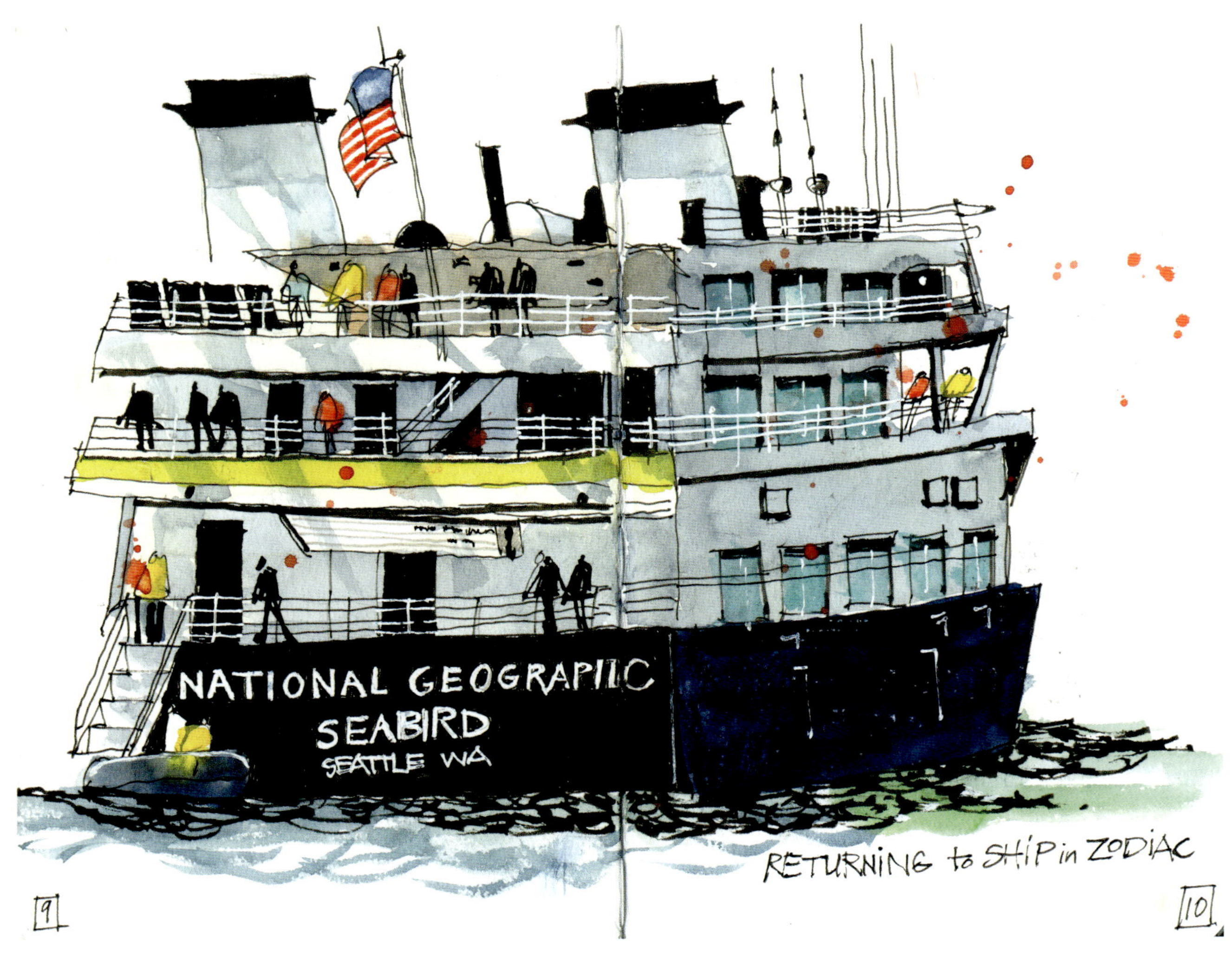

The *National Geographic Seabird*, seen from an inflatable Zodiac boat.

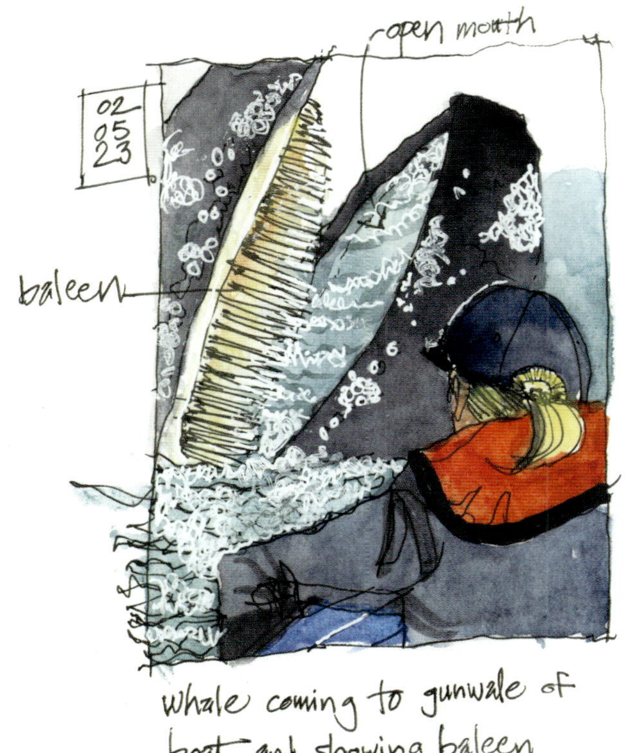

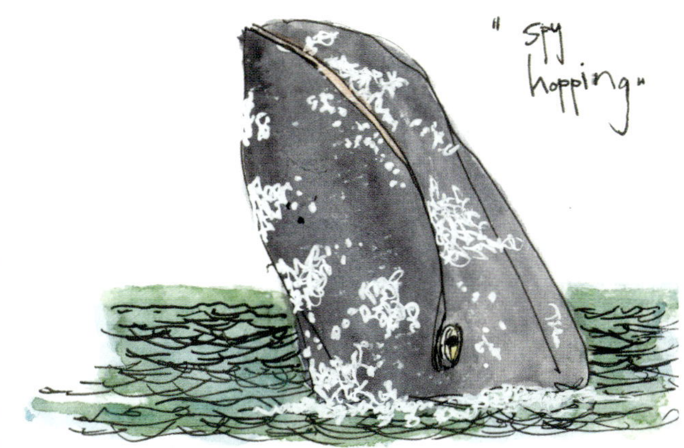

Whales cruised along the surface with backs exposed, raised flippers and flukes out of the water, and engaged in a behavior called "spy-hopping," where they'd slowly raise the front third of their body vertically out of the water to take a look around, then slide back down. No one seems to know why they do this. That's okay. The natural world should always have some mystery to it.

The grays are inquisitive during mating season; both adults and calves approached the boats. Others were "spy hopping," presumably to have a look around at the world above the surface.

Our first excursions in the pangas were a lesson in sketching from small open boats in choppy seas—a humbling experience. Gray whales seemed to be everywhere we looked.

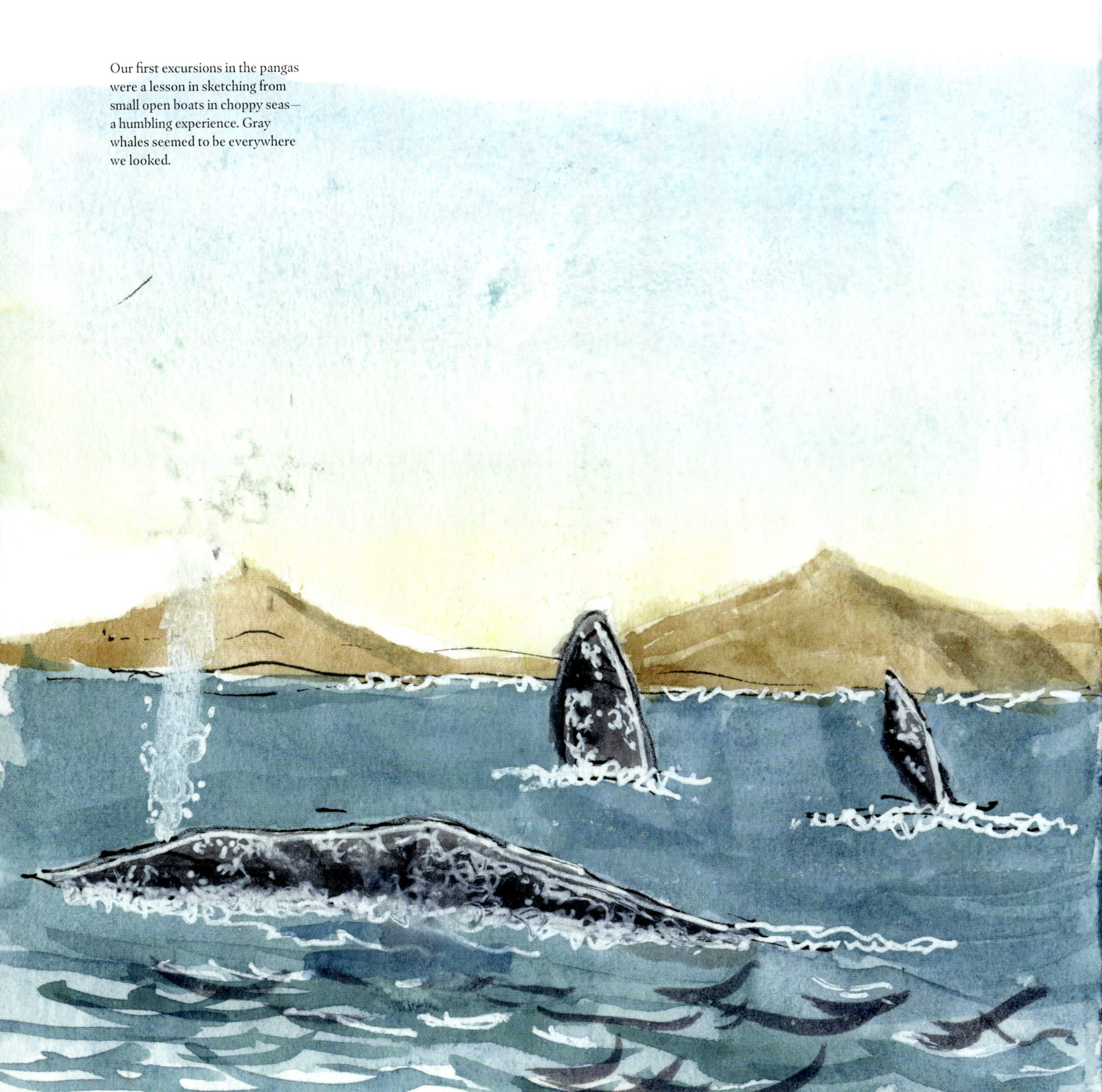

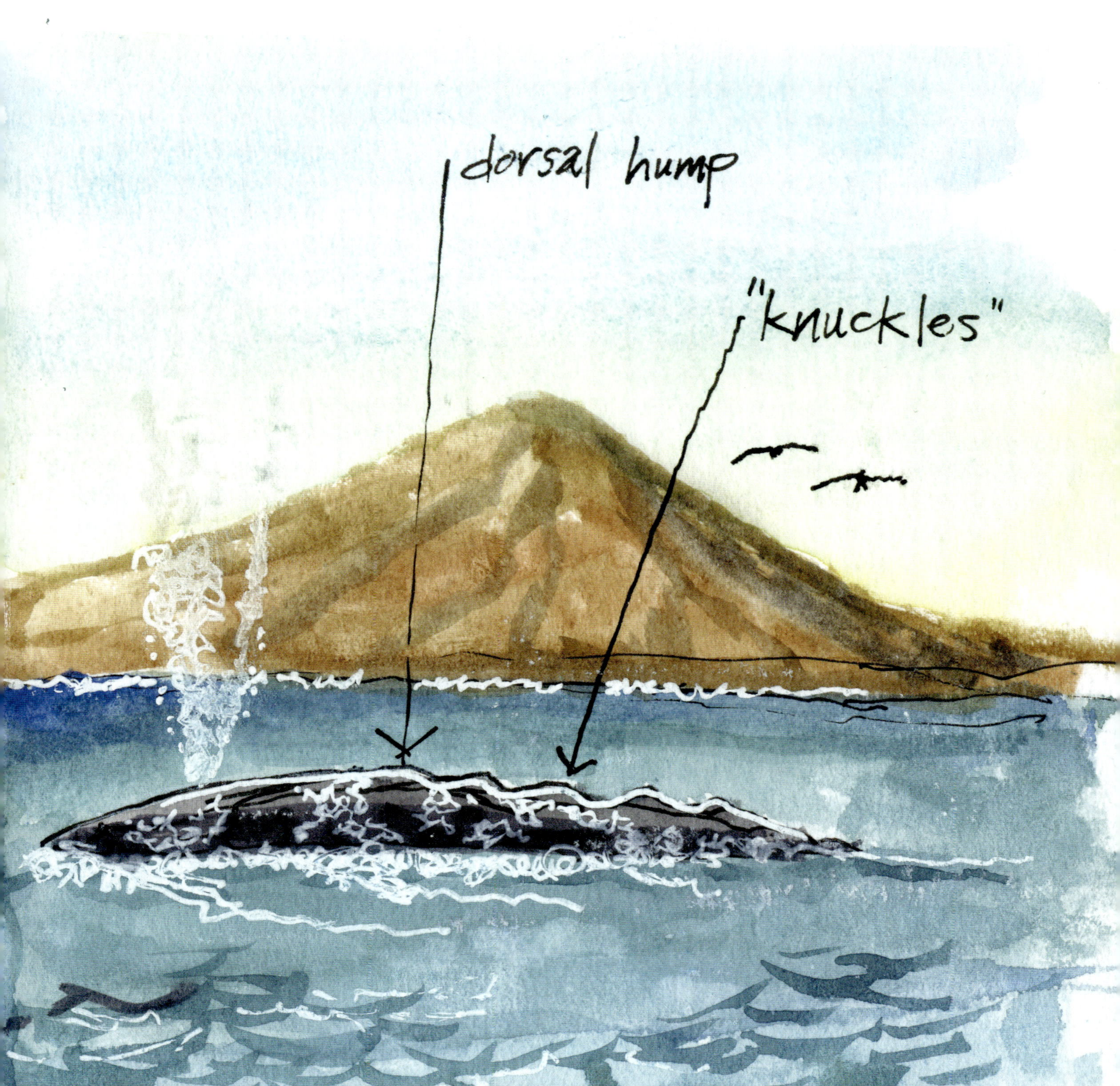
dorsal hump
"knuckles"

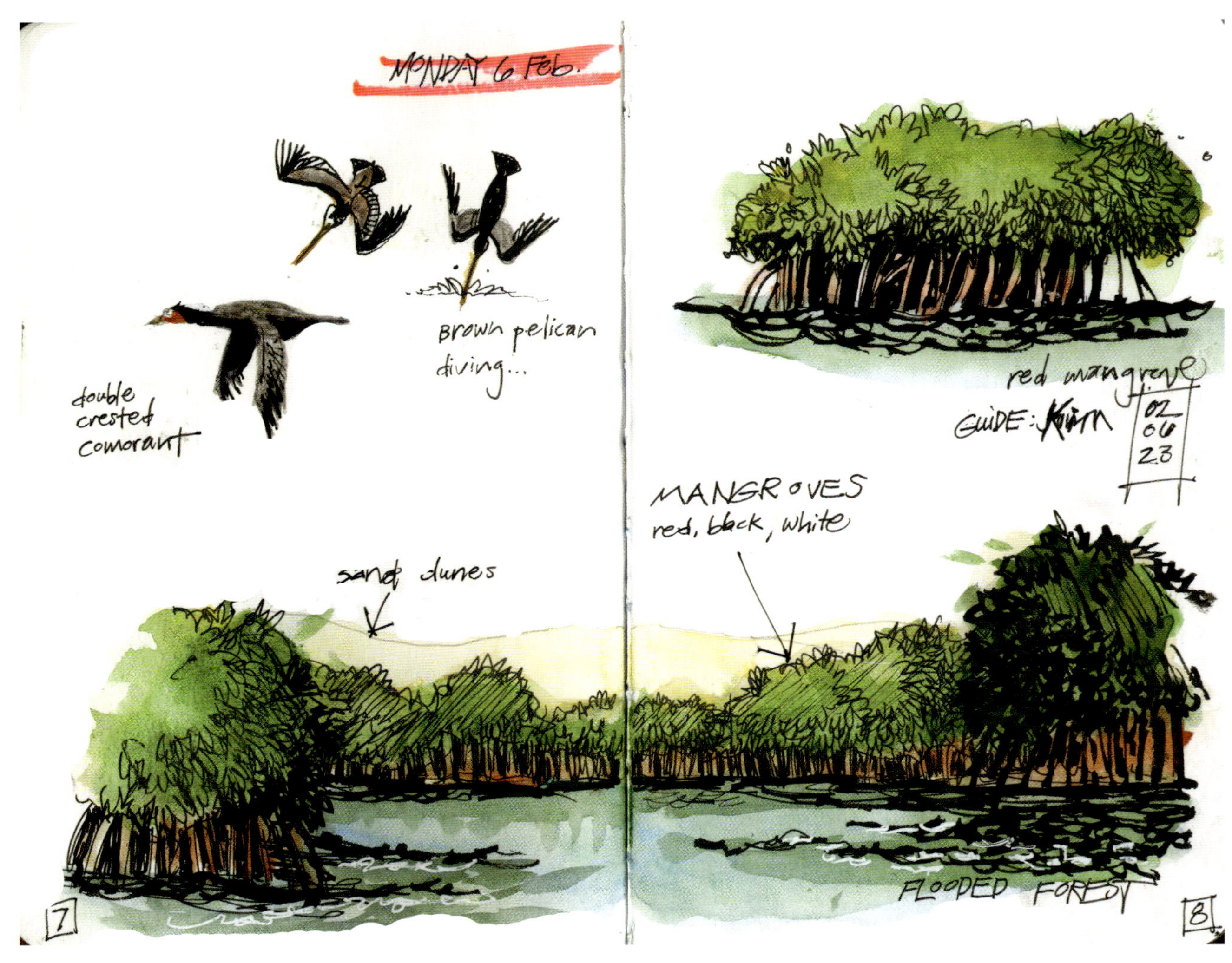

Expeditions into the mangrove ecosystems were great opportunities to watch seabirds feeding.

Chasing the whales or moving in close is strictly forbidden by regulations, but no one told the whales. Magdalena Bay is thought to be the only place in the world where the whales seek close human contact. The calves came alongside our boats one after another, surfacing to get a look at us, allowing some rubbing on the skin. It felt like smooth, slippery wet rubber. One opened its mouth wide, exposing its baleen, close enough to touch but a very bad idea that might get you an early plane ticket home.

The whole close encounter experience felt surreal, and is in fact very rare. None of the other groups that departed later in the day had similar contact.

We had several more morning excursions with naturalists over the course of the week, encountering many more whales, including mature cows with their calves swimming on the surface and against the current to strengthen the calves for the long migration back to the Bering Sea. I continued sketching them from the boats, along with mangroves, sand dunes, brown pelicans, and thousands of double-crested cormorants. The *Seabird* had a lounge area, and I spent several afternoons there adding watercolor to my ink sketches, often accompanied a bright 10-year-old girl—the only child on the trip—who would arrive early save me a seat next to her so that we could draw together. When we weren't painting, she'd take Patti by the hand and run to the latest fascinating thing she'd found on the ship. Over time, more and more passengers would come by our afternoon table to watch the sketchbook drawings evolve, asking questions and chatting among themselves.

At one point late in the week, after perusing my sketchbook in process, the ship's lead naturalist approached me. "I don't know how you do your business," she said. "But would you be interested in doing something with us? Lead some classes? Have you worked with children? I know the people who make these decisions. If we can make a copy of your sketchbook, I'll send it to them, and we'll see what happens. Maybe nothing. But who knows?"

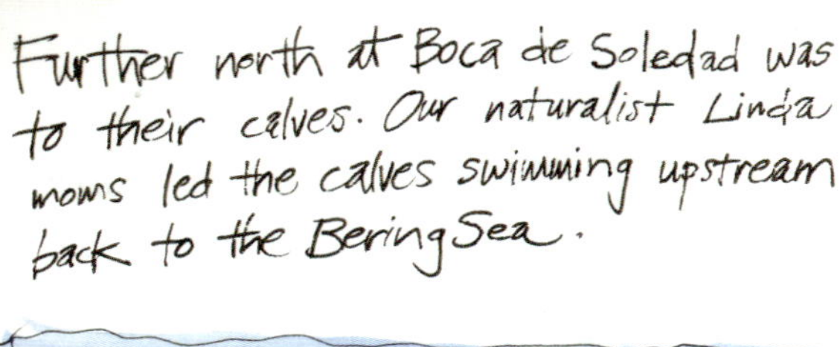

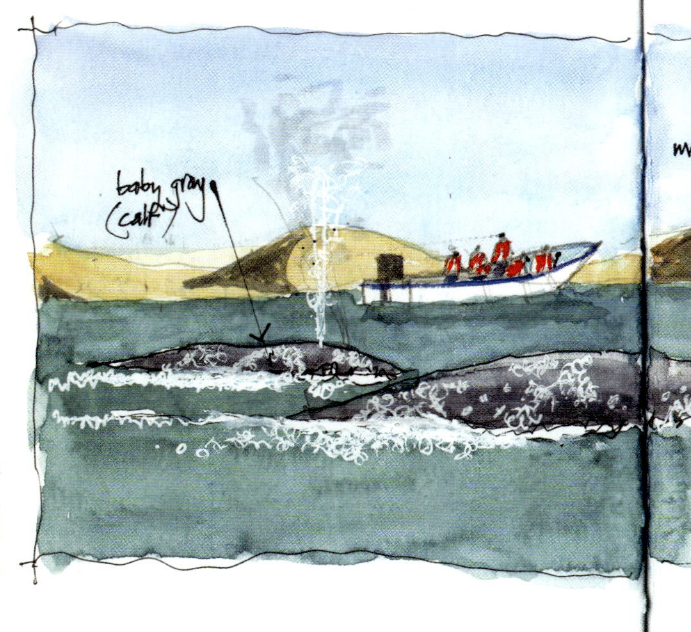

The momma grays (called "cows") and their calves spent time swimming together against to current to build strength for the long journey back to the Bering Sea

WEDNESDAY 8 Feb.

Another run to Boca de Soledad to see moms → and calves. This pair passed directly under our panga – the drawing based on photos by Joe Menn. Naturalist: Linda

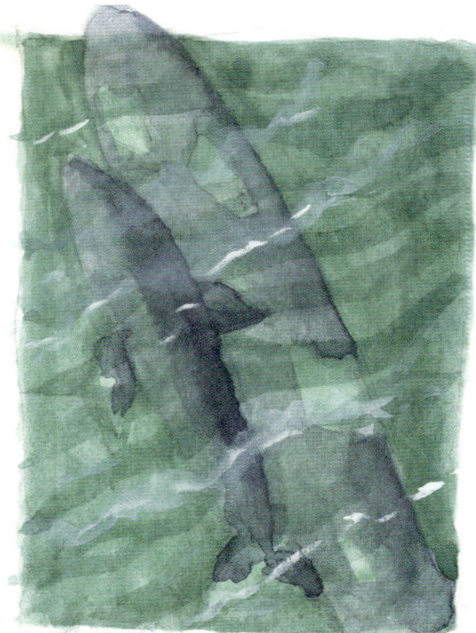

About 200 yards of beach packed with double crested comorants ↓

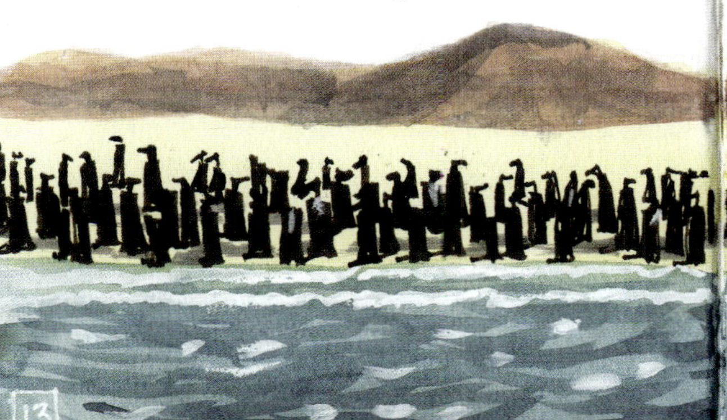

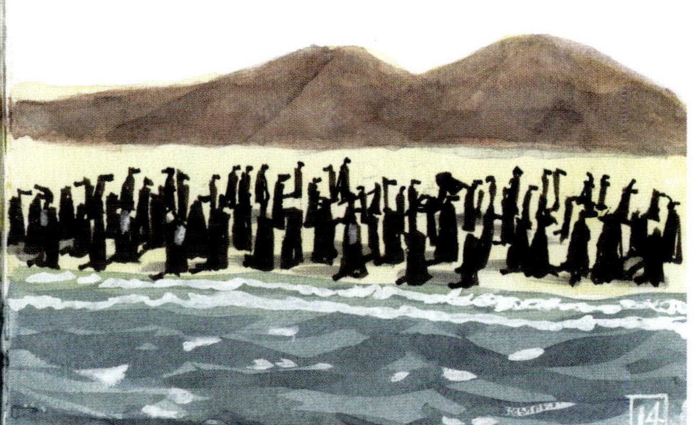

A cow and calf swimming under our panga, and hundreds of cormorants packed along a beach, apparently doing nothing in particular.

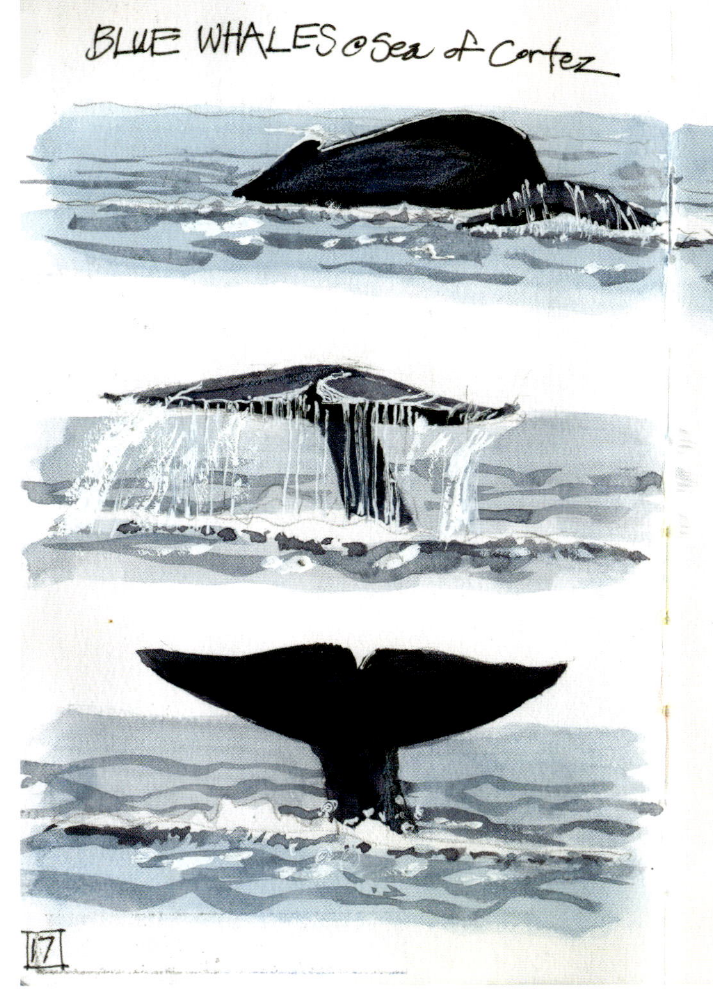

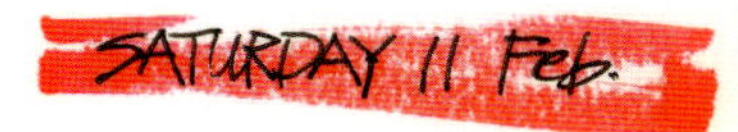

Friday 2/10 was supposed to be our day to search for blue whales off Loreto, but 18 mph winds closed the harbor. Next day was departure day, but guide NECKY had us meet him at the marina before dawn to get in a whale search before afternoon flights. We departed in darkness, watched dramatic sunrise, and eventually sighted 3 blue whales spouting, diving and fluking. These were some of the most dramatic moments of the expedition.

Spotting three enormous blue whales in the quiet of first light on the morning of our departure was a spine-tingling, unforgettable experience.

Our last morning of the trip was back in Loreto on the Sea of Cortez, with only two other travelers. High winds and waves had scuttled our blue whale excursion planned for the day before, so this was it—last shot. We met our guide Necky, a longtime local partner of NATGEO, at the marina long before dawn. We departed in a panga in darkness, watched a dramatic sunrise over the coastal hills, and were escorted for a while by dozens of dolphins racing and leaping across the surface. Rain drizzled on us occasionally, but hey, that's what we signed up for. And when I'd normally be having my first cup of coffee in our warm, dry living room, we spotted another boat drifting near the shore—a hopeful sign. As we turned towards the boat, an enormous tail fluke broke the surface of the water and slowly descended back under the sea. Over the next two hours, we spotted three blue whales, first the long back only slightly above the surface, then the beautiful arching of the back and dorsal fin rising out of the water. The wide fluke breaking the surface to follow the arched back was the breathtaking finale, with seawater pouring off it like waterfalls. At the top of the arch the tail was vertical, then reentered the water to power the whale to feed in the depths. This heartbreakingly beautiful mammal, likely 300,000 pounds and up to 100 feet long, moved as gracefully as anything in nature. These were some of the most dramatic moments of the expedition.

The sketchbook that emerged from this adventure was different than most—small, dog-eared, and often multiple drawings per page, all heavily annotated with arrows and notes. It was a real journal of the experience and what we learned along the way. And to some extent, it changed how I thought about sketchbooks and all they could be. And its more approachable design and drawings have inspired many to tell me they'd be carrying a sketchbook on their next journey.

And the pitch to NATGEO? I haven't gotten a call. But as the naturalist said, "Who knows?"

Reintegrating Work And Play

I was once asked in an interview if I thought my quick, rough sketches and preliminary studies were worthy of being final pieces in and of themselves. "Do you ever consider them actually better than the more finished works?" And of course, for my tastes, the roughs usually are better. I mentioned that I had a few artist friends who kept me honest when my "more finished works" were losing the life and spirit of the rough stuff. One of those friends used an on-the-spot drawing of a market tent I'd hurriedly drawn in Nairobi to make the point:

"This really embodies the style of yours I fell in love with—the expressive and flowing realism. The looser style has a vibrancy and energy to it. It communicates a lot more emotionally and energetically. I feel pulled in, and like I'm witnessing your inner voice as an artist, and a sense of joy that's captured in the making."

And there, in four sentences, she nailed it. She had simultaneously bitch-slapped me and held up a mirror. I had to think about why the rough sketches looked so much more alive. I found myself thinking about child's play. That is, when I think of the drawing I'm jumping into as play—unselfconscious, without judgement—the joy I'm feeling comes out in the work. My guard is down, I'm having fun, and it shows.

When I draw out of a sense of obligation and angst—say, for a commission—that shows too. I tighten up and second guess. The resulting piece inevitably looks a little (or a lot) stiffer, overworked. It becomes like taxidermy, an okay simulation of the thing on the outside, but dead inside. When I'm really on having fun, the moves and the lines come rushing out of me before I have time to think about them. The difference can be astounding.

So, it's helpful to get your head in the right place. When I'm drawing, the medium or tools aren't the secret. Rather, it's when I feel like I'm playing that the drawing comes alive.

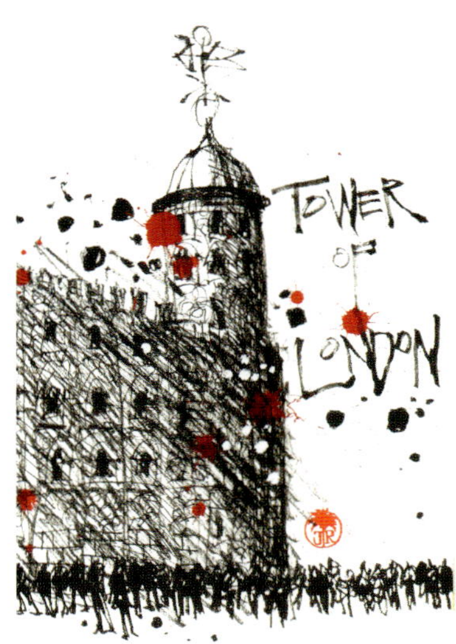

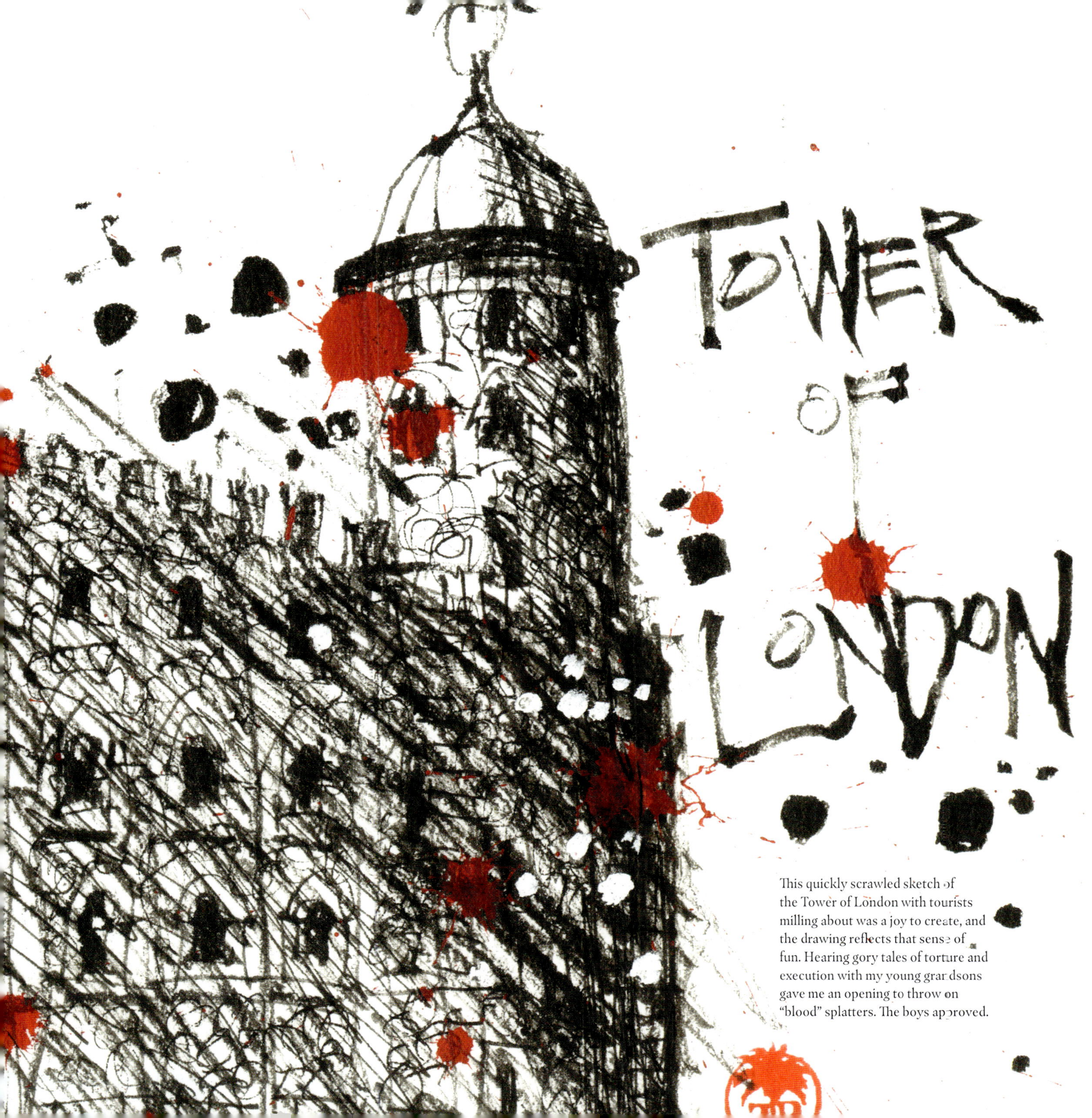

This quickly scrawled sketch of the Tower of London with tourists milling about was a joy to create, and the drawing reflects that sense of fun. Hearing gory tales of torture and execution with my young grandsons gave me an opening to throw on "blood" splatters. The boys approved.

The Sketcher's Code

Keep it loose.

Relax. Imperfection is a virtue. Avoid the temptation to start with a careful pencil underdrawing, then painstakingly refining it. Go straight to ink. If a line is way off, don't start over. Draw again on top of it. Yeah, two lines. Or three, until you're okay with it. Is the building on your page leaning? Does one of your figures have three legs? Don't fix them. This ultimately results in a sketch that feels more alive, like a human being really did it. We can better see your emotions and identity as an artist. We don't want a perfectly rendered reproduction of a scene. We want you.

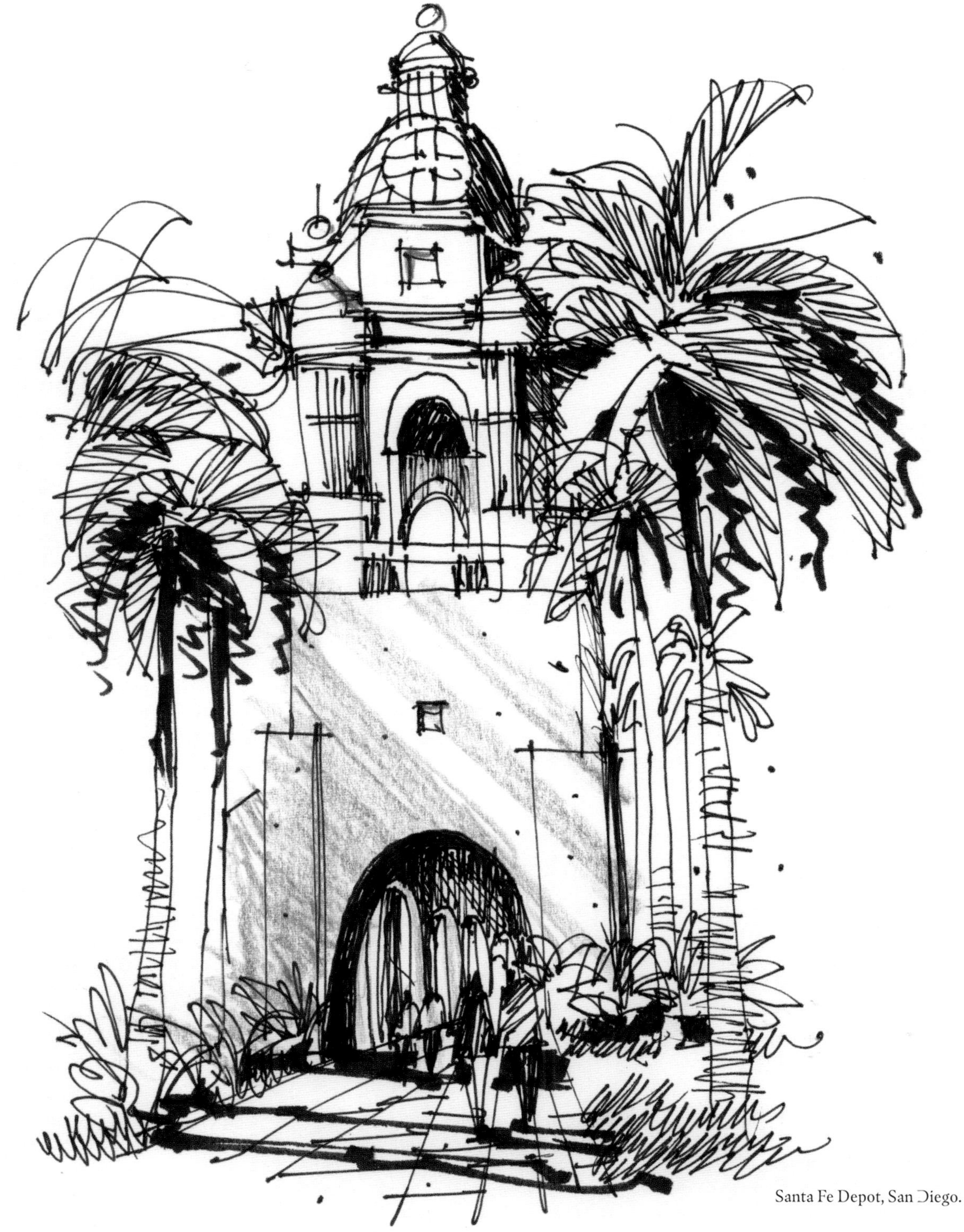

Santa Fe Depot, San Diego.

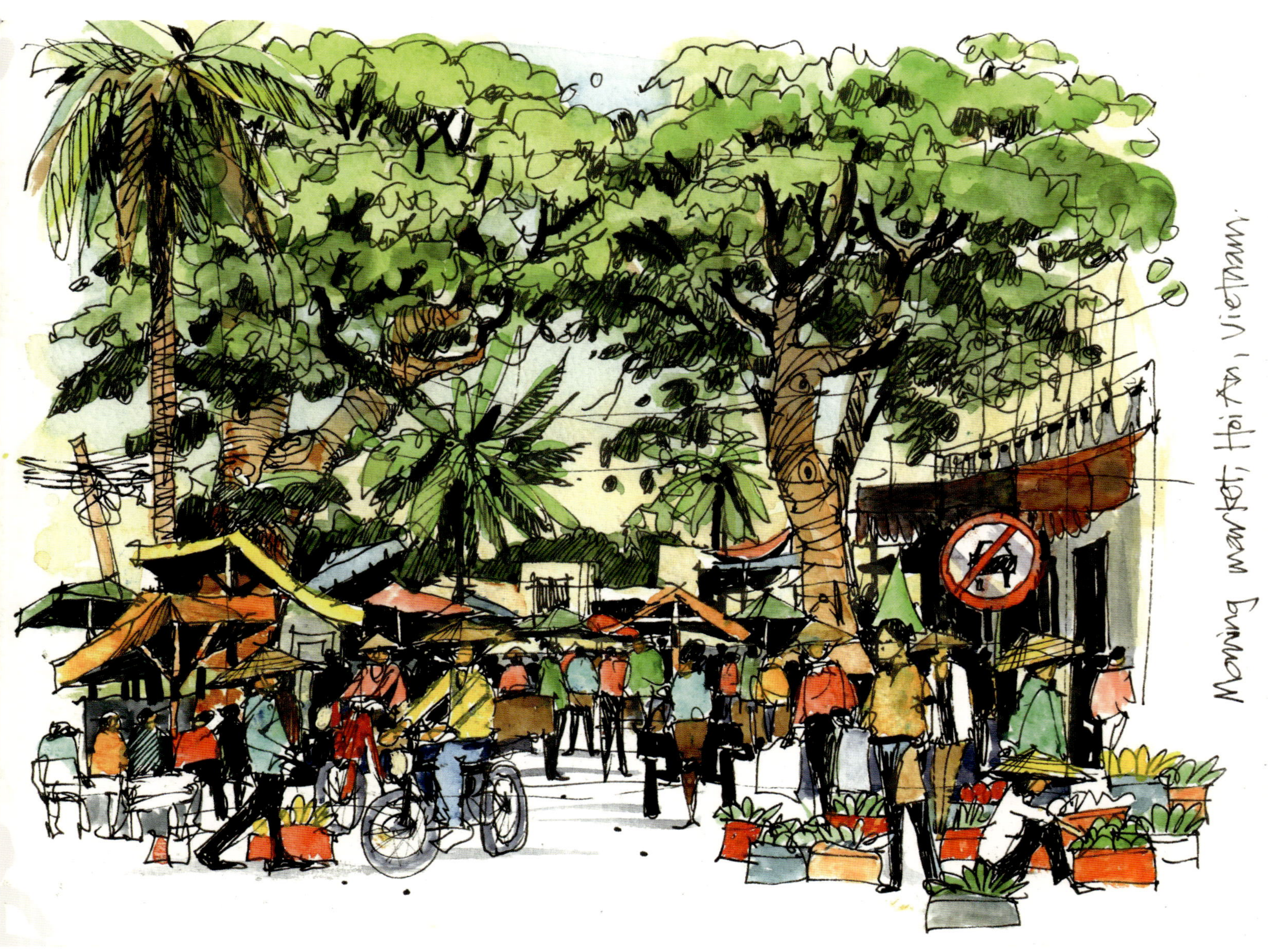
Morning market, Hoi An, Vietnam.

CHAPTER 6

Vietnam: Ambushed by Beauty

IT HAPPENS A LOT. Just for a few seconds, maybe a minute or two, my mind becomes lost in memories of Vietnam—air heavy with heat and humidity, lush tropical vegetation filtering golden sunlight onto Saigon streets wet from afternoon rains. I remember smells of flowering trees and incense sticks and of mouth-watering food being cooked on small grills along the sidewalks next to bins of tropical fruits, peppers, garlic, live crabs, and fish. I hear endless rivers of motor scooters zipping along crowded streets. I see solitary farmers tending to rice paddies, families working together in market stalls, elders practicing tai chi in the park, and young people laughing in clubs in the evening. I literally salivate remembering the smell and taste of the bahn mi sandwich at Banh Mi Phuong in Hoi An. I remember the beautiful young hotel greeter in her crisp, white *ao dai* tunic, waiting in the lobby to see what I'd drawn that day. I see centuries-old shop houses, small residential boxes stacked atop each other like building blocks and beautifully draped in vines, grand buildings that are vestiges of old French colonial rule, and scars of war—all growing out of a fascinating, very complicated, and often tragic history. I didn't expect to fall in love with Vietnam, but the rich mix of impressions from the other side of the world has my heart, and won't let go.

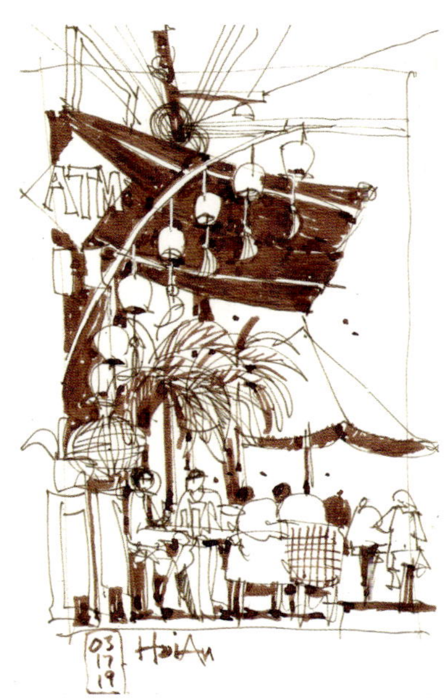

My first real insight into the culture was gleaned from simply learning to cross a busy city street in the heart of Saigon, always filled with the continuous flow of thousands of motor scooters. Our guide explained, "Look briefly at oncoming traffic, raise a hand to signal you are crossing. Without hesitation, look forward and step into the street.

Opposite: Commerce spills into the streets in the early mornings at Hoi An's Central Market, one of the best places to experience the culture and connect with the locals.

Top: Streetside café tables, Hoi An.

Walk directly across at a steady pace. Do not slow down, speed up, turn around, back up or change course. Above all, do not stop!" We watched with mouths agape as he stepped off the curb and into the speeding melee to demonstrate.

Here's the thing: the scooters didn't stop or even slow down as he strode across the street. Rather, they adapted to the intrusion immediately and, as he walked, swirled around and past him like a fast-moving school of fish. No horns, yelling or road rage, just flow. Avoiding carnage meant that all the scooter riders—men, women, young, old, poor, and well-to-do—had to think as one in the moment, each making quick but smooth adjustments to the moving pedestrian and each other without slowing down. It was a marvel of almost instinctive understanding and cooperation. It was amazing—and terrifying—to watch. I studied the guide's method carefully, emulated his moves dozens of times in the course of our visit, and was almost always successful. But the real lesson of the moment, and of history, was the Vietnamese's ability to adapt to obstacles with single-minded purpose.

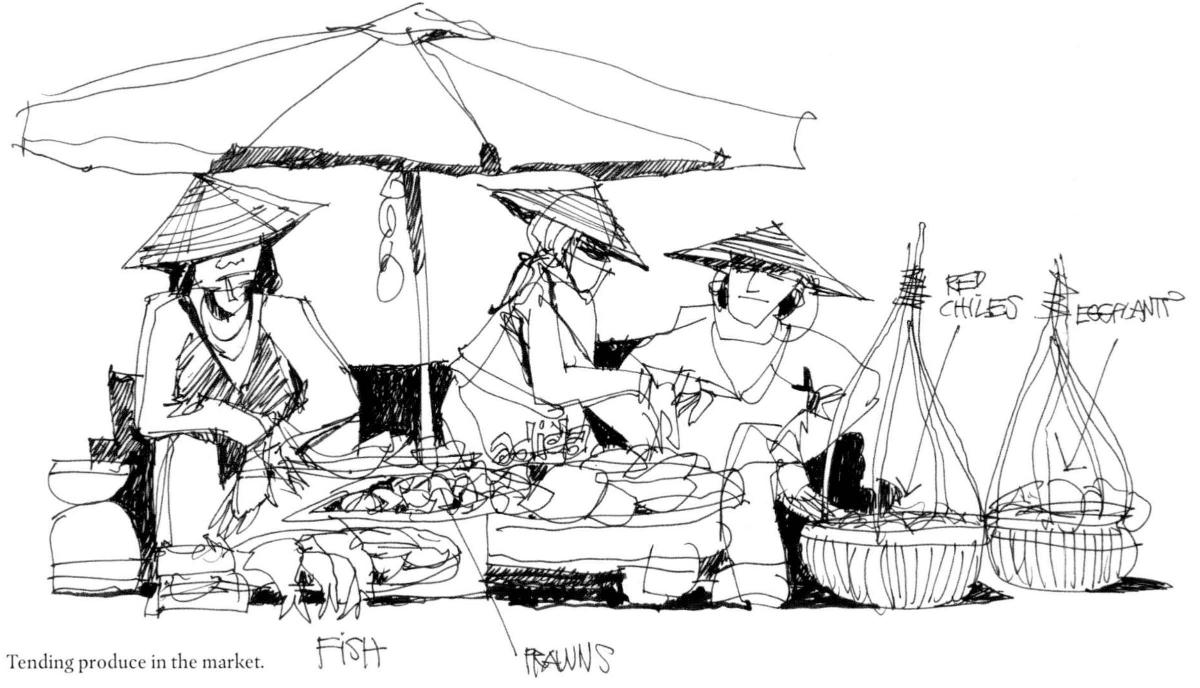

Tending produce in the market.

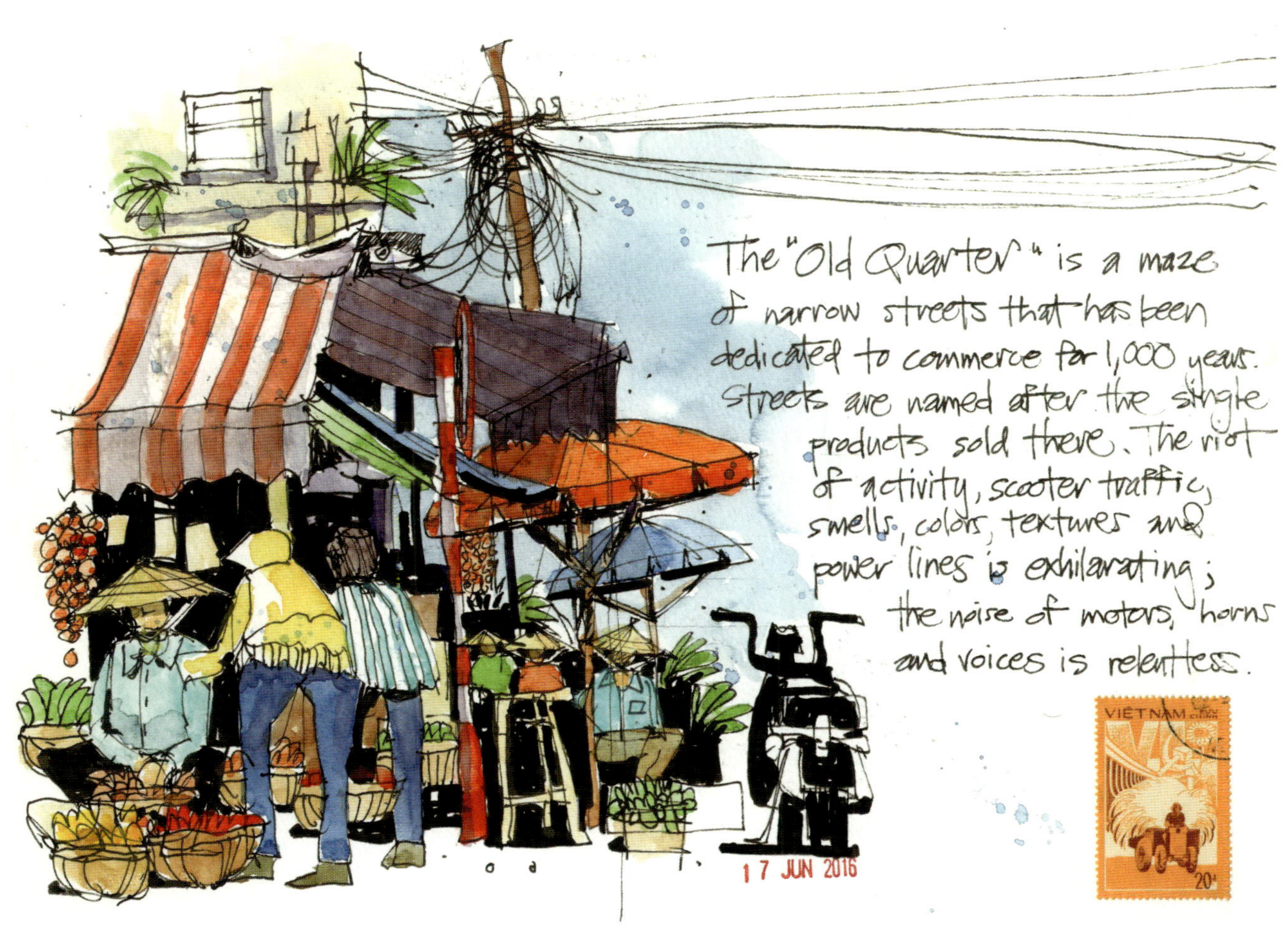

Corner commerce on a narrow street in Hanoi's Old Quarter.

While in Saigon, I arranged to meet with Chien Bau, a successful architect and founder of Urban Sketchers Vietnam. We were joined by local sketcher Phong Khieu, and the three of us spent an afternoon sketching together in the heart of the city, in the streets and later from the balcony of a bar offering seats, shade, and cold beer overlooking a performance hall. As we drew together, Chien offered some of his insights into the city's more recent history and changes and said he'd show us around the city that evening.

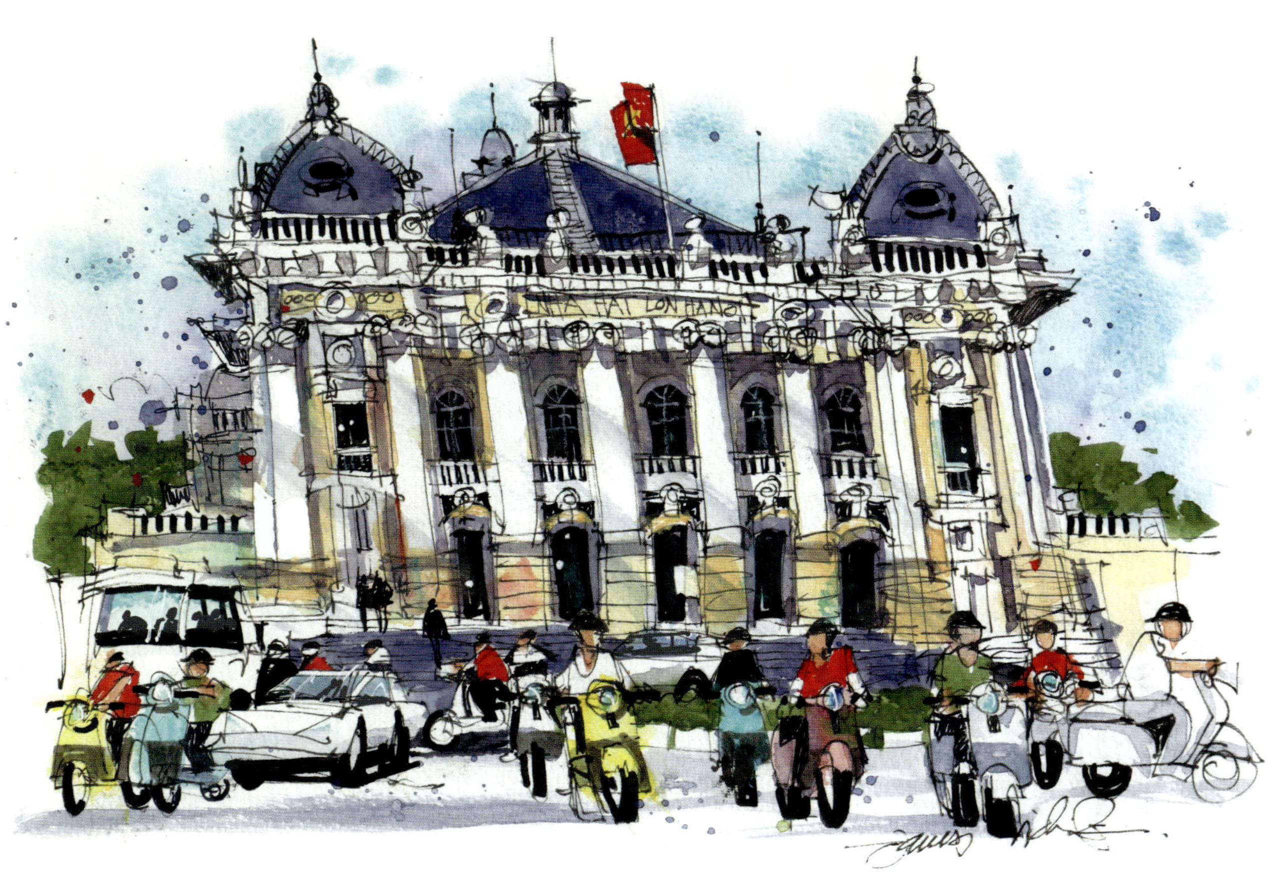

The elegant backdrop for the sea of circling scooters and cars is the Hanoi Opera House, erected by the French colonial administration between 1901 and 1911.

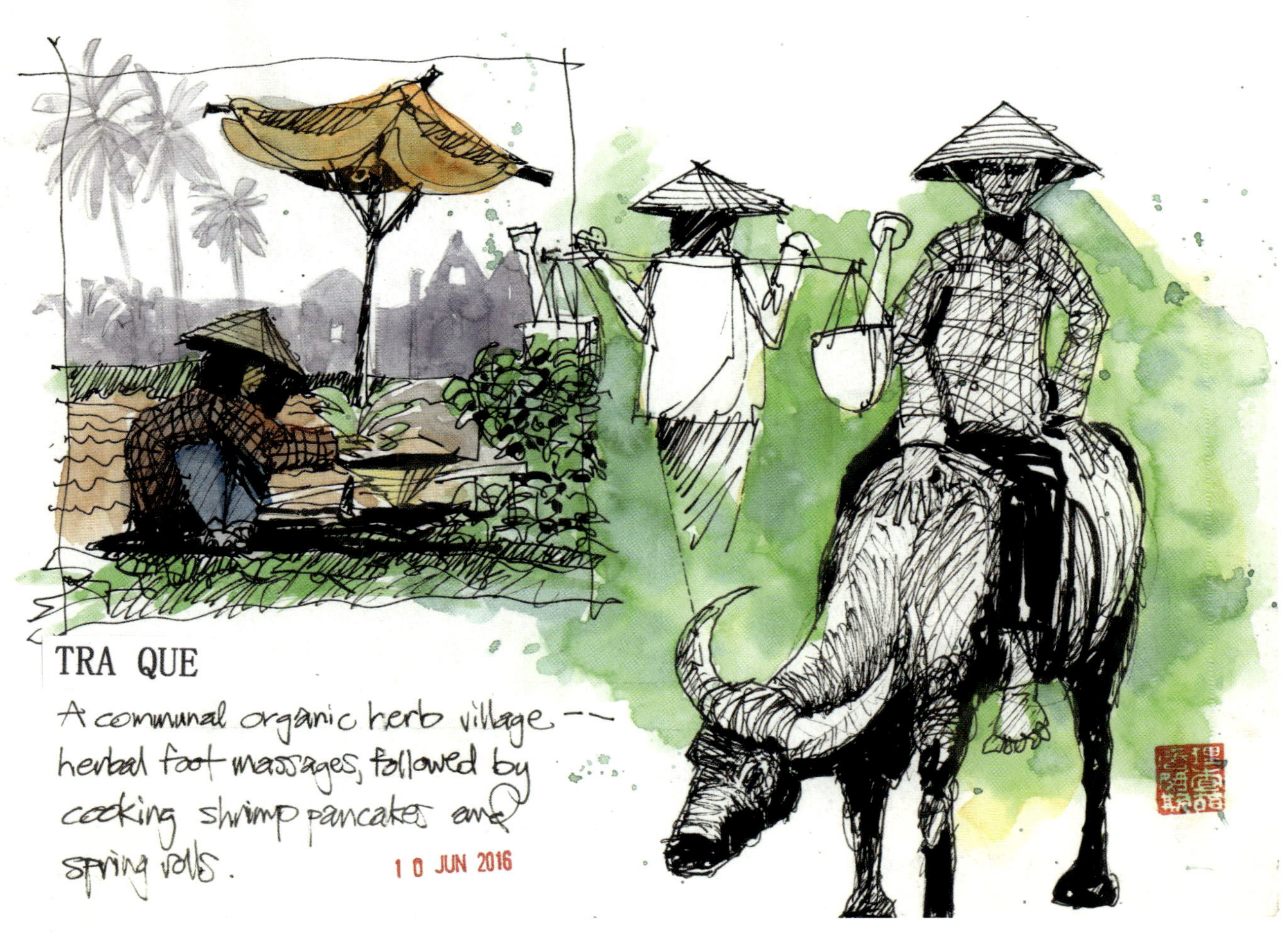

A couple of hours later, in what could have been a scene from an adventure film, Chien wheeled into our hotel porte-cochere on his muscular vintage Russian motorcycle with sidecar. As the vast majority of Saigon traffic is small scooters, this classic behemoth stood out and turned heads. (We were later amazed but not surprised to see a photo of Anthony Bourdain on the same bike with Chien taken a couple of years earlier.) Patti quickly claimed the sidecar; I climbed onto the bench seat and rode behind Chien as we slid into the flow of scooters and sped off into the nighttime streets.

For a generous tip, you too can capture the authentic experience of a man atop a water buffalo on the side of the road. If the line is too long, come back tomorrow; he'll be in the same spot.

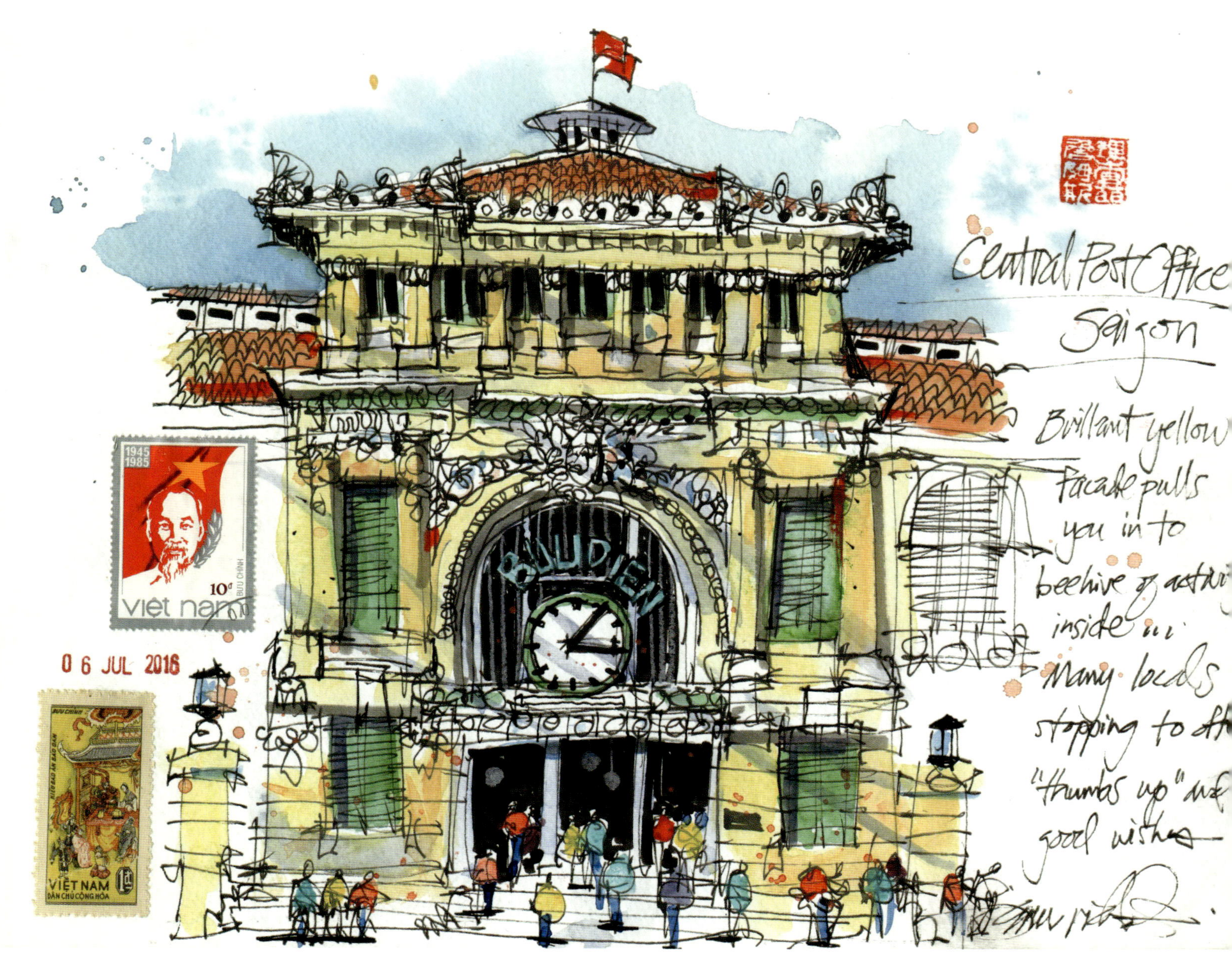

The Central Post Office, Saigon.

The ride on this vintage monster of a motorcycle was exhilarating, with night wind in our faces, the deep rumbling of the engine, constant weaving in traffic and young scooter riders honking and pulling alongside to have a look at this strange scene. Chien took us down tree-lined boulevards, past parks and monuments and pointed out many buildings that were key sites in the city's history, especially during the years of what the Vietnamese call 'The American War." We pulled over and stopped at gates of The Independence Palace, a 1960s modernist building that had been South Vietnam's war command center and the residence of the South Vietnamese President during the war. Chien spoke a little about the role the building had played during the height of the conflict—history he knows well, as his father was a soldier in the North Vietnamese Army. Standing next to his motorcycle, Chien pulled out his cell phone to show us an old black and white photo. It was

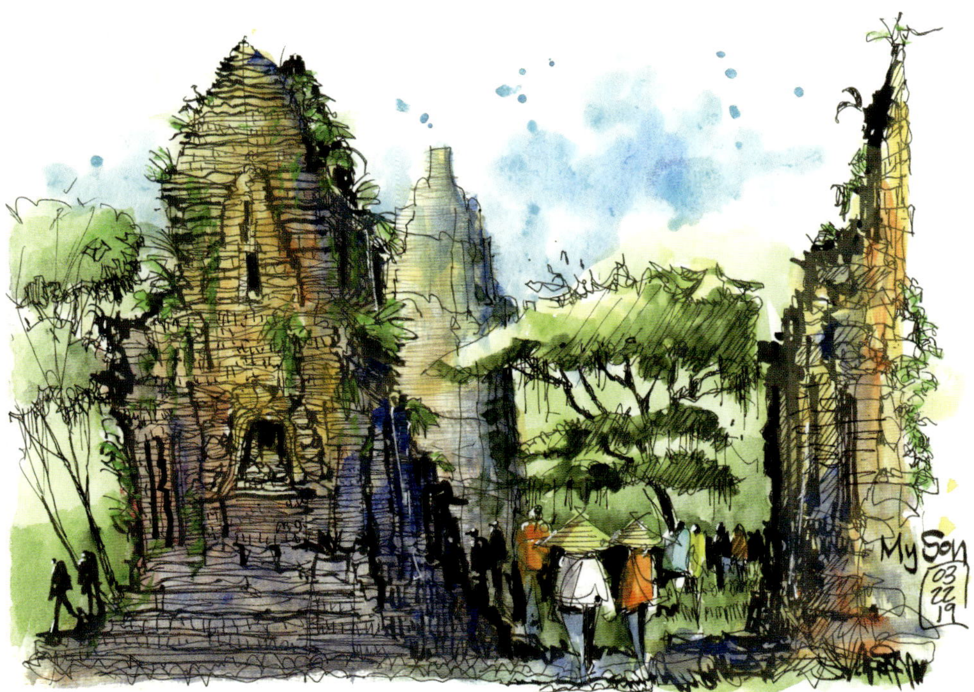

The My Son temple ruins in the jungles of the Central Highlands predate better known Angkor Wat in neighboring Cambodia by eight centuries. Much was destroyed by carpet bombing during the war, but the relics retain a majestic presence and timeless dignity.

a North Vietnamese tank, waving the flag of the revolution, crashing through the palace gates on the very spot we were standing—April 30, 1975. "This moment," he said, "was the end of the American War."

The ride on this vintage monster of a motorcycle was exhilarating, with night wind in our faces, the deep rumble of the engine, constant weaving in traffic and young scooter riders honking and pulling alongside to have a look at this strange scene.

This took a moment to sink in. As a college student I'd seen the photos in *LIFE* magazine and watched clips of this event on the evening news. This spot and what happened here are forever burned into the American psyche and into the history of the late 20th century. The scene in front of us now couldn't have been a bigger contrast: serene, the grounds well-manicured, and the building—now a museum—dramatically lit as a symbol of reunification of north and south.

After a few moments, we reboarded the motorcycle and again merged into the scooter traffic to retreat to a pub, where we meet friends, have a beer together, and smile as Chien shares with us his love of American muscle cars and classic rock music.

The next day, our group traveled a couple of hours to the heart of the Mekong River Delta, where we boarded several small rowboats and glided slowly along the waterways, past wooden stilt houses enshrouded in the thick vegetation, fishing nets hung from wooden stakes like submerged tennis nets across streams, and small villages along on the shore. I was able to grab some quick thumbnail sketches of the passing scenes from the boat. This was nice—the slow pace, quiet and lushness of the landscape were a welcome contrast to the high urban energy of Saigon.

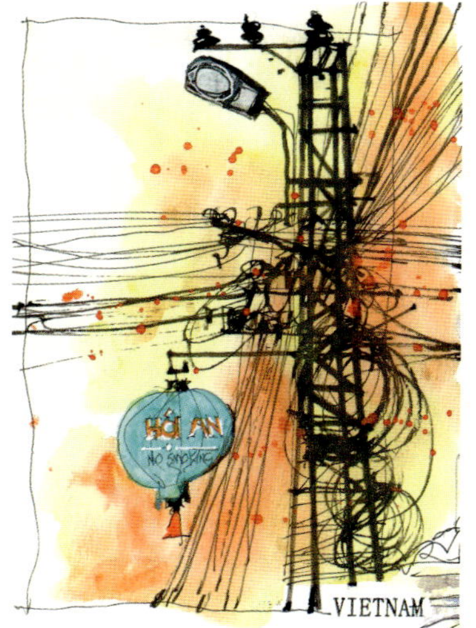

Famously tangled power, telephone, and cable television lines are arguably one of the most iconic symbols of Vietnam. Yes, the paper lantern really said, "No Smoking."

Our rowboats landed at one of the villages, where women under a large thatch shelter were weaving strips of water hyacinth into baskets, boxes, and other goods. As usual, I was moving about the room and scanning the village, looking for sketch opportunities. I was surprised, and admittedly somewhat pleased with myself, when a beautiful young woman moving through the shelter smiled demurely and, with downcast eyes, softly and discreetly stroked my athletic and abundant midsection

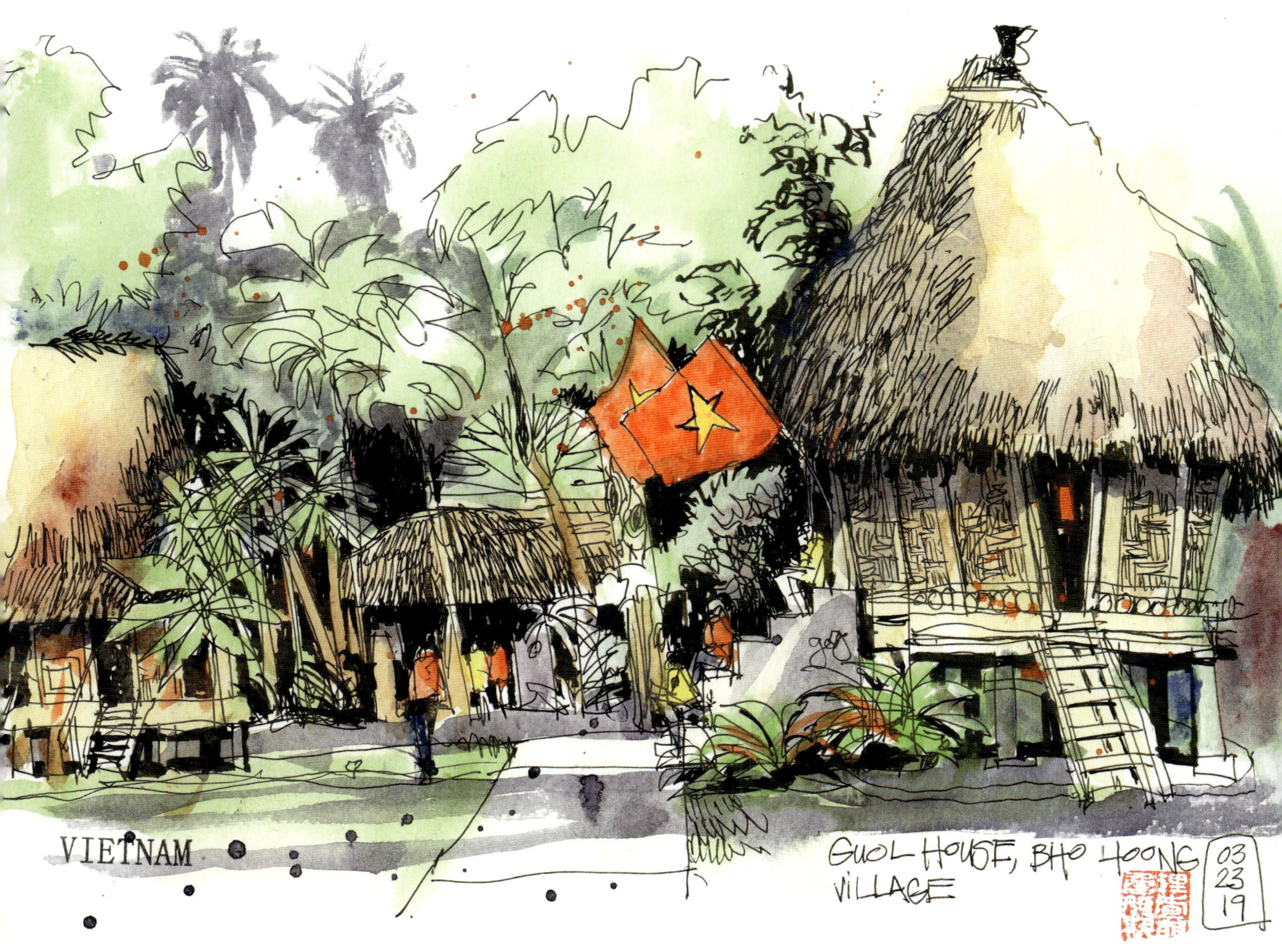

The structure on the right is the central meeting house of Bho Hoong. It faces the sacred open space of the village, where once a year a water buffalo is sacrificed in a traditional ceremony and dance to bring good fortune to the village and its people. Yes, I absolutely joined in the dance.

A shaft of light from an opening at the top of Huyen Khong cave dramatically illuminates a statue of the Buddha, who smiles serenely on the scene.

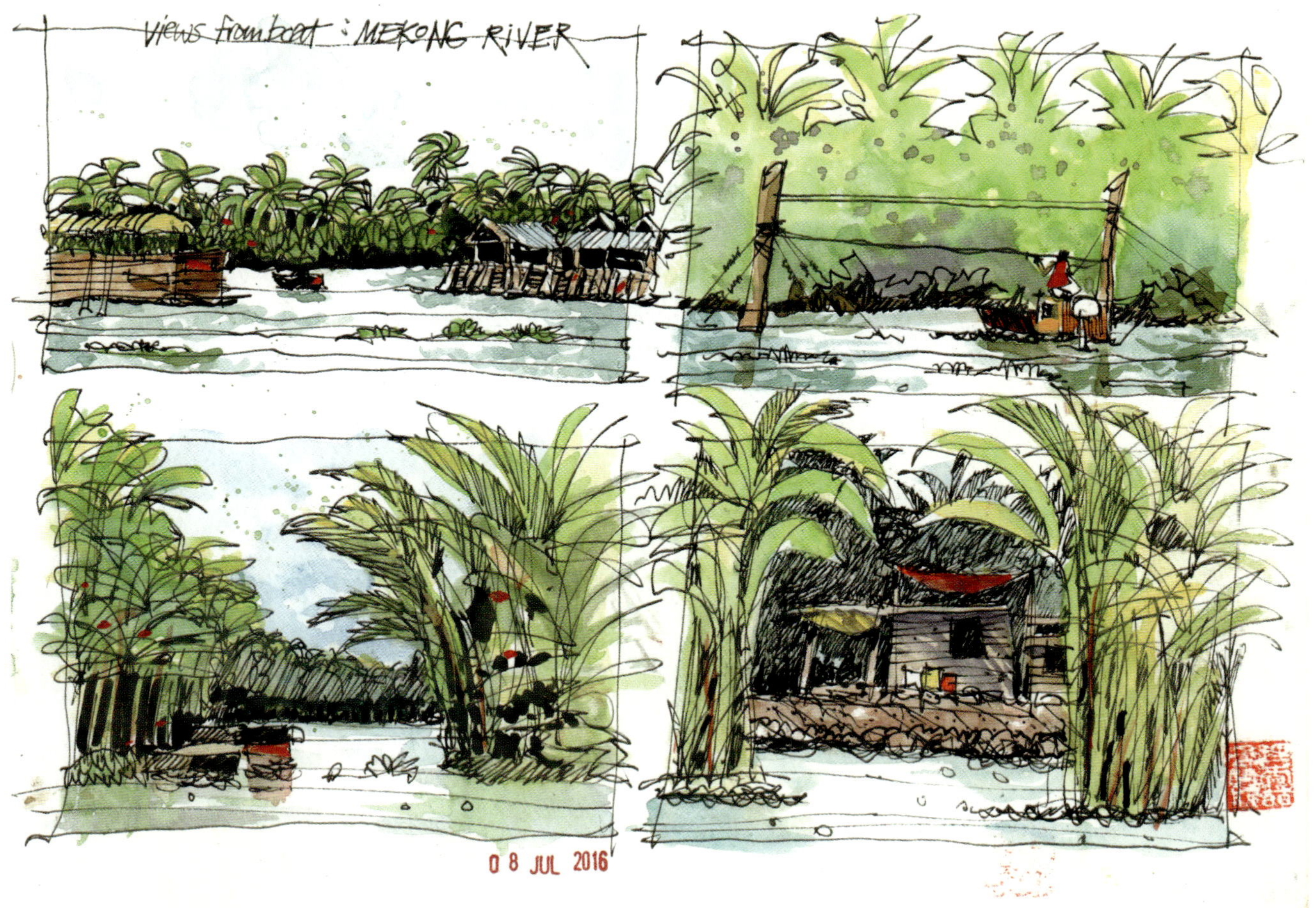

as she walked past. Okay, this is unexpected, I thought, but not completely unwelcome, looking around to see if anyone had noticed. All good—I was in the clear and had plausible deniability. And, I reasoned, that was that—until another attractive young woman made the same discreet move minutes later. I'm embarrassingly ignorant of rural (or urban) Vietnamese culture, but it was obvious these girls were into me! But stay cool. No need for an international incident here.

When reboarding the boats, I pulled the guide aside, told her what had happened, and that I was apparently a thing among the young women of the village. "Oh yes," she said. "It's good luck to rub the belly of the Buddha."

These quick impressions capture an unfolding sequence of views as our small boat moves down a tributary of the Mekong River south of Saigon.

A sketch map of the ceremonial heart of Bho Hoong, a remote rural village of the Co Tu ethnic group in the Central Highlands.

My Vietnam sketches have sent many people my way, and most have expressed appreciation for the window they provide into the place and its culture. One of the most poignant was a letter sent by a sometime travel companion and American veteran of the Vietnam War. He had been a U.S. Navy Seabee during the conflict, building camps, bridges and roads, and through those assignments saw much of the country. He had told me early on that he wasn't interested in traveling with us to Vietnam. "I've been there." Later, he told me that he feared that the ensuing years and modernization had resulted in a disheartening loss of the

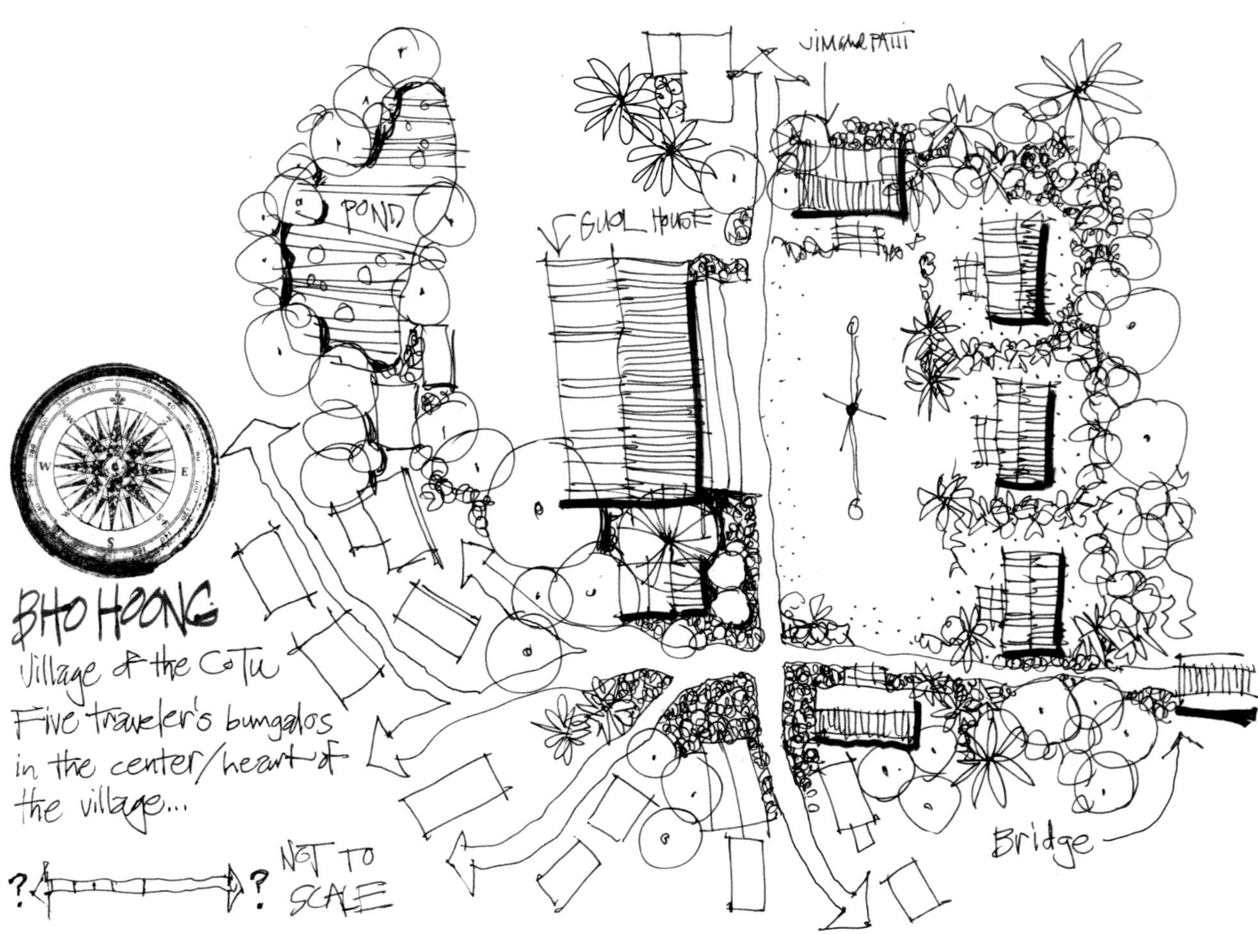

culture and character he had remembered. After seeing my sketchbook, he was inspired to pull out his photo album of black and white photos from the war. He sent me copies, and wrote, "I was pleased to see in your sketches that the spirit of the country I remember still exists...You brought out the inherent beauty of the culture." At the end of the day, it's that beauty of the landscape, the people, and the culture that lives in my memory, and calls me back.

A procession of Buddhist monks chant in unison at the Thein Mu Pagoda.

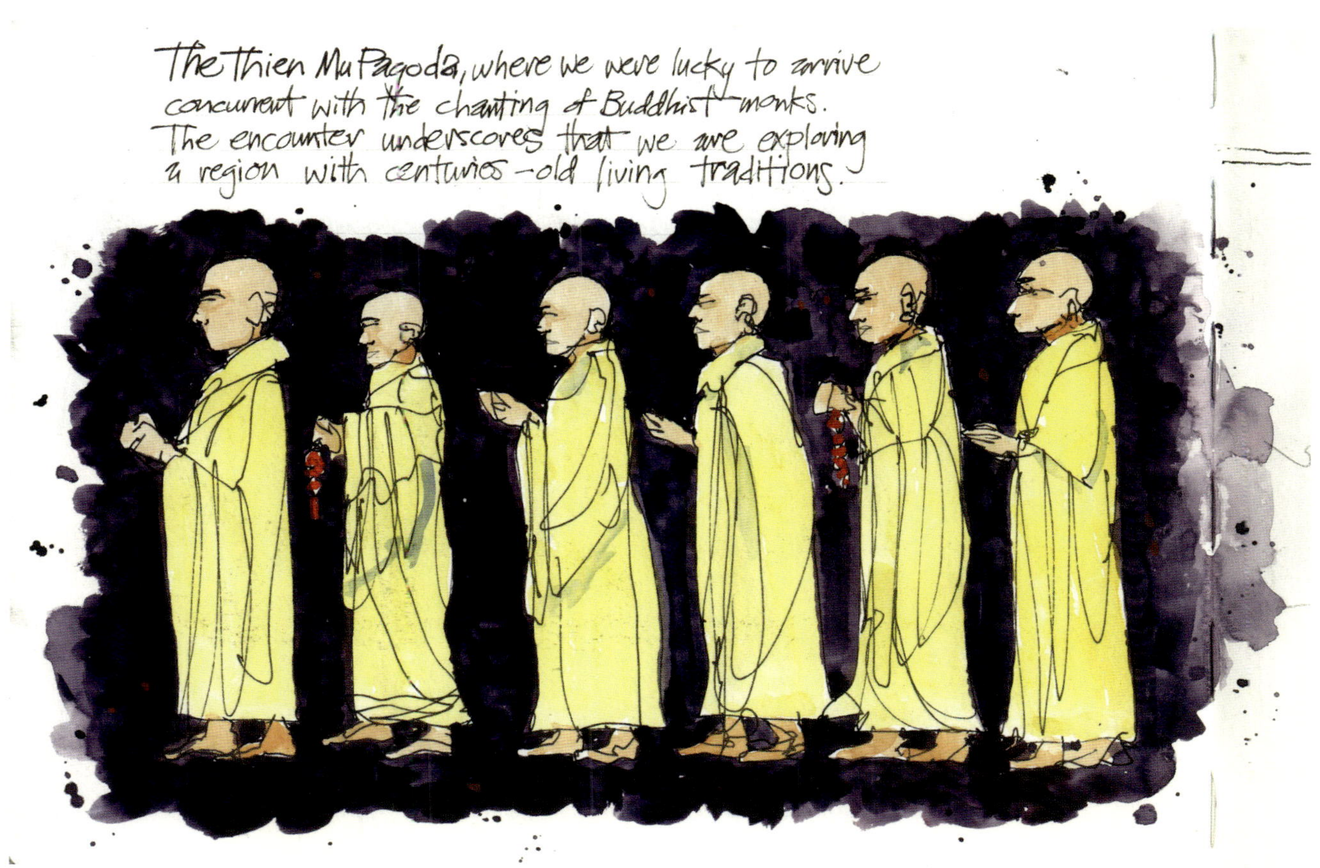

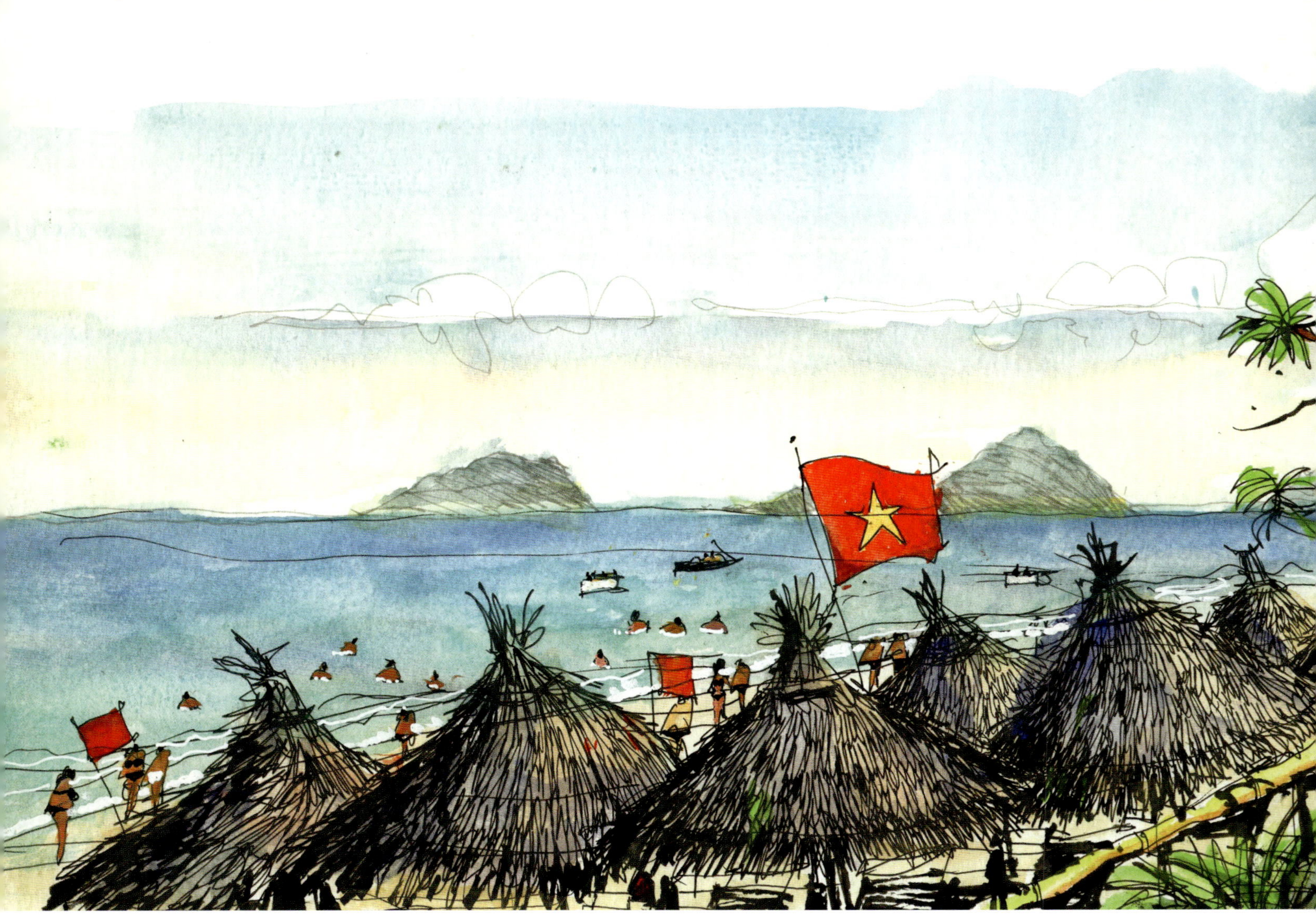

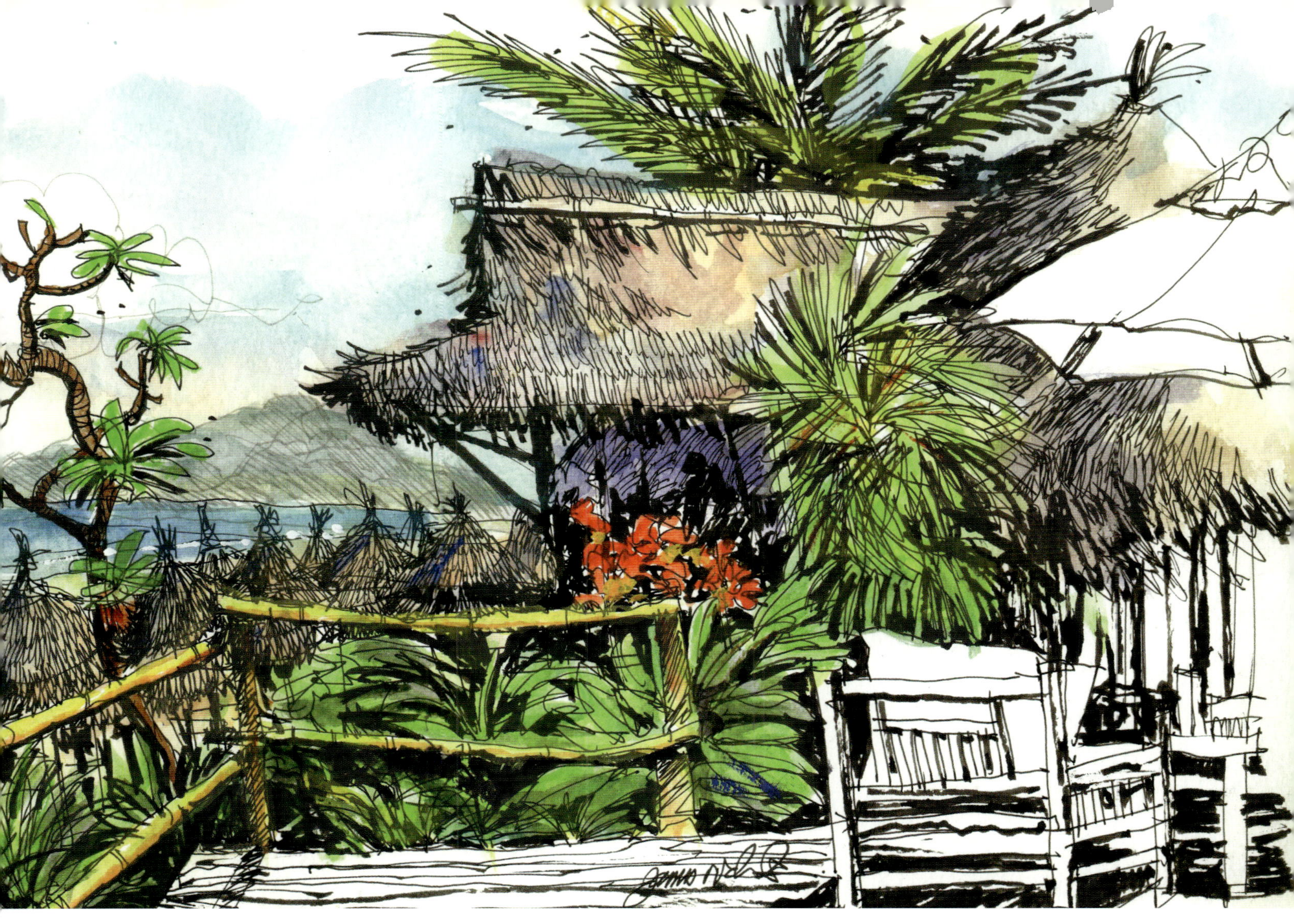

This beautiful white crescent of sand at Danang was dubbed China Beach by U.S. soldiers during the Vietnam War, and was the first landing spot for American combat troops. It's now An Bang Beach, with luxury resorts and public beaches looking out onto the breathtaking views.

On location: sketching the Da Nang Cathedral

This sketch outing with Chien and about 40 Vietnamese students followed a short lecture and panel discussion at Da Nang Architecture University. I arrived a little late at the meeting point—Da Nang Cathedral—so my sketching decisions were driven in part by a compressed time frame. I decided to draw a relatively simple front view, so perspective would play little part in the image. A sense of depth, however, is always important, so a dramatic foreground element came to my rescue.

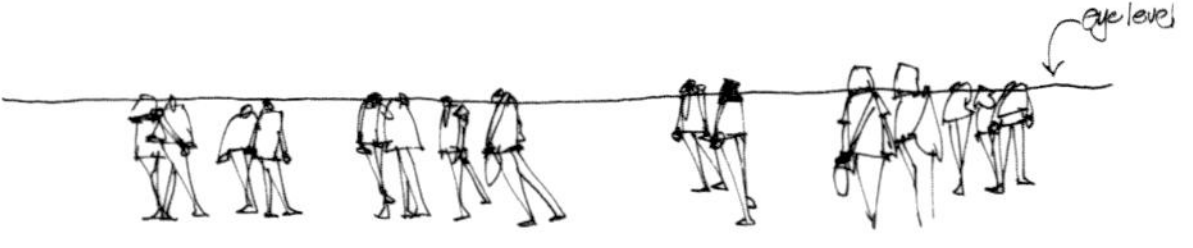

As always, I began by locating my eye level line on the page, and used it to place a few people in the frame.

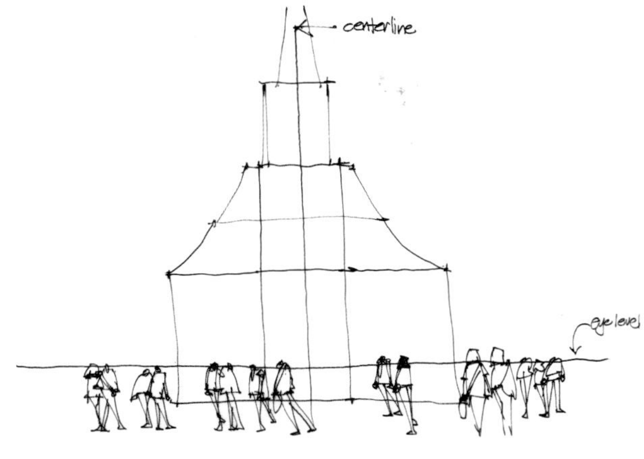

Next, I added the basic geometry (rectangles, triangles) of the big shapes to situate the composition on the page. I decided not to try to include the entire steeple, but rather to crop it at the top.

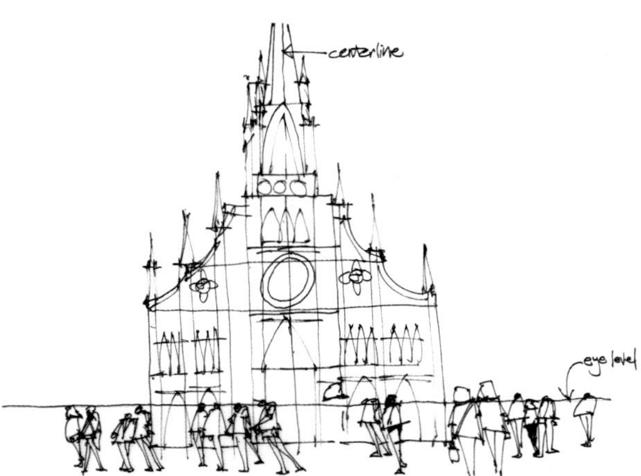

I subdivided the big shapes with their smaller interior shapes, a simple process.

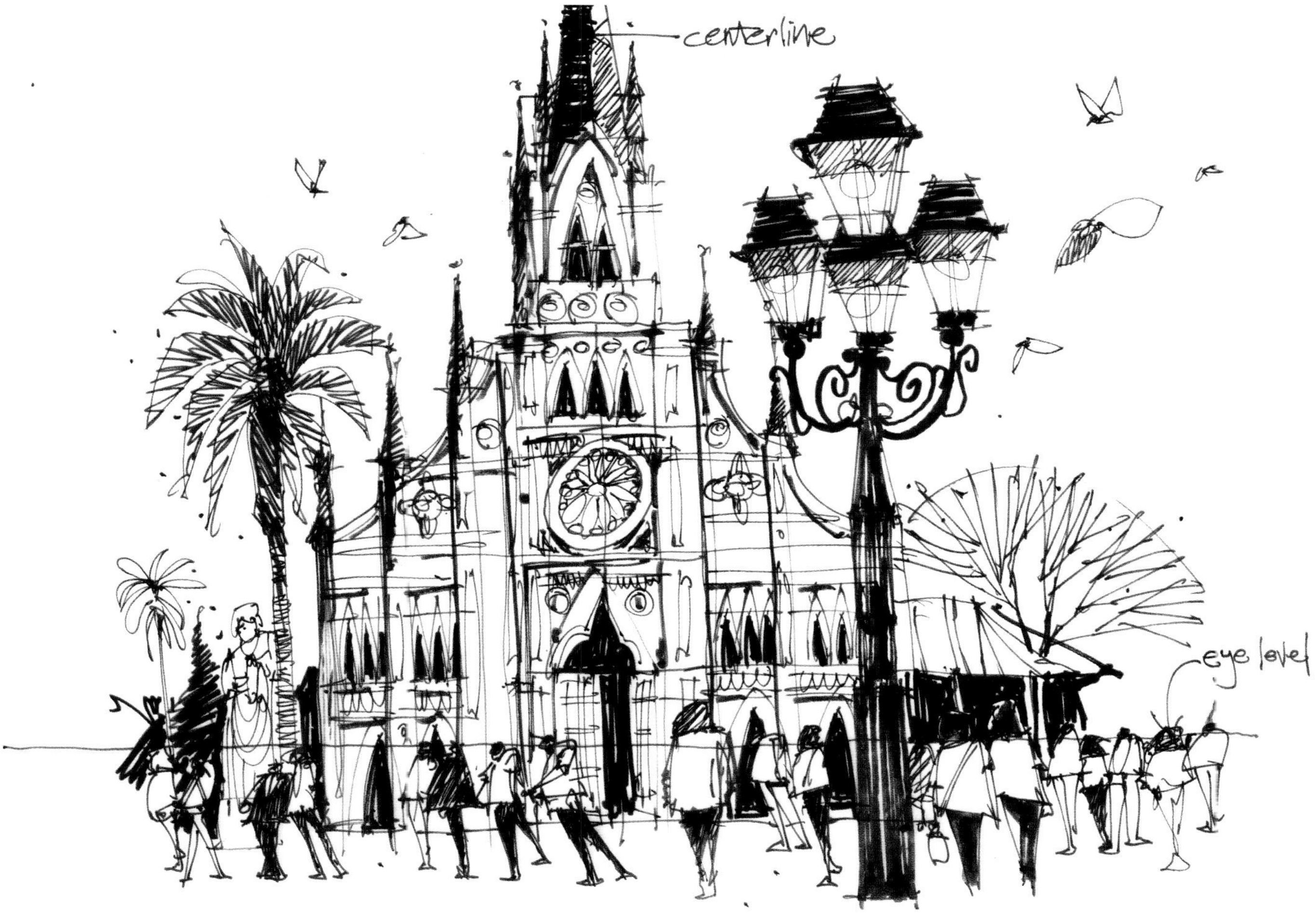

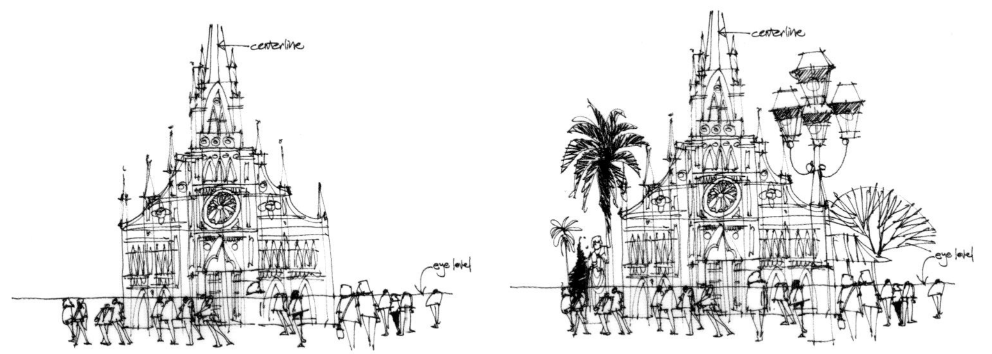

With the geometric framework in place, I quickly added details—greatly simplified—with a fine line pen to hint at the visual richness of the façade.

I shifted an ornate streetlamp from the surrounding forecourt into the sketch, pulling it deep into the foreground to enhance an illusion of depth. The trees hint at the tropical sense of place.

Finally, darks add contrast and vitality, bringing the scene to life.

The Sketcher's Code

Don't touch the monkey!

There are some things you shouldn't have to tell a grown-up not to do. Don't touch the monkey! They're not cute pets that ride on your shoulder like in the movies, they're disease-ridden little pickpockets that bite. Don't drink the homemade wine with a dead snake in the jar (it's a thing along the Li River in China). Don't go with the lady who sees you sketching in the plaza and sits down to engage you in conversation while stroking your thigh. Seriously, I've got to tell you these things? Don't let your inner adult leave the room just because you're in a place where you think nobody knows you.

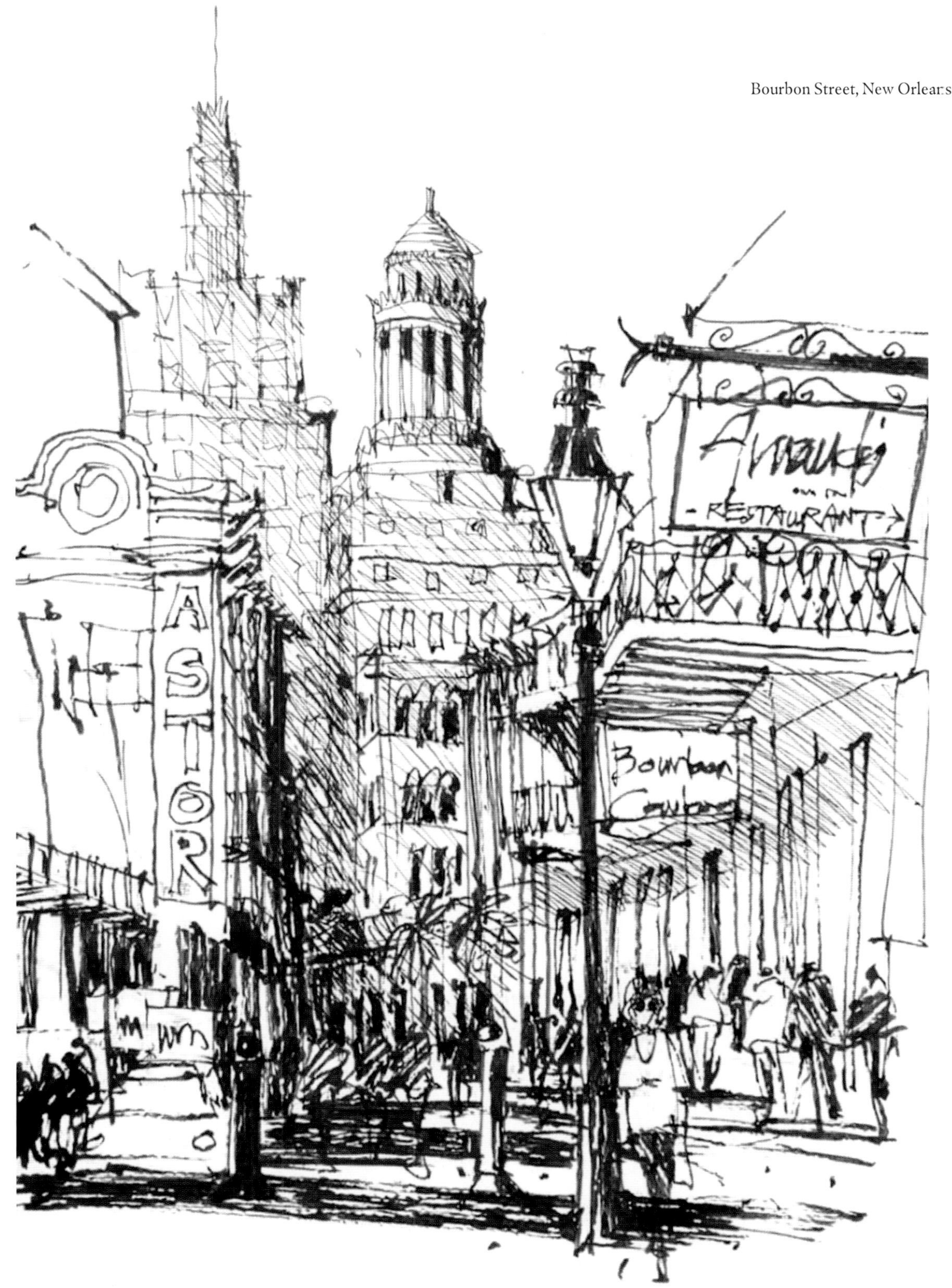

Bourbon Street, New Orleans.

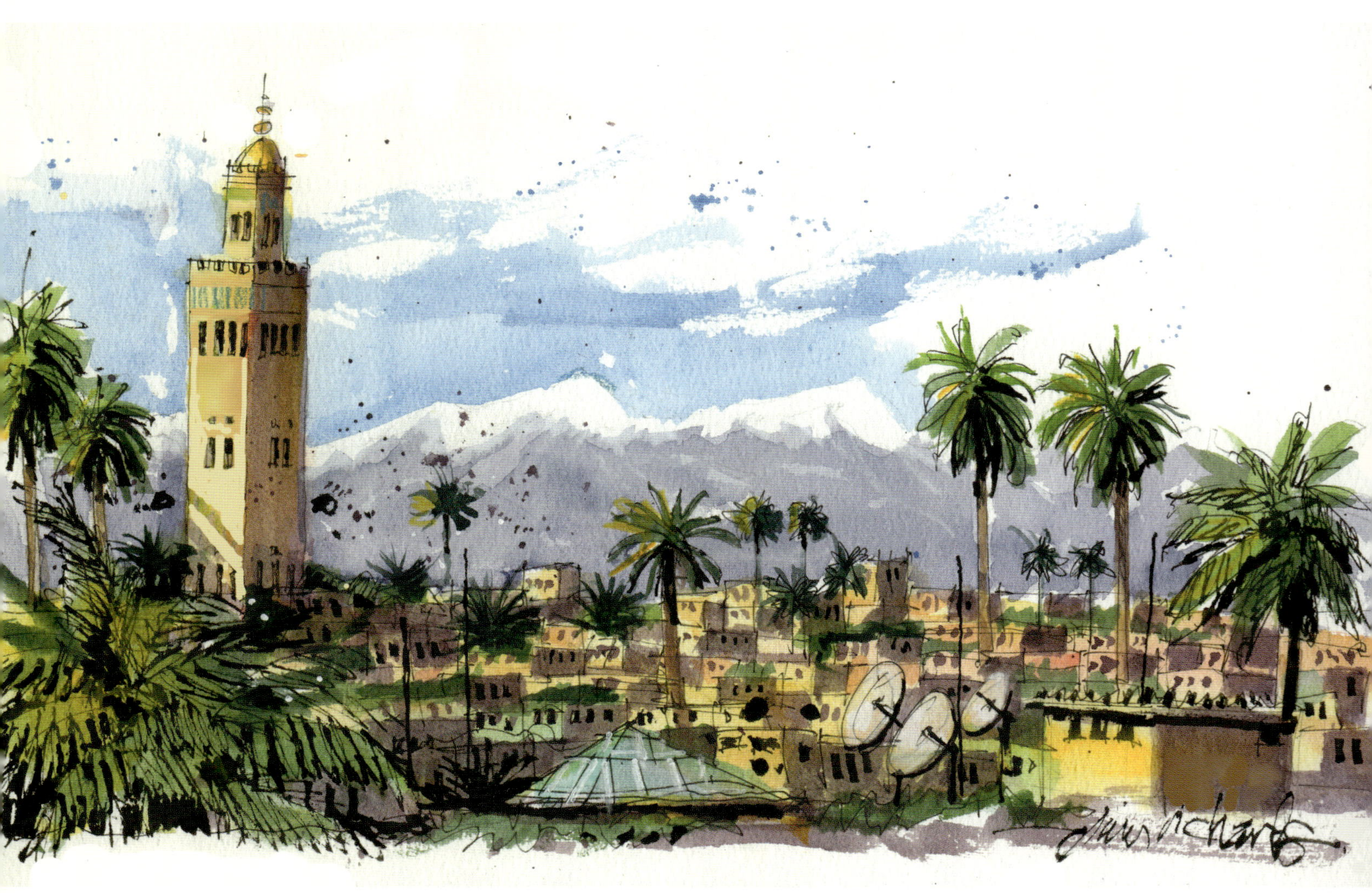

CHAPTER 7

Morocco: Looking for Different

My first impression of Morocco was reading an account of Keith Richards' 1967 journey there to be inspired by the exotic culture and music, make off with bandmate Brian Jones' girlfriend, and smoke hashish. I was a teenager at the time, and to me this sounded like Homer's *Odyssey.* So, years later when Karolina sent me a draft itinerary for a sketching excursion there, I knocked over a chair rushing across the room to sign the contract. I sensed adventure. I wanted to explore and sketch a place that felt exotic. And the thing is, the more places around the world start to look and feel the same, the more we look for what's different. Morocco is an adult dose of different.

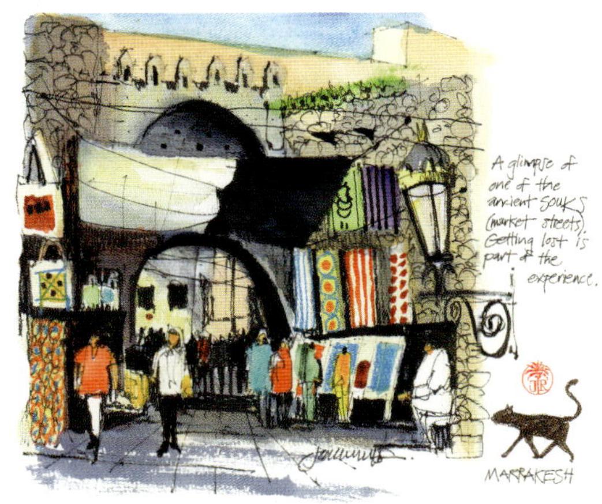

For our Morocco adventure, I led 15 artist travelers in exploring a pretty good swath of the country. Most of our group had at least some experience in sketching. All had done a bit of travel. None had been to Morocco.

Ah, Marrakesh. We drew in Jemaa el-Fnaa square, the central open marketplace, among merchants, food vendors, snake charmers, and monkeys trained, in one way or another, to separate tourists from their money. We drew in souks, the crowded, narrow market streets where craftsmen practiced trades and crafts largely unchanged for hundreds of years, while motorcycles honked and wove their way through the slow-moving crowd. These narrow streets are a sensory overload—fabric, wood, jewelry, bells, rugs, bottles, ceramics, shiny bits of metal, most hung together vertically, not so much a market display as an organic curtain of rich colors and textures that line these dark interior streets.

Opposite: The Marrakesh cityscape on a clear day, with the High Atlas Mountains seen in the background.

Top: A walk through the souks is a step back in time.

Everywhere is the smell of dust, donkeys, spices, baking bread, and smoke from grilling food. It was exhilarating. I defy anyone not to think of Indiana Jones here, but this ain't a movie set. It ain't Disneyland. It's Marrakesh, and it's the real deal.

And the thing is, the more places around the world start to look and feel the same, the more we look for what's different. Morocco is an adult dose of different.

Emerging from the souks, we sat at café tables and drew our views of bustling streets and squares. Anywhere we paused to sketch, we were immediately approached by one to a half dozen hawkers wanting to sell their treasure du jour. If you need to, you can be firm in declining, but you really can't get huffy about it. After all, it's an ingrained part of the culture you came to see. And if you're drawing in their public marketplace, it's just part of the gig.

I turned down a quiet side street to explore off the tourist path and came on a jaw-dropping scene: a line of overhead fabric canopies loosely strung across the road, earthen walls, wooden stalls, cooking fires, and gorgeous, angular shafts of light piercing the dust and smoke between the canopies. It was a surreal scene. A group of men watched me from the side of the street. When I raised my phone for a photo, a young and clearly agitated young man hurried towards me. "No! No photo here! Who are you? Show respect! Nothing unless you ask permission! We are not monkeys in a zoo! Leave! LEAVE!"

I was stunned. I'd never had anyone react with rage to my walking and sketching. But it was the camera that set him off. With that iPhone, I was just another voyeur tourist on his residential back street. I tried to show him my sketchbook, but the ship had already sailed. I should have known better. Hell, I did know better. Read the room. This wasn't an Instagram moment. It's their home.

It's a message about respect. For tourism—even artist travelers—to coexist with authentic places and peoples, the visitor should have some genuine understanding of the place and culture, and treat both with respect. It requires a mind open to receiving something from the experience, rather than simply taking away.

Leaving Marrakesh, we traveled east through passes in the High Atlas Mountains, across the desert plains and into gorges, sketching

Opposite: This busy promenade linking the striking Koutoubia Mosque, the largest in the city, with the Jemaa el-Fnaa marketplace is a world- class sketching location.

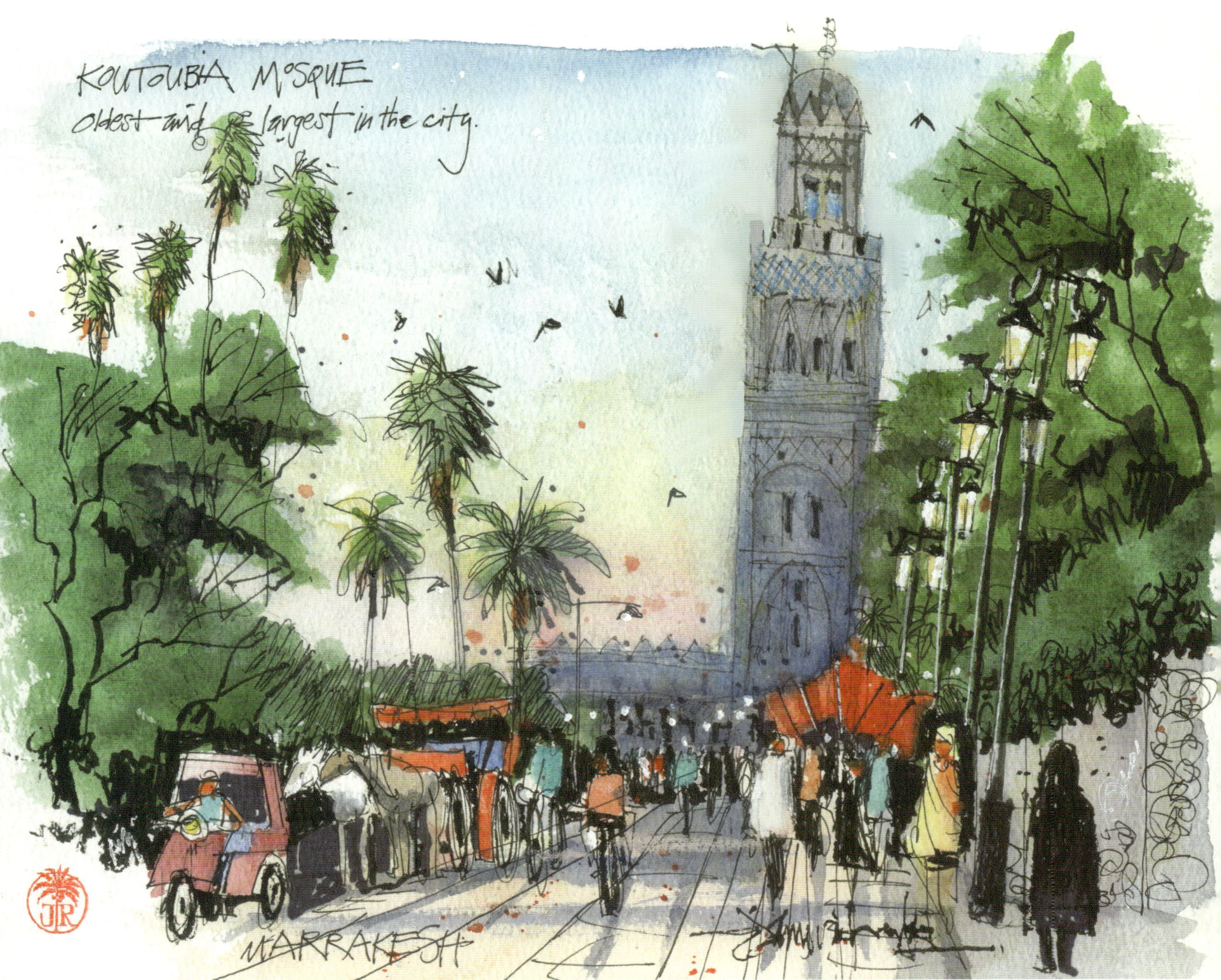
KOUTOUBIA MOSQUE
oldest and largest in the city.
MARRAKESH

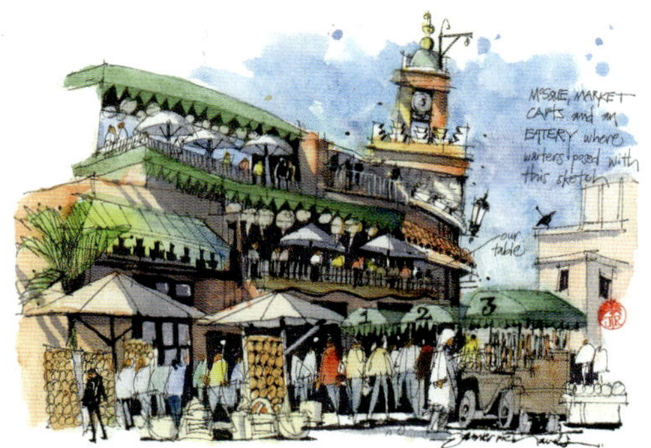

oasis settlements shrouded in date palms and rushes, villages of stone and earth that seemed to have grown out of the rocky outcrops, goats in trees, and bustling roadside markets teeming with locals buying and selling. At one village, Berbers in bright blue traditional dress appeared, certainly to offer to pose for photo ops. As often happens, they immediately became transfixed with this group of intensely focused strangers sketching their village. As the drawings progressed, each a different, personal take on the scene, there was chatter, laughter and high fives.

The following afternoon, reddish dunes appeared on the far horizon. This is why we came east, to experience the Sahara on its westernmost fringe. A few hours later, we were trekking deep into the dunes in a camel caravan to experience the intensely red Sahara sunset, and the stars starting to appear in the darkening, deep cobalt blue sky.

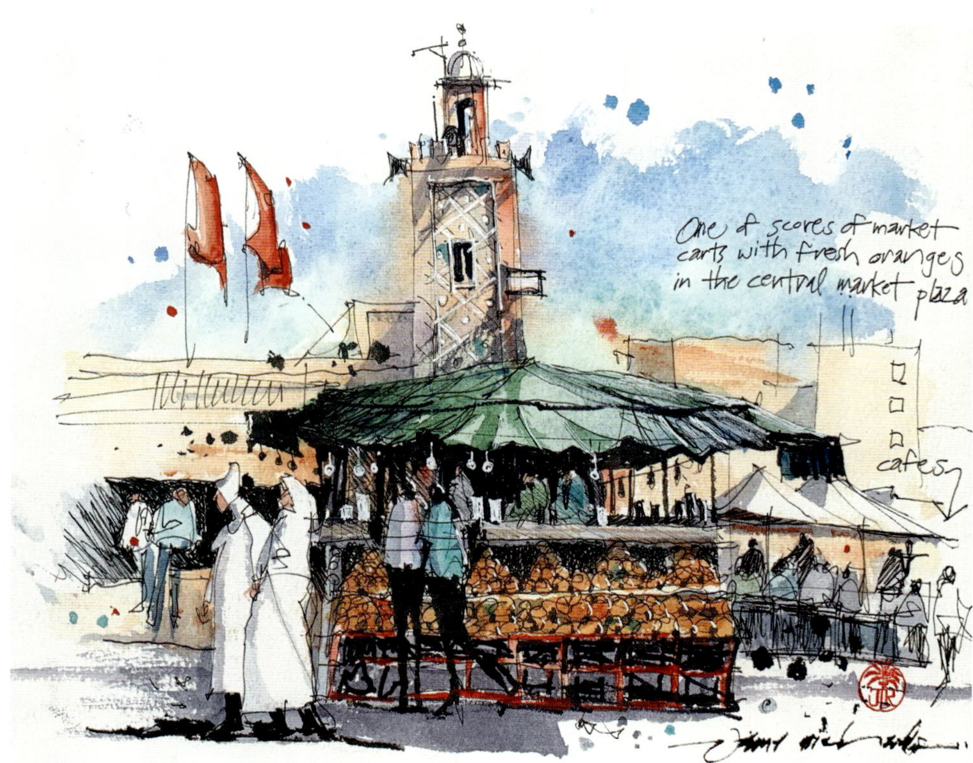

Top: A restaurant occupies the upper deck, overlooking Jemaa el-Fnaa Square. A waiter took notice and posed for a photo with my sketch.

Right: A mosque, interesting characters and one of dozens of fruit stands in Jemaa el-Fnaa Square made for a striking sketch composition.

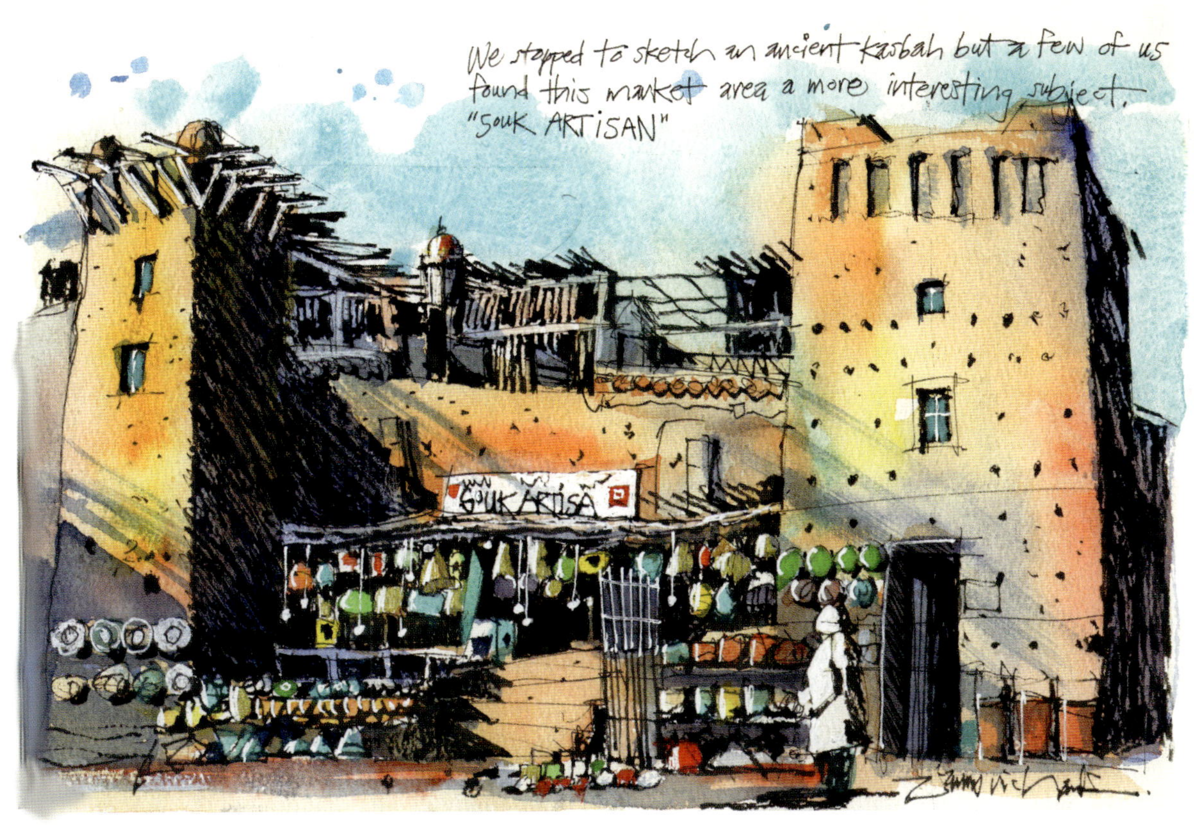

This souk artisan's riot of texture and color beckoned from the roadside, demanding to be sketched.

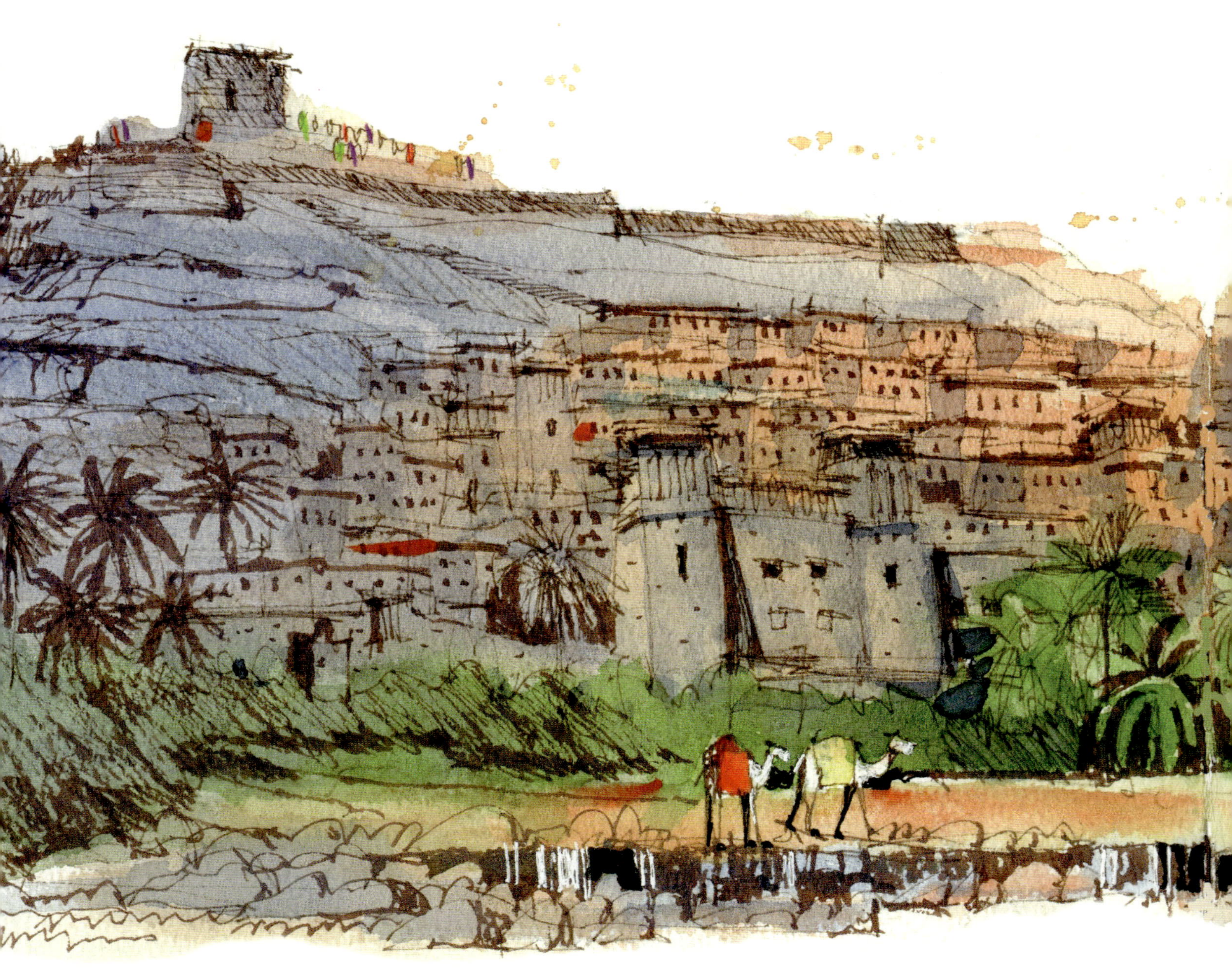

Aït Benhaddou is a *ksar*, or a fortified earthen clay village along the old caravan route between the Sahara and Marrakesh. Over one thousand years old, it provided settings for *Lawrence of Arabia, Gladiator, The Mummy, Game of Thrones* and many other films and television shows.

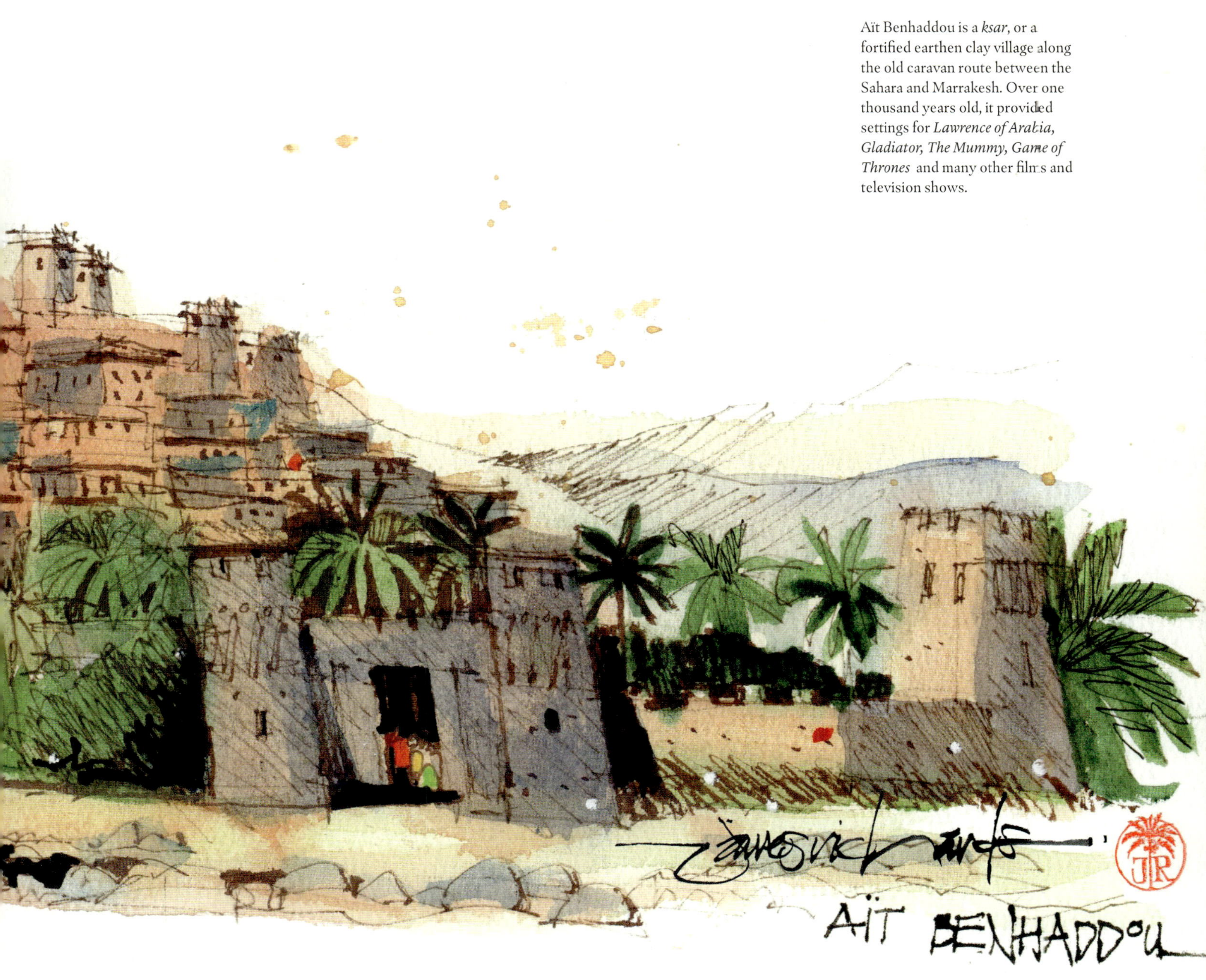

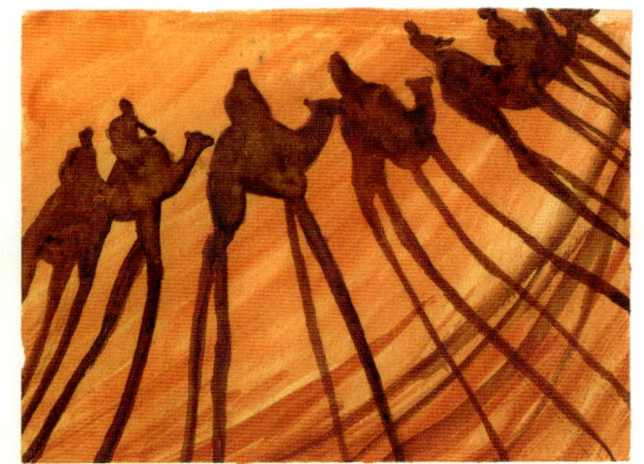

Shadows on the dunes of our Saharan camel caravan about 30 minutes before sunset.

Late in the evening, a few of us quietly hopped into 4-wheel drives for what I was assured was a strictly off-itinerary field trip into the desert night. Several minutes later we arrived at a small cluster of earthen buildings. We could see flickering light from a fire on the walls and hear music as we were taken to an open-air courtyard, where 15 or so people sat in a circle around the fire. Seven musicians sang over a hypnotic rhythm from their handmade drums and finger cymbals, all in a haze of bonfire smoke with a hint of hashish. Eventually, the musicians rose to move to the rhythm. The outsiders joined in, forming a dance line around the fire. It could have been a scene from hundreds of years ago, but here we were, dancing in the thick of it.

Our last road trip destination was Essaouira, a beautiful old port city of white and blue buildings and stone walls perched on the rocky edge of the Atlantic. This was once a fortress for the Phoenicians and later the Portuguese. Our group sat on the top of the seawall, capturing the dramatic stretch of coast where the city abruptly meets the Atlantic, clinging to the rocky shore and reflecting the beautiful coastal light in what looked like a scene from another time. When I finished my panoramic watercolor sketch, I followed my nose along the waterfront, past old wooden boats and working fishermen, through a massive stone gate to the bustling fish market.

I've loved the sights, noises, and smells of real working fish markets since I was a boy in New Orleans, when the fresh catches came in daily to a part of the French Market that now houses praline and t-shirt shops. Here the market is open air. The seller's carts, tables, and crates are shaded by tarps and umbrellas. The ground is very muddy, with potholes of standing water. The tables are packed with fresh eels, sharks, skates, red snapper, saber fish, squid, sea urchins, and several other species I was clueless about. I stood in the mud and sketched from an out of the way spot, trying not to impede movement or commerce.

Like much of Morocco, the whole scene felt like going back in time, so it felt natural to emulate the feel of an old N.C. Wyeth illustration for an adventure book. The drawing is recognizable as Essaouira and takes me back to that place, but it also takes me back to boyhood daydreams of travel and adventure. On those occasions when this happens, I have a feeling of having come full circle, from reading and imagining as a boy on my bedroom floor to exploring new horizons with the sense of purpose that drawing and discovery can bring. It feels like I was meant to be here to drink in the experience, to draw it, and to share it with followers from other parts of the world—vagabond artists, armchair travelers, and maybe a kid on the bedroom floor dreaming of sketching the world.

The fish market in Essaouira

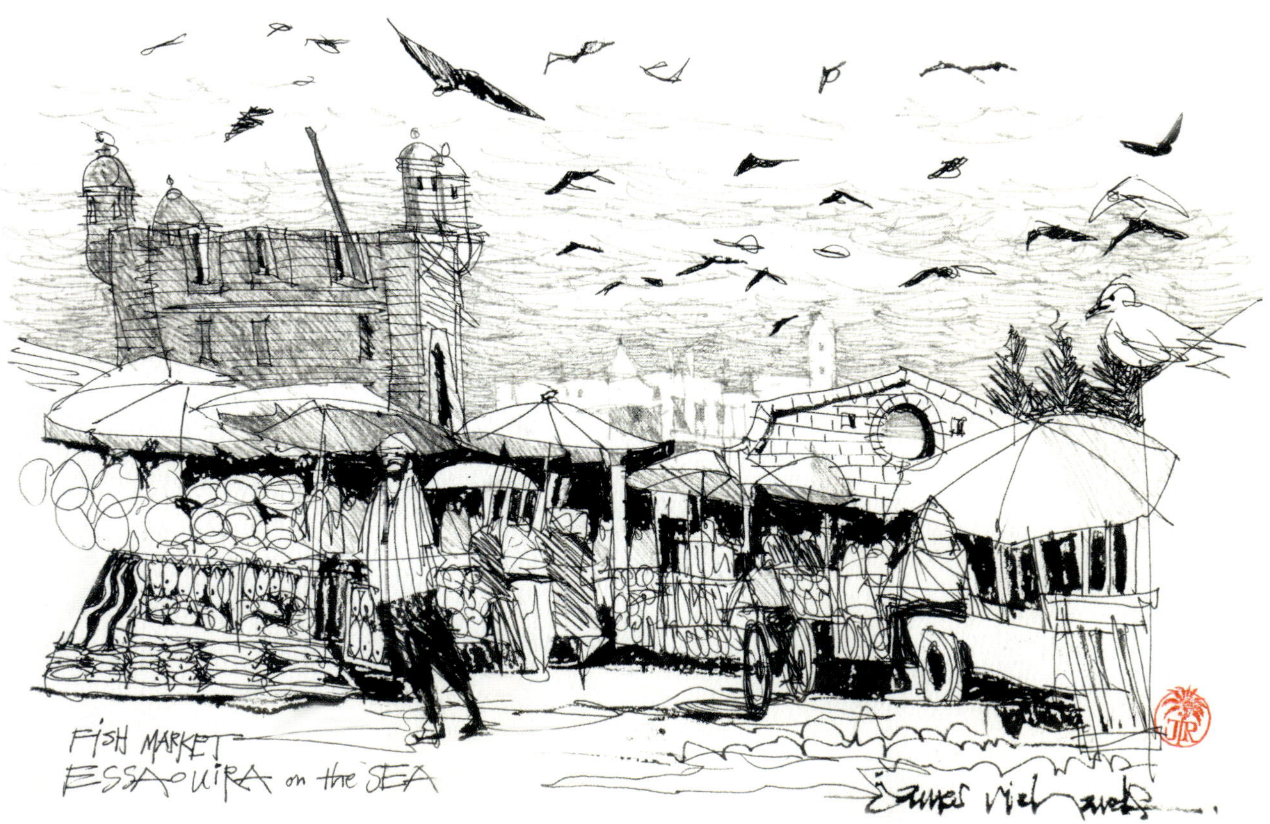

Searching for the Genuine

For me, few things are as disappointing as showing up in a new location expecting to sketch a place that feels exotic, or at least that still has some traces of authenticity, and being assaulted by the same strip shopping centers, KFCS, dollar stores, chain hotels, and billboard ads that I just left back home (I've let Starbucks slide because they have nice restrooms).

I'm looking for what I call "real places" — vibrant cities, traditional towns, villages, or pockets of wildness that retain a sense of authenticity, with roots in their native landscape, history, cultures, and regional building traditions. You can sense an integrity that has somehow remained intact through decades or centuries of growth and change. They have a character that's distinctive, like nowhere else.

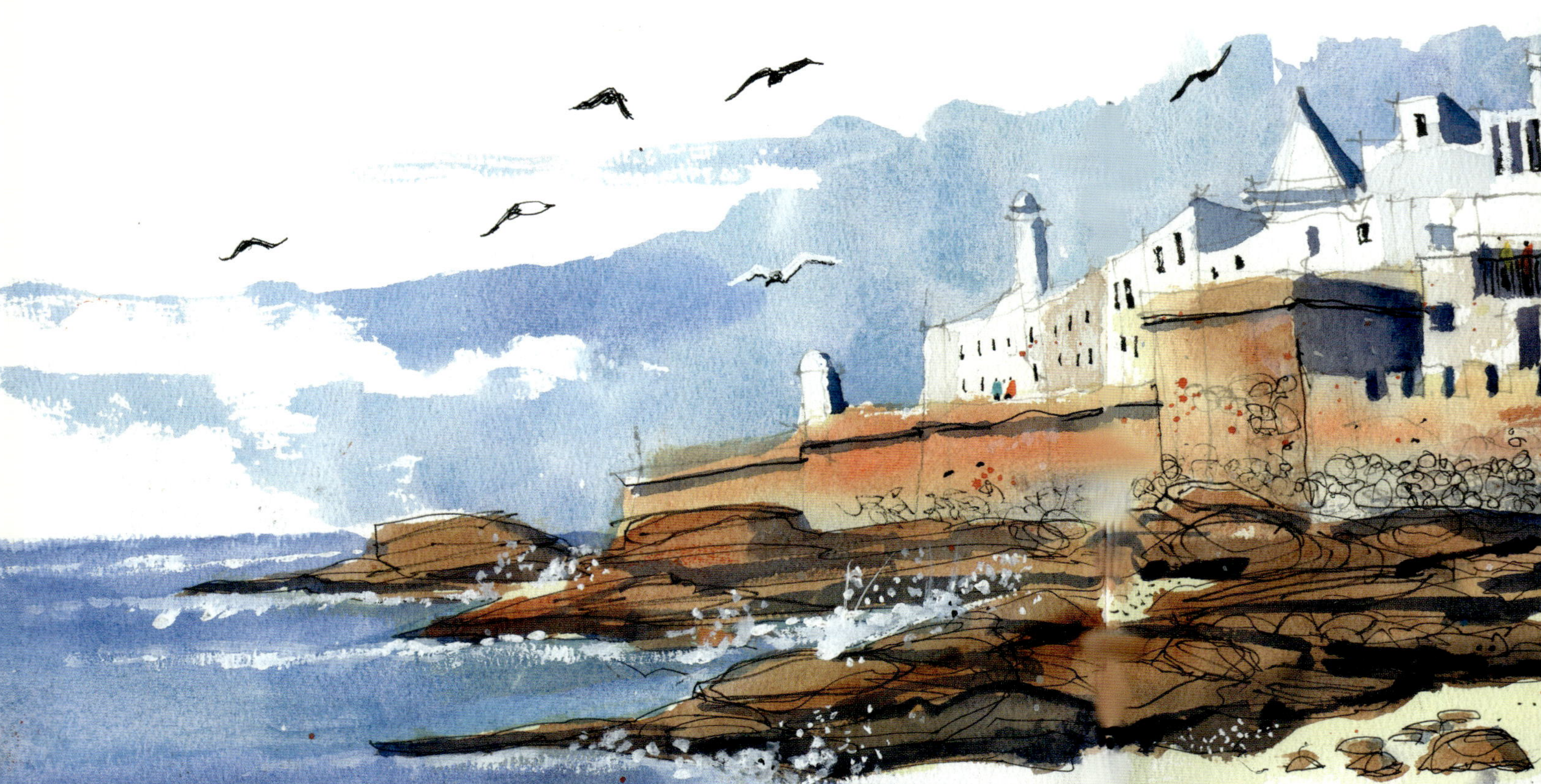

Essaouira's white townscape perched atop the rocky Atlantic coastline.

These are increasingly rare qualities, and I believe we're hardwired to be attracted to such places. And as images from cave paintings to millions of selfies around the world testify, it's human nature to try to document our own personal experience of memorable places.

At best, the sketches I create there have their own sense of the genuine, almost all having been drawn on the spot and in the moment. They convey something of the energy of the time and place in which they were drawn and reflect all the imperfections and idiosyncrasies that are the nature of the real thing. I'll sometimes rework one in the studio from a rough field sketch, always with the intent of preserving the spirit of the on-location work.

The best of these take on a life and energy of their own, becoming a unique fusion of place, pen, and personality of the recorder. The result is a unique, creative expression of a particular instant. Something is born in that moment that didn't exist before, and that magic can't come together in exactly the same way again. That's the genuine. And that's the definition—and the rush—of creative work.

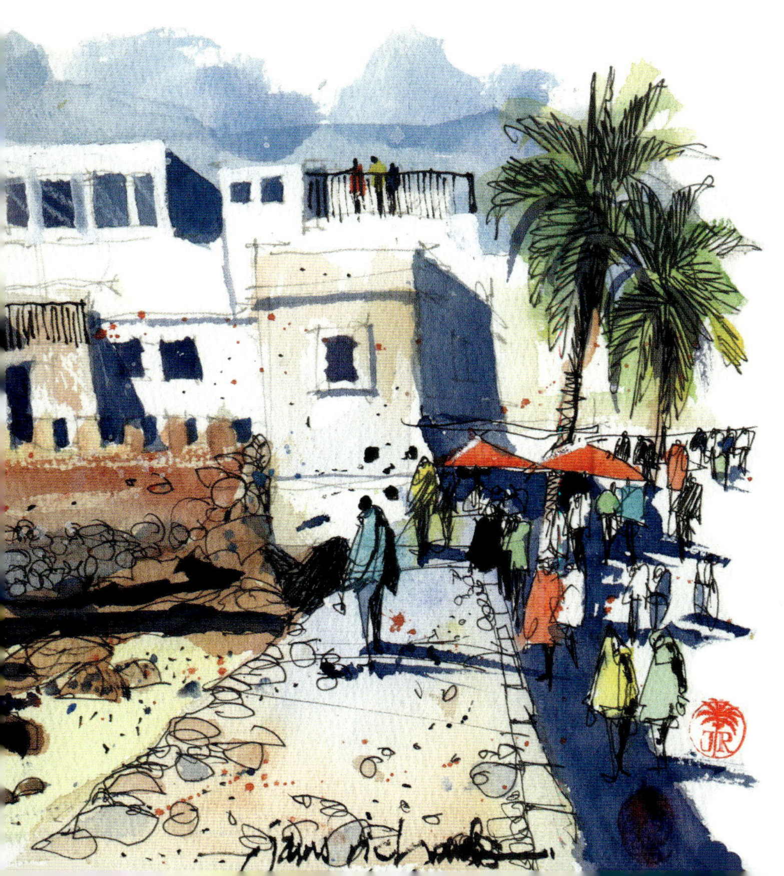

The Sketcher's Code

We don't need no stinking rules.

I sketch left-handed with a fountain pen. I have for years. But no one ever taught me how to do it correctly. Over time, I found my own way of working, committing the deadly sins of working right to left and pushing the pen as much as I pull it. The drawings are great. But I still worried that someday, someone would discover that I had no idea what I was doing.

Then I remind myself that Jimi Hendrix played a right-handed guitar upside down with his left hand. With his technique, experimentation, and imagination, he invented sounds we'd never heard before, like something from another dimension, and changed music and culture forever. As far as I know, no one ever approached the stage and said, "Excuse me sir, but you're not doing that correctly." And I'm reminded of a hard-earned lesson: that our personal idiosyncrasies and perceived limitations aren't a burden. They're our gift.

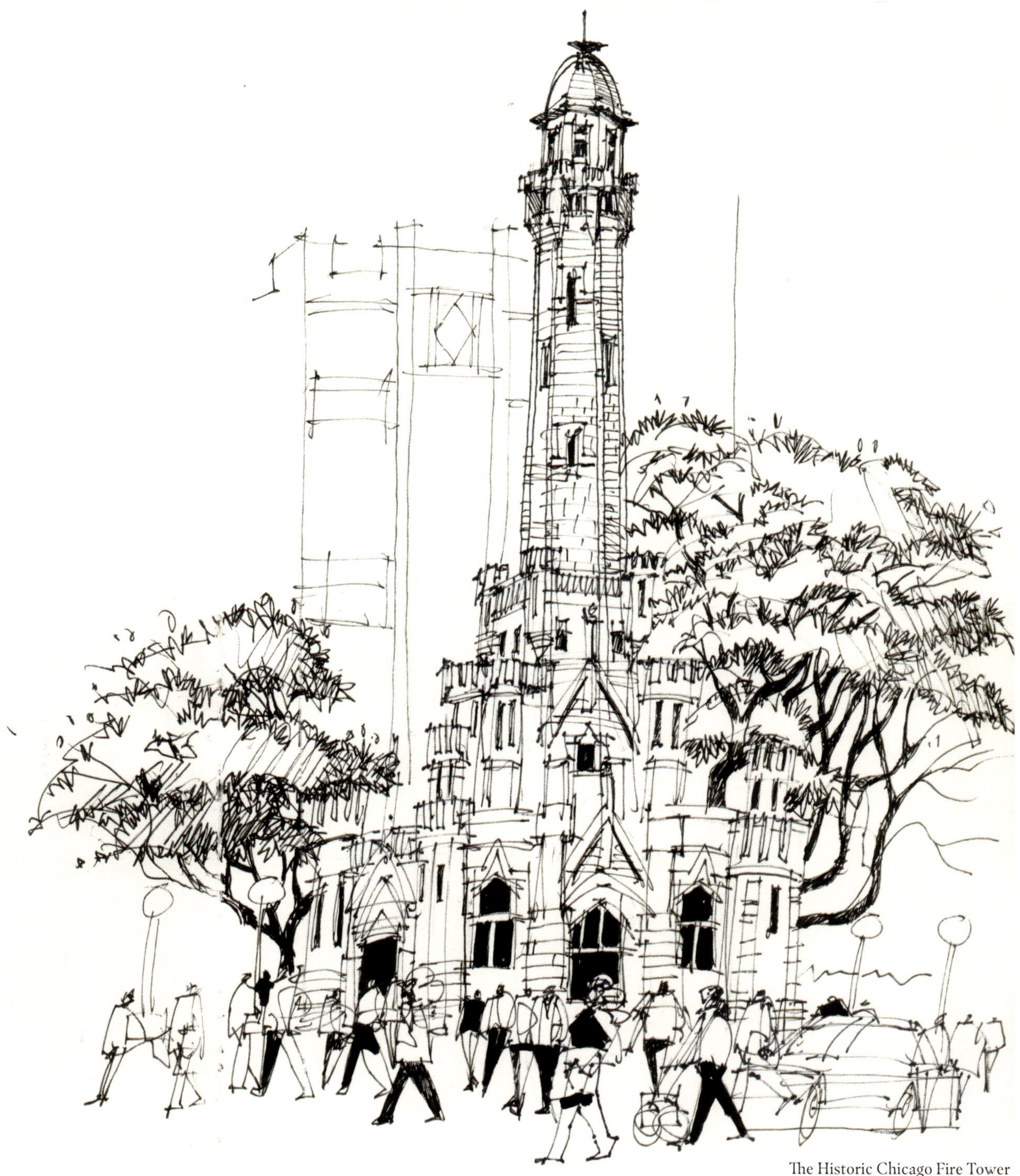

The Historic Chicago Fire Tower

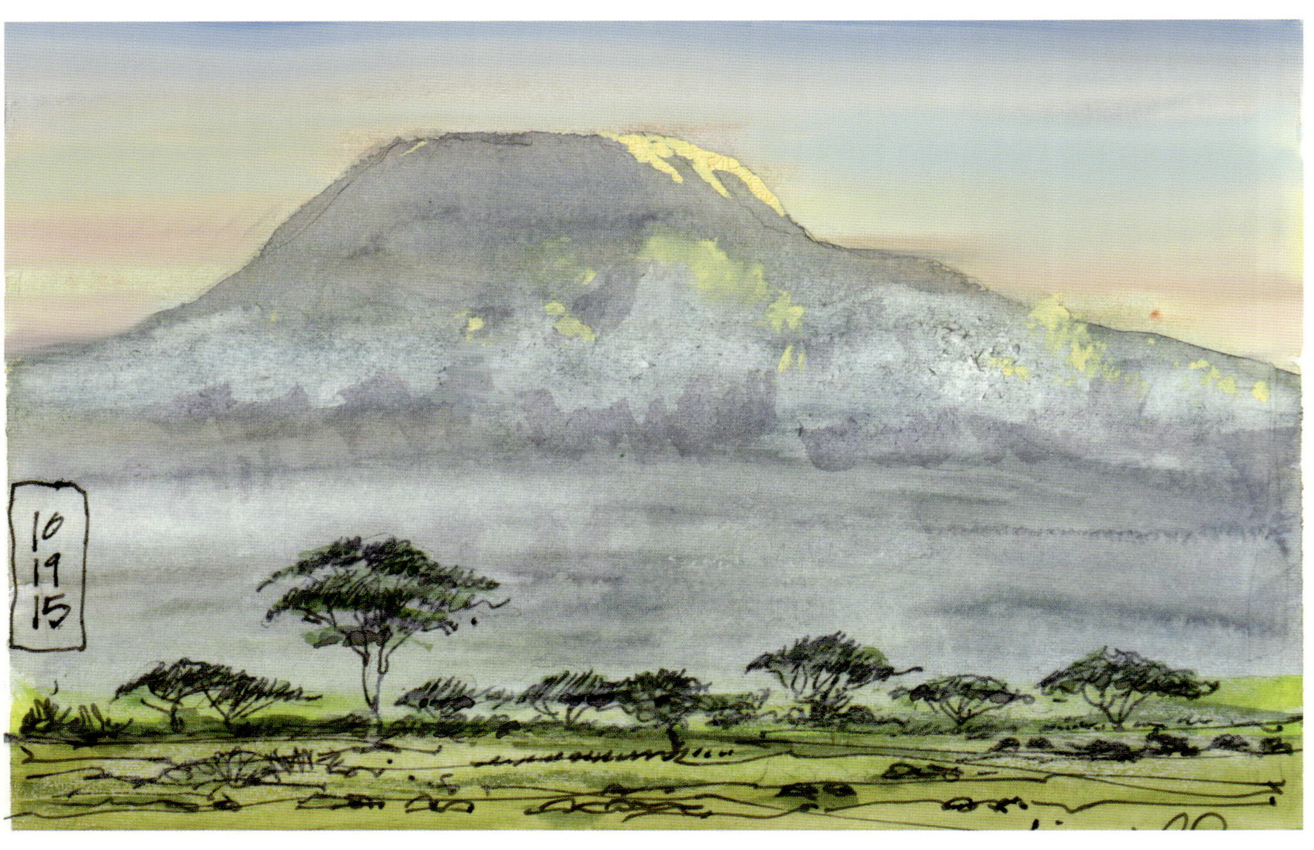
10
19
15

CHAPTER 8

Kenya: Through Ancient Eyes

AFRICA HAD BEEN the Holy Grail on my travel list since I was old enough to watch 1940s adventure movies on Saturday afternoon TV. Many were set in the "jungles of Africa" which, I learned later, were actually Florida, Hollywood back lots or any of dozens of locations that had nothing to do with my childhood imagination's notions of a dark, mysterious continent. Kenya, especially, held a fascination for me, stoked by reading the accounts of Theodore Roosevelt's safari expeditions there, the fictional and real-life stories of Ernest Hemingway, and Karen Blixen's autobiographical *Out of Africa*. I'd been fascinated since high school by the work of the Leakey family of world-renowned paleoanthropologists, whose discoveries in Kenya's Olduvai Gorge and its environs established eastern Africa as the cradle of humanity. And my desire to experience the majestic presence of Kilimanjaro had long been a dream, hoped for but seemingly out of reach. Yes, Kenya's grip on me was strong and longstanding. So, when my friend and fellow sketcher, architect, and professor Gathogo Githatu asked if I would come to Nairobi to keynote an international conference, teach a drawing workshop, and lead university students on their first on-location sketch outing, there was no question in my mind. This was it. When a dream calls, you go.

My first memory of Nairobi is of the sprawling Maasai Market, where tribesmen and women had spread their curios, jewelry, paintings, fabric, wood carvings, and the occasional giraffe hair bracelet or gazelle horn on blankets, hanging from branches or from makeshift frames under the

Opposite: Kilimanjaro emerges from its shroud of cloud cover at sunset in Amboseli National Park.

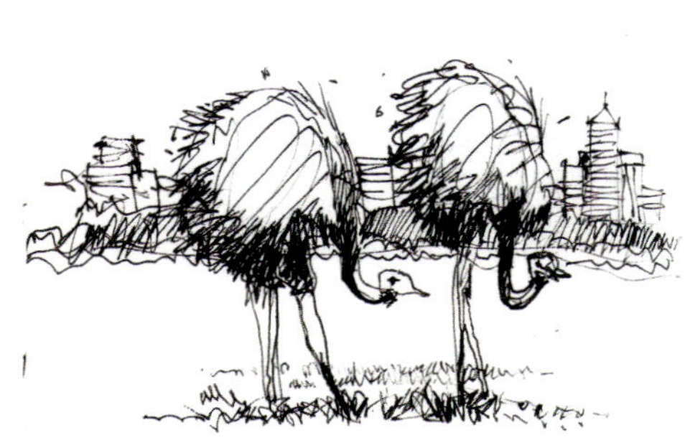

shade of trees along a stream. None were particularly pushy, but if you showed the slightest interest or even took a second glance, our guide quickly tossed the item into his burlap bag. Later, under a large tree, the treasures were spread on the ground and the tribesmen gathered to negotiate prices. They quickly determined that my negotiating skills consisted of, "I have money. You have stuff. I give you money. You give me stuff." Done. The Grown-up's no-bullshit bargaining, on the other hand, quickly struck fear into their hearts, and they tried to avoid her at all costs.

"Papa, look at this," they'd whisper. "I make good price for you."

"Nah, man, you gotta talk to Mama."

"No, no, no! No Mama!" they'd hiss. "Papa, please, look, good price."

"Sorry, man" And any semblance of joy drained from their face as they shuffled towards Patti, heads down, like lambs to the slaughter.

Arriving at the Jomo Kenyetta University campus, we were led to a large room full of excited students, with what looked like a couple of hundred drawings pinned to the walls. "Come take a look," Gathogo said. And on leaning in, I saw that the student drawings were skillful interpretations of my own, copied by the students from my book to aid them in learning their secrets. I couldn't believe the sheer number and quality of the drawings, and the outpouring of love from the students showered on

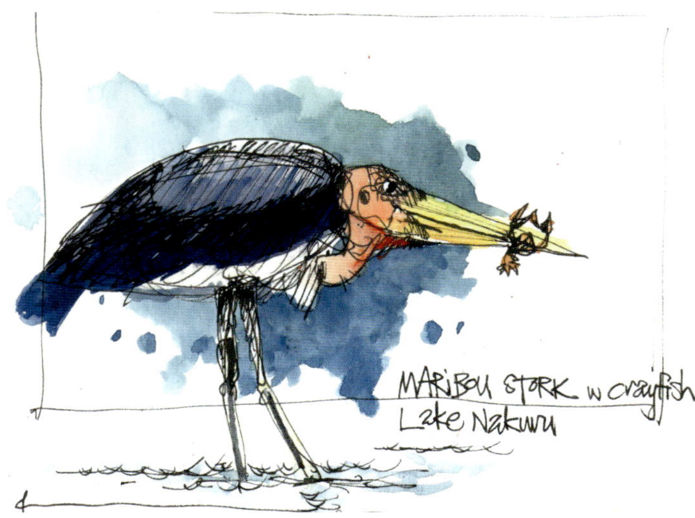

Top: Ostriches, Nairobi National Park.

Right: Marabou stork with a crawfish Lake Naikuru.

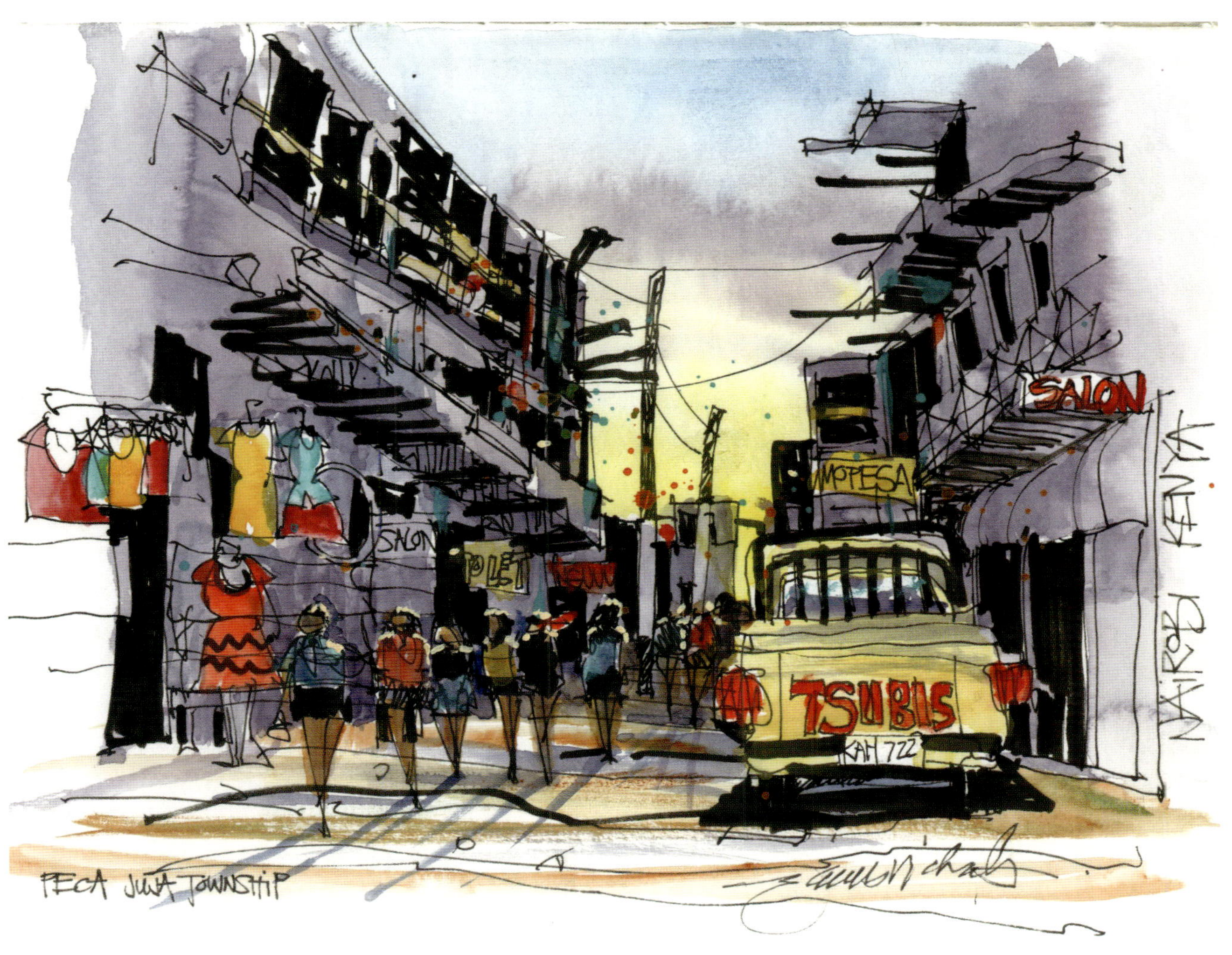

A narrow earthen road in the heart of Peca Juja township, the site of our sketch walk with faculty and students.

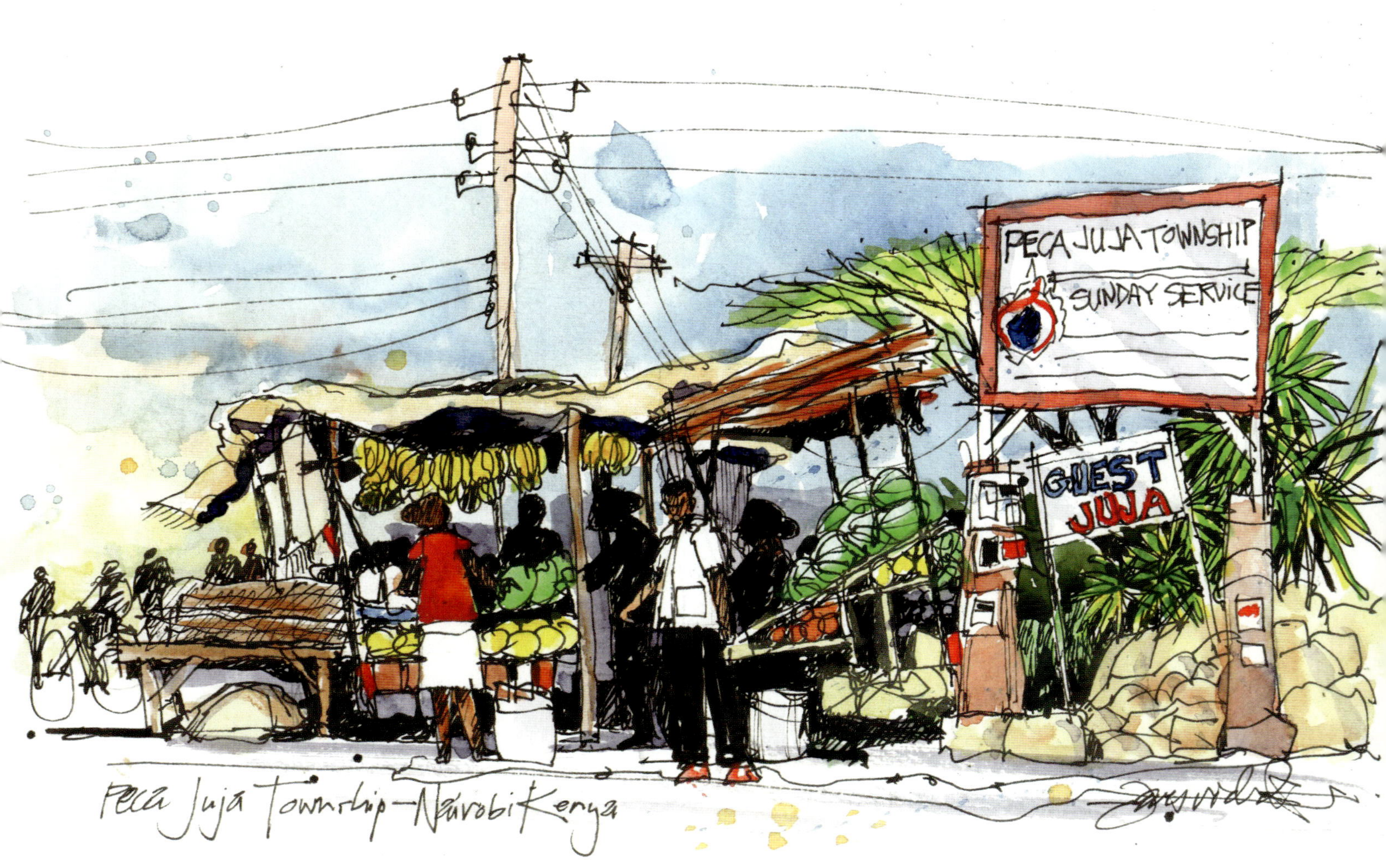

A market stall in the township immediately outside the university gates.

Patti and me as we took it all in. And this is the thing—when you make something that's true to yourself and put it out there in the world, you never know how it's going to impact people you've never dreamed of meeting. That makes all the effort and the years leading up to it more than worthwhile.

After delivering my keynote to academics from across Africa, a large group of students and a few faculty gathered at the university gate for their first on-location sketching experience. I'd done some scouting earlier and made a few preliminary sketches of this little corner of Juja Township with its dirt streets, market stalls, dogs, motorbikes, cattle pulling carts, and children running barefoot in the road. I showed the group a couple of my very simple sketches to try to diffuse their angst over drawing in public, and to show that their everyday surroundings made great sketching subjects. Everyone jumped in—they seemed hungry for it, like drawing together was scratching some creative itch. There was intense focus, lots of laughter, and "aha" moments as students started to buy into the idea that this reintegration of work and play

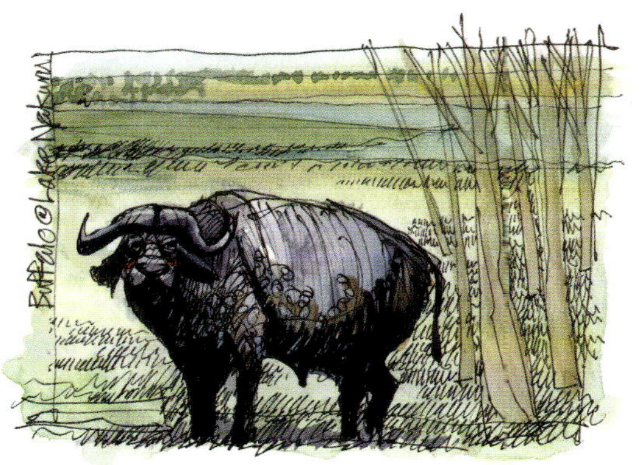

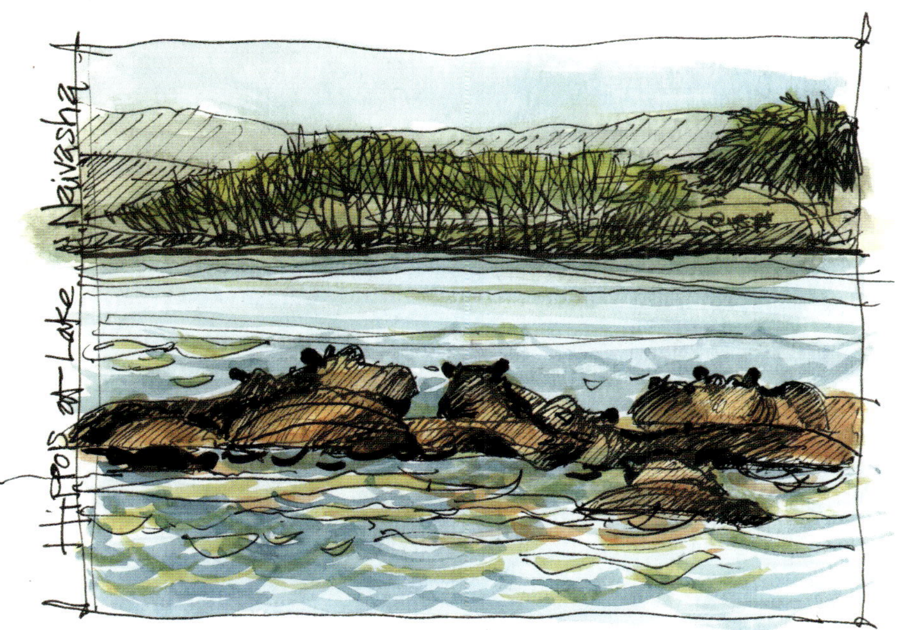

Top: An old cape buffalo bull near Lake Nakuru.

Left: Hippos uncomfortably close to our small skiff on Lake Naivasha.

was just part of living a creative life—their creative life. Patti and I were swamped by those kids in the street, who clamored to see my drawings and have their photo taken. Yeah, for my money, this is what urban sketching is all about.

We left Nairobi with our new guide Dennis in his Land Cruiser, repainted a bright chartreuse that could probably be seen from space, and headed out on a sketch and photo safari that crisscrossed the southwest quadrant of Kenya. Nothing I had read or seen prepared me for the scale and majesty of the landscape. In the course of our ramblings, I sketched a panorama of the Great Rift Valley from a high bluff and hippos and flamingos from a dangerously small boat on Lake Naivasha. We slowly made our way through packs of baboons to encounter large herds of cape buffalo and two of the elusive white rhino near Lake Nukuru and spent two days exploring the breathtaking savannahs of Maasai Mara, teeming with wildlife and littered with white bones of animals that had died in that spot, their carcasses lying where they fell.

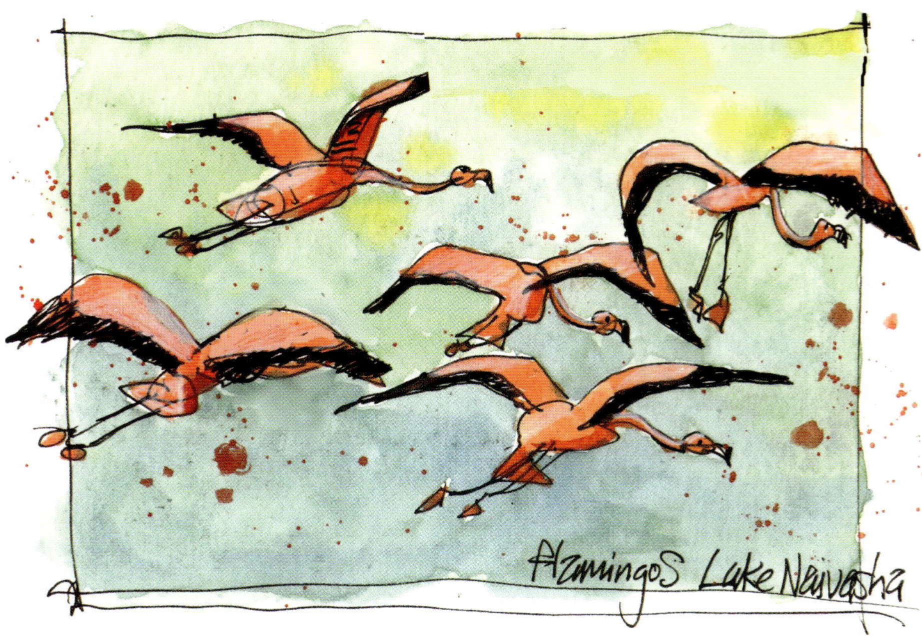

Flamingos on Lake Naivasha, quickly doodled as they took off to put more distance between themselves and our small boat.

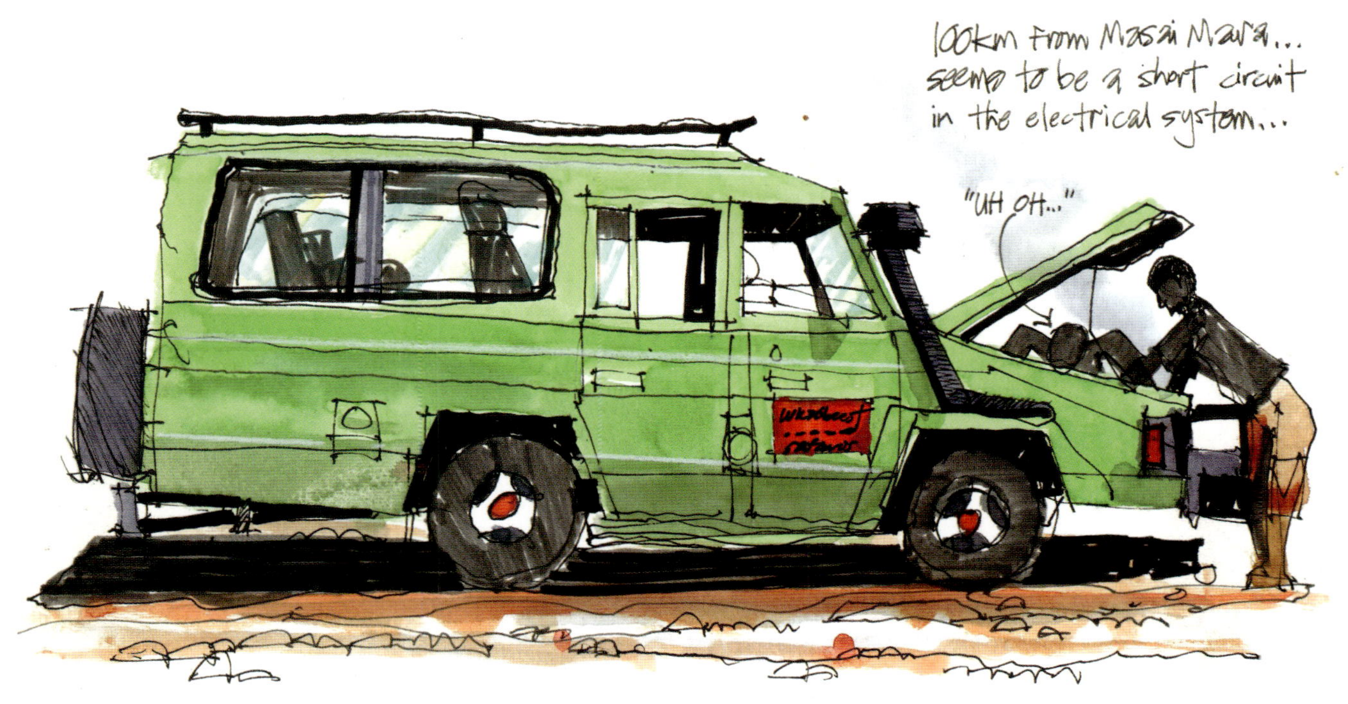

In a crisis everyone pitches in. I made myself useful by sketching the scene as our guide and his friends pondered the possible causes and solutions for our ailing engine.

Crossing the Mara on a very rough dirt road, and at a point roughly 100 miles from the last town and our ecolodge destination, our old Land Cruiser heaved, sputtered, and slowly rolled to a stop. *This probably isn't good,* I thought. Call AAA? Not likely. Either our guide can sort this out or we'd better get ready to spend the night out here. I'd been told that you really haven't experienced a safari until you break down and are stranded in the middle of nowhere, so at least we got to check that one off the "must do" list. Dennis opened the hood, leaned across the fender and fiddled with the engine a bit, and emerged clearly bamboozled. He called a friend in the town we'd passed through over an hour ago to bring a few parts and a buddy who knew these vehicles better than any of us.

I felt oddly at home there—a place long forgotten by countless generations of ancestors and far removed from my own daily life—but that seemed to claim some primal part of me, as something deep within the recesses of my mind seemed to dimly remember it.

Still waiting a few hours later, we heard bells. A young Maasai girl was herding goats across the plain. I saw no signs of a village in the vastness from which she'd come. I saw nothing in the direction she was headed. She crossed the road just yards away, paying us no attention. When she glanced towards us, I pointed to my cellphone camera. She hesitated, then stopped and faced me, as goats crossed the road behind her. I took the shot. When I waved thanks, she stood her ground, expressionless, extended her arm and opened her palm—clearly not her first rodeo. I don't remember how Dennis and his friends fixed the Land Cruiser, or how long it took. But I'll never forget that young Maasai girl, perfectly calm, confident, and capable, alone on the savannah with her goats.

At our new camp, we were woken long before dawn by teenage Maasai girls driving cattle, and often watched by vervet monkeys in the trees. We were terrified by 2am screams of a herd of panicked elephants, attacked by gawd-knows-what as they moved up a riverbed just feet below our tent on the bluff above. We traded stories in the small mud hut of the son of a Maasai chief, whose neck was adorned by gifts from "many girlfriends," and who enjoyed conversation but quickly became bored with my sketchbook. Hot days were often capped by relaxing with a cold Tusker beer, brewed in Nairobi and a proper complement for

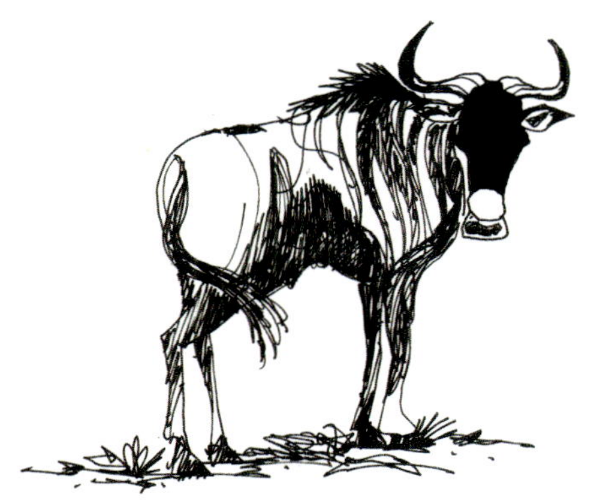

A wildebeest, Amboseli National Park.

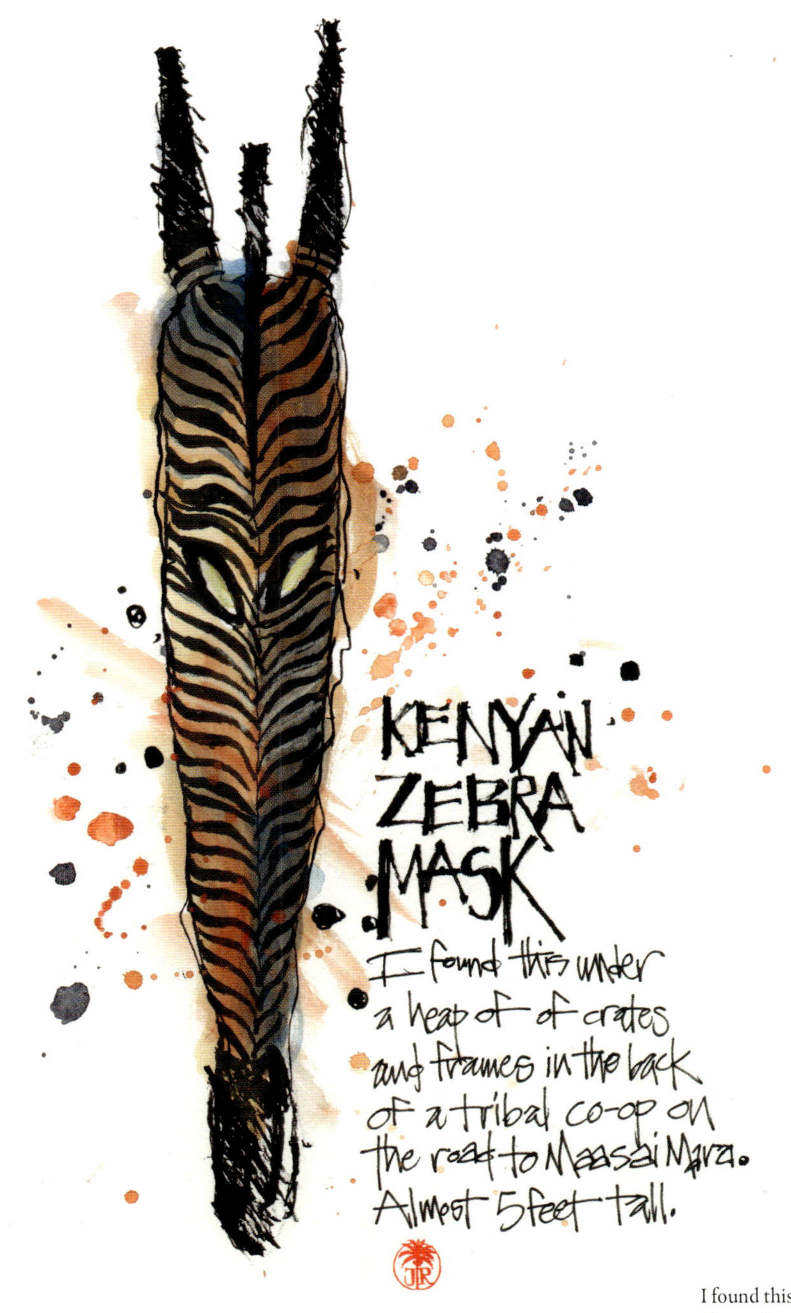

I found this wooden zebra mask, almost five-feet tall, in the back of a tribal co-op building on the road to the Maasai Mara.

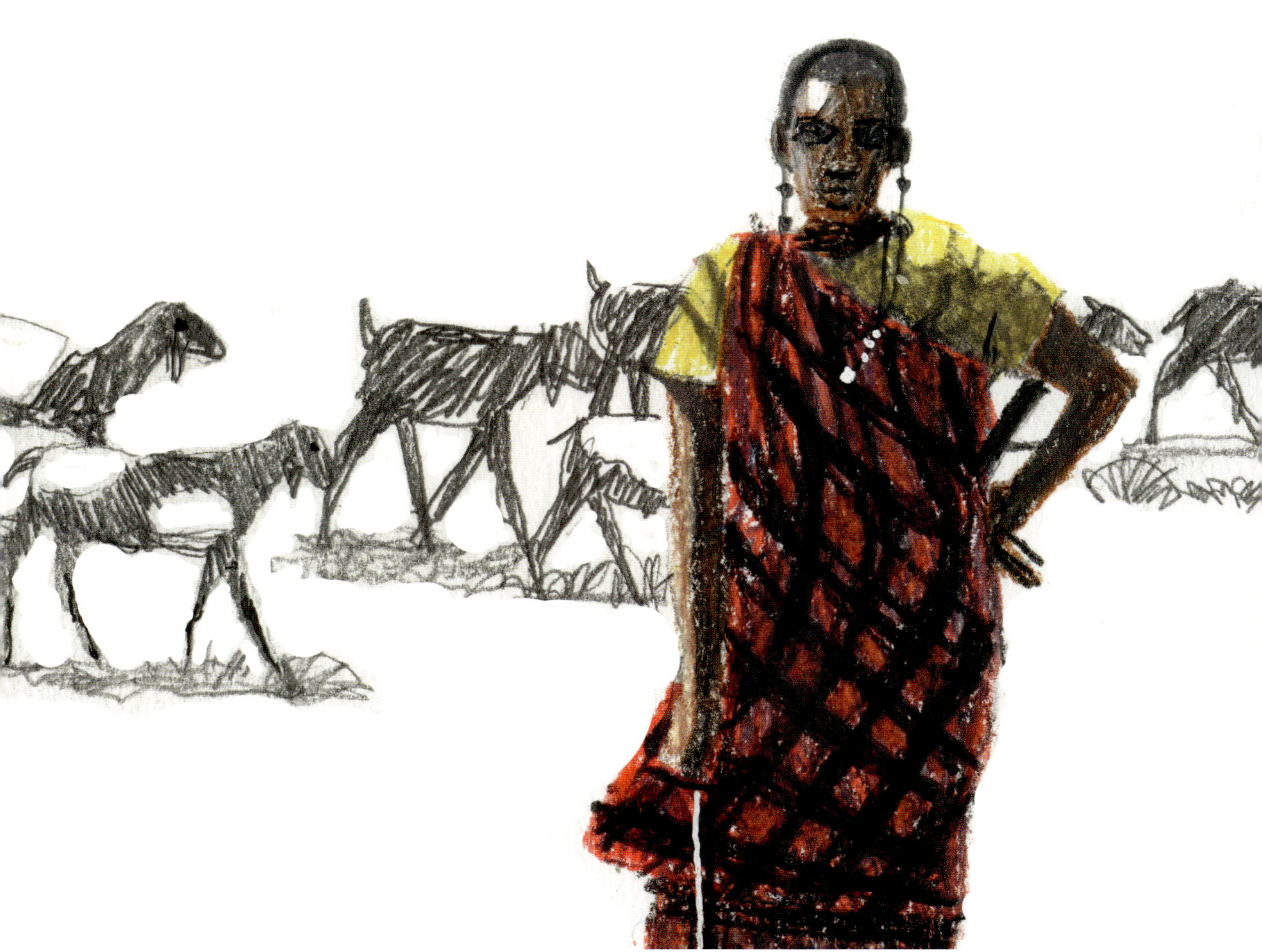

The Maasai girl and her goats.

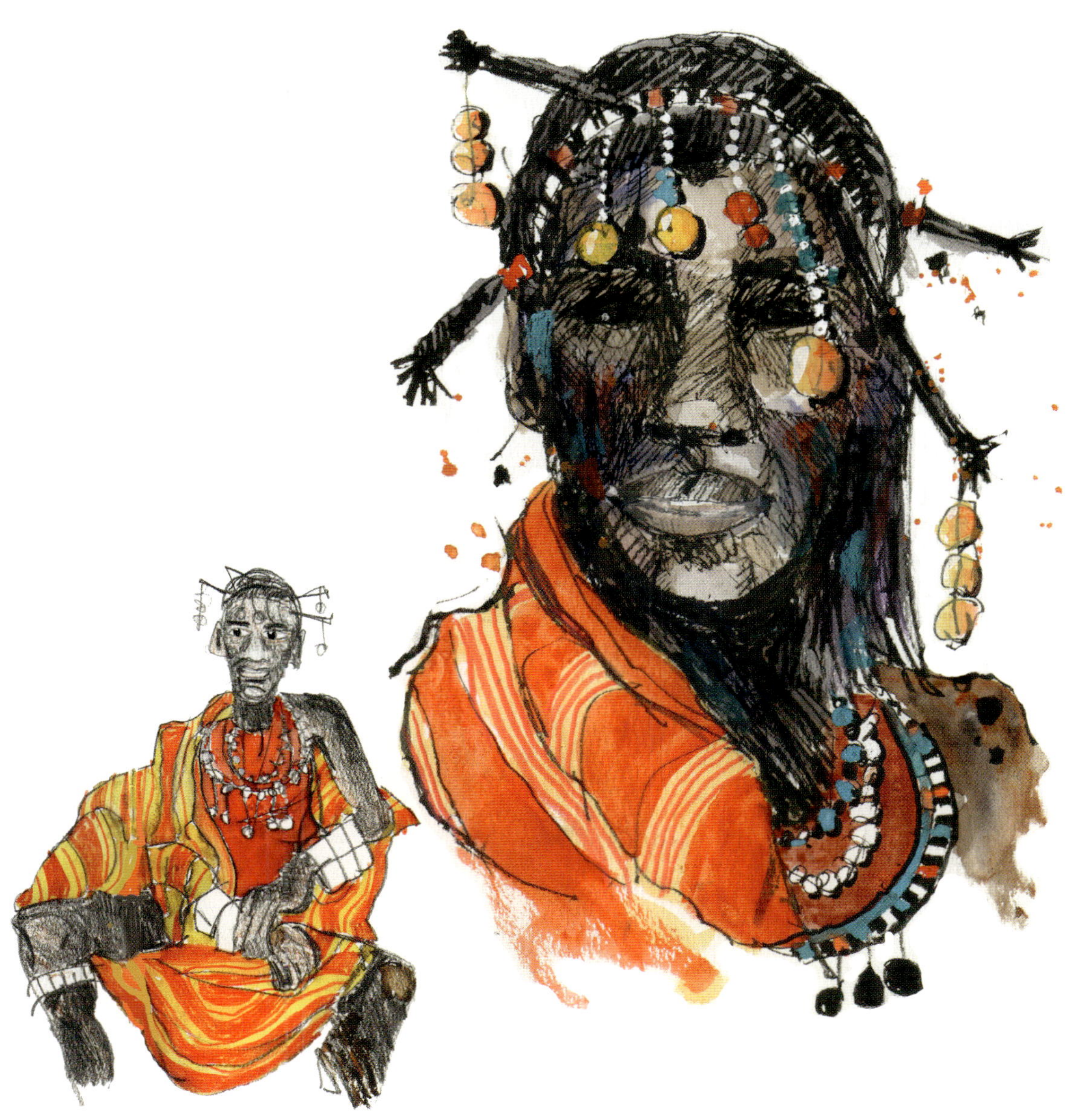

The son of the Maasai chief, who asked many questions, but was unimpressed with my sketchbook.

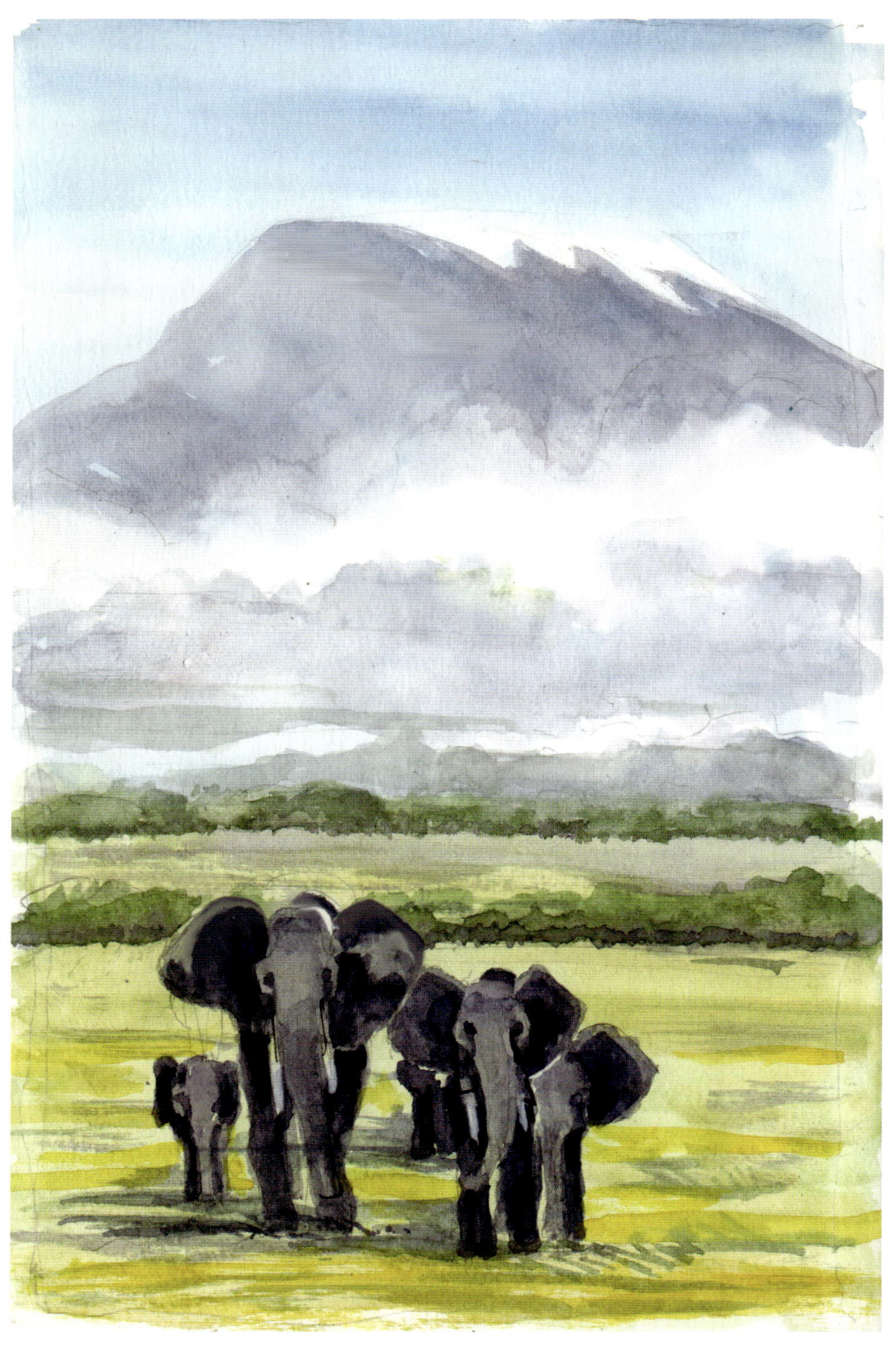

Elephants slowly ambling towards our Land Cruiser with Kilimanjaro as a majestic backdrop.

contemplating the sunset and our extraordinary surroundings. And yes, among herds of elephants, zebras, and wildebeest in primordially beautiful savannahs of Amboseli National Park, Kilimanjaro finally emerged from its perennial cloud cover, overwhelming the surrounding landscape. Leaving the Land Cruiser in an area teeming with wildlife was forbidden by Dennis—lions know the roads and the places and times that vehicles are likely to stop—so when I saw THE dramatic composition I wanted to capture, I had Dennis back up to the sweet spot, and popped up through the sunroof to capture the view in my sketchbook. That experience will make my life's highlight reel.

I remember having a recurring feeling that I was looking at these landscapes through ancient eyes—that I was seeing some of the same impressions seen by ancestors who had climbed down from the forests and stepped onto these savannahs upright, and eventually migrating northward along the Rift Valley to spread into what became the Middle East, Europe, Asia, and points beyond. And I felt oddly at home there—a place long forgotten by countless generations of ancestors and far removed from my own daily life—but that seemed to claim some primal part of me, as something deep within the recesses of my mind seemed to dimly remember it.

Trying to adequately describe the Kenya experience has been elusive. One word that keeps coming to me is transformational--that is, if you allow it, Africa changes you. For my part, I left with a deep feeling of connection to these places I'd never been, to people I'd never met, and to the broad, sweeping history of mankind, as seen from the unbelievably powerful setting of its origins. The experience pulls at me in ways I can't explain. Part of me is called to return. Part of me never left.

Where it began

My first glimpse of the Great Rift Valley was from a broad overlook just outside Nairobi, perched between—not too surprisingly—a fuel stop on one side and a souvenir shack on the other. But the grandeur of the sweeping view wasn't diminished in the slightest by these distractions and was heightened by an understanding that this magnificent vista was just a tiny slice of an ancient geologic feature stretching from Lebanon in the north through Ethiopia, Kenya and Tanzania to Mozambique to the south. Some of the oldest hominid fossils on the planet were found to the south of us in Olduvai Gorge, with evidence of the pre-human primates dating to 2 million years ago. So here, stretching out before us, with its mountains, rivers, broad savannas, tribal villages, and small towns, was what is widely accepted as the very cradle of mankind, and the Great Migration route out of Africa to the Middle East and beyond.

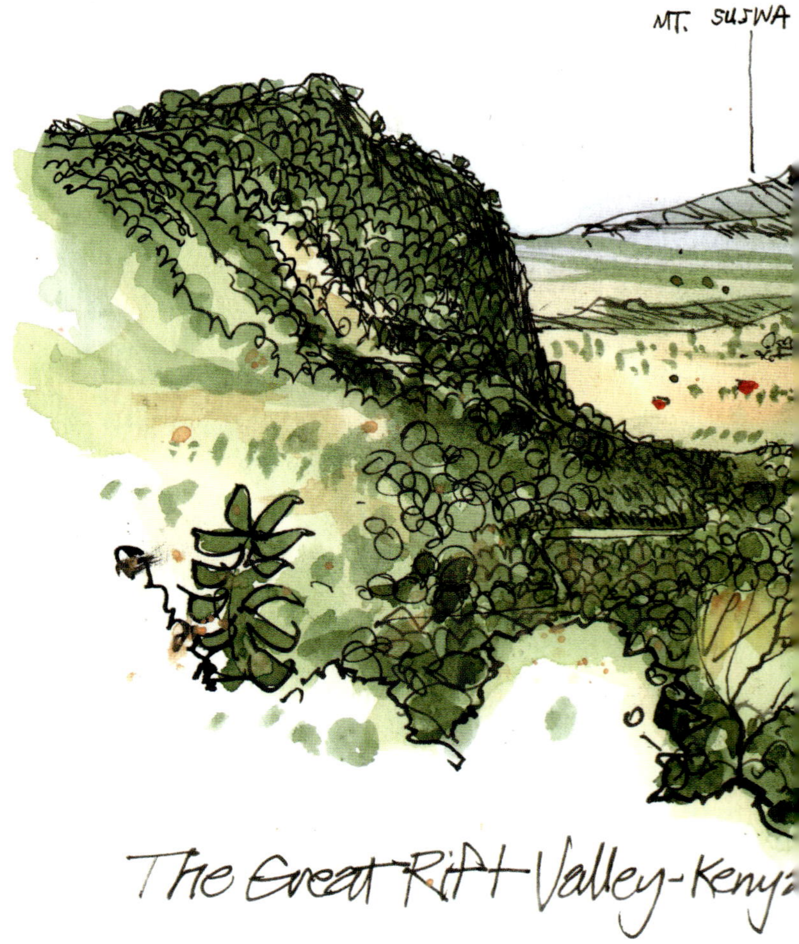

The Great Rift Valley-Kenya

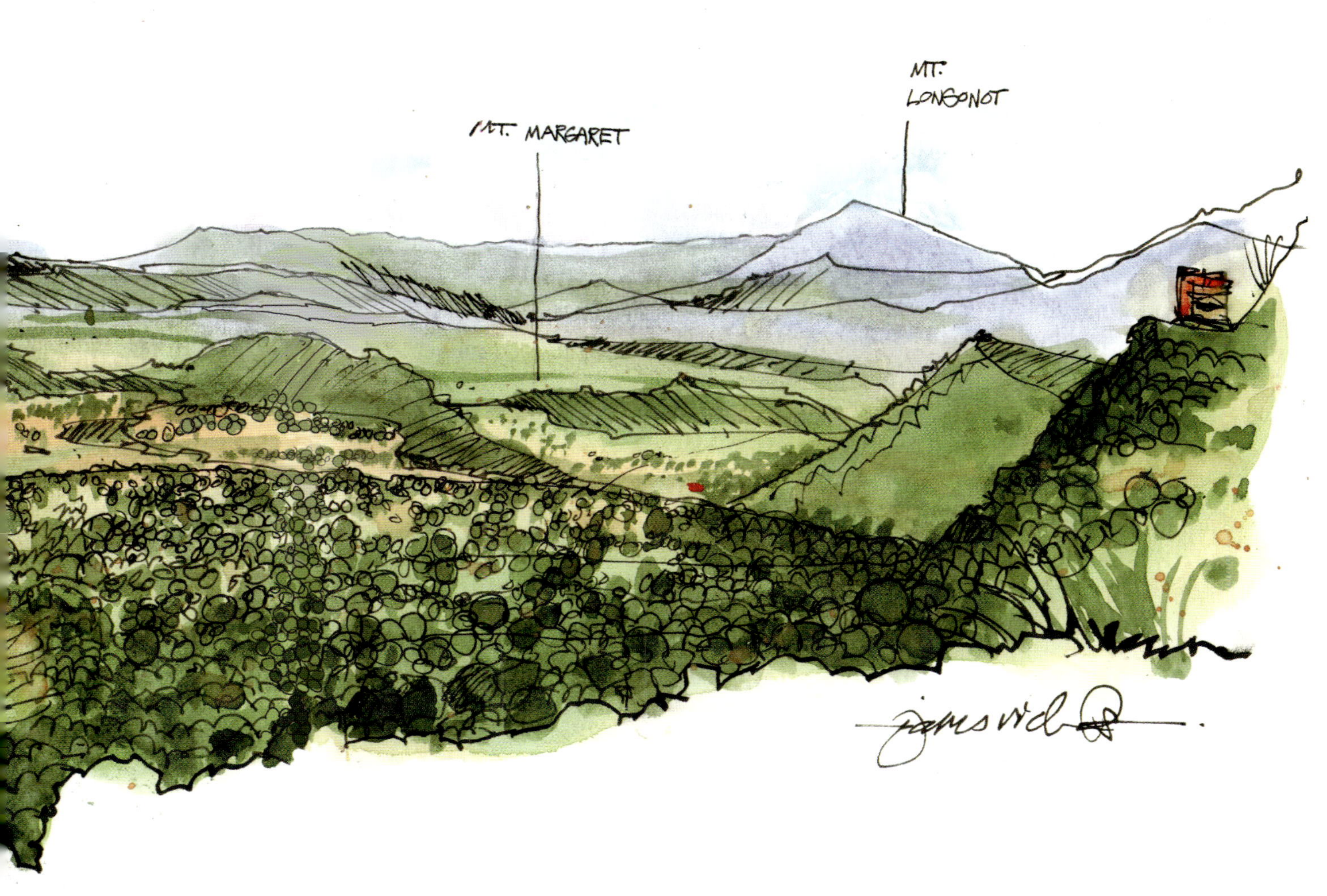

A breathtaking panoramic view of the Great Rift Valley from a roadside overlook. The mountain names were provided by a local who took a break from hawking souvenirs to watch my progress and offer some insider knowledge.

The Sketcher's Code

Be cool.

It's important to be courteous to locals and to visitors. If you're sketching in a public place and someone looks over your shoulder, don't cop an attitude and ignore them or wave them off. Locals created the place and culture that you've traveled to experience. It's not a theme park, it's their home. Do the right thing. Engage them. Be curious. Ask questions. That can open the door to connections and stories that can make you a better artist. And a better person.

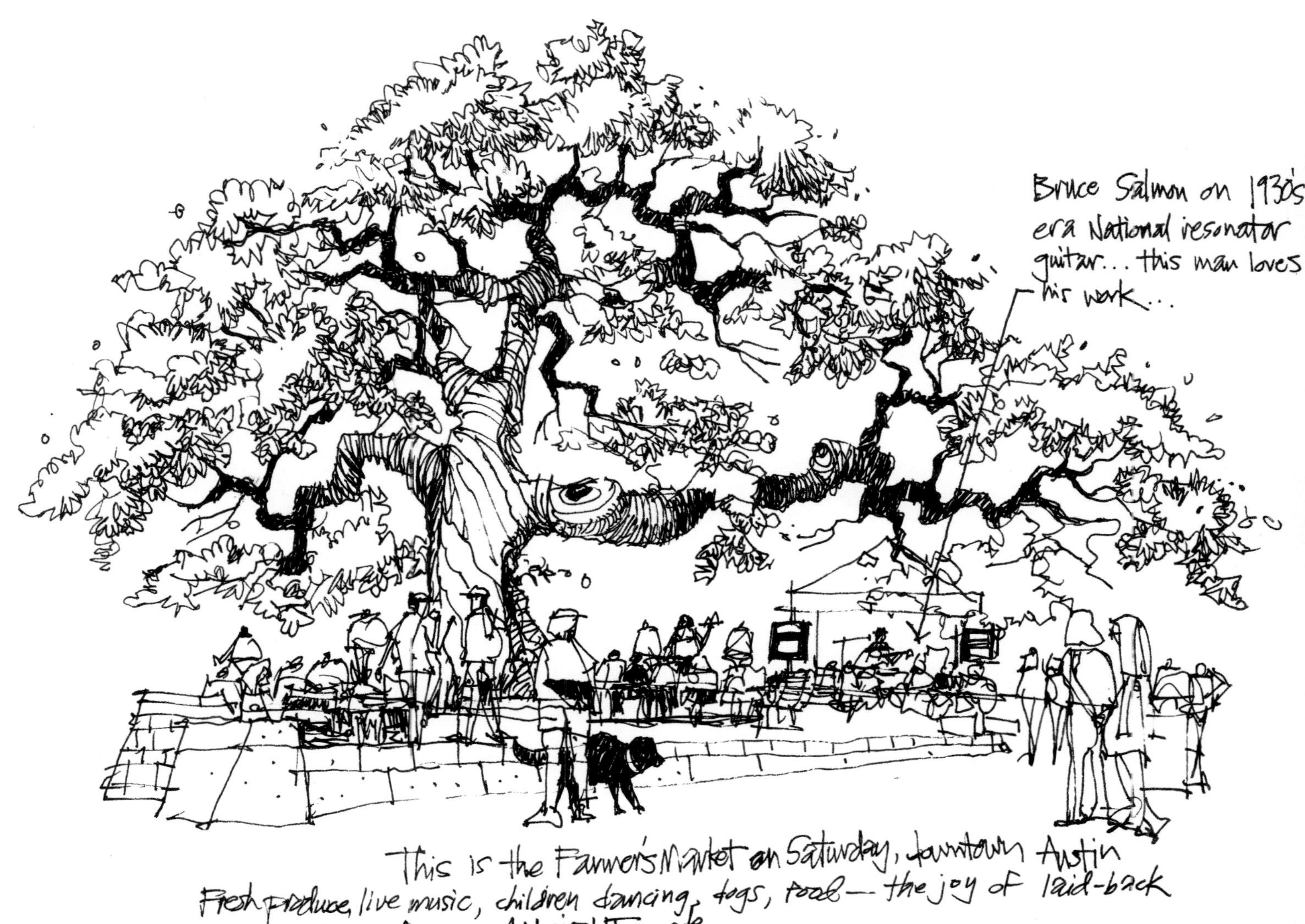
Bruce Salmon on 1930's era National resonator guitar... this man loves his work...
This is the Farmer's Market on Saturday, downtown Austin
Fresh produce, live music, children dancing, dogs, food— the joy of laid-back urban life under an ANCIENT oak..

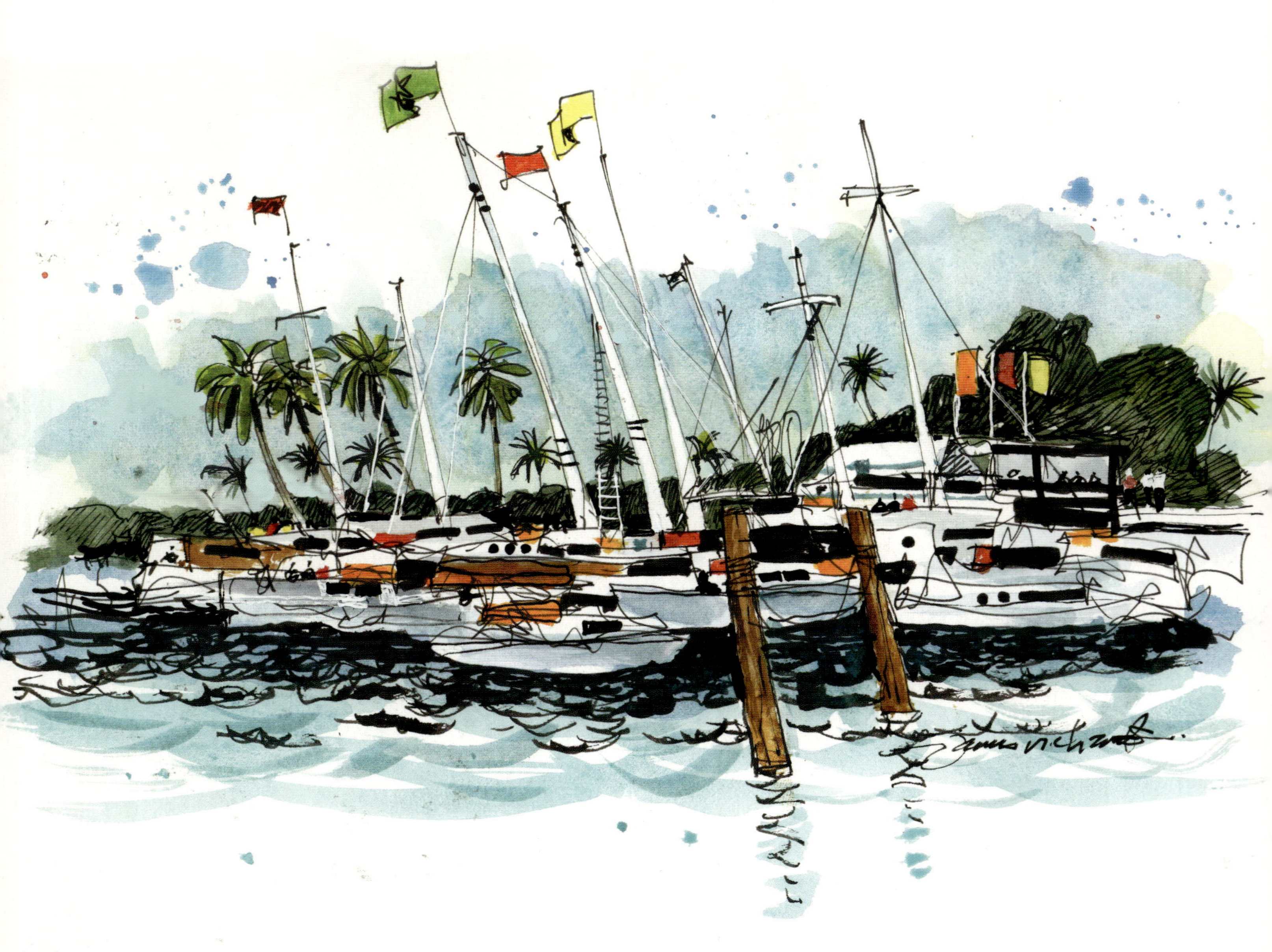

CHAPTER 9

Key West: The End of the Road

KEY WEST IS CLOSE TO HOME, geographically and spiritually. Considerably closer to Havana than it is to Miami, it's a short drive and a three-hour ferry ride from my home on Siesta Key. It's the gateway to Cuba and the Caribbean, both of which are strong cultural influences there. Given the island's famously accepting culture and history shaped by pirates, wreckers, smugglers, writers, musicians, and all manner of eccentrics, I feel very much at home wandering the streets with a sketchbook, making drawings and visual notes while exploring the funky streets, old neighborhoods, marinas, cafes, and bars. I've spent a good deal of time here, and I try to return as often as I'm able, because no place recharges my creative batteries in the same way that Key West does.

Arriving on the island for the first time, we jumped into a cab and traded small talk with the driver, a laid-back, long-haired storyteller with more than a passing resemblance to "The Dude" in *The Big Lebowski*. I asked how long he'd lived here, and he started in on a story that we would hear variations of from more than a few locals:

"I've been here over 40 years. Came down right out of high school in the '70s to explore and party for a week or two. I'm from Shreveport, man, I'd never seen anything like this. So fucking beautiful. The people were easy and laid back. There were some real characters. It was easy to make friends. It was cheap to live here then. I worked a few jobs. It felt like complete freedom to me—paradise."

"I never went back."

Opposite: Key West Bight Marina.

"After a few months, my dad sent my best friend down to talk some sense into me and bring me home. He never went back either."

When it's full of tourists, it's easy to forget that Key West is still one of only a handful of American towns that is truly unique, which is one reason it has historically attracted characters as singular as the place itself. Its most remarkable characteristic is its southernmost, isolated location, literally at the end of the road. You don't pass through Key West. You have to want to be there. And it is seemingly a different world, with its own laid-back culture and outlaw attitude far removed from life and more conservative standards of behavior on the mainland. It's only about four miles long and a mile wide, surrounded by gorgeous turquoise water, which darkens to a rich cobalt blue as the sea deepens further from shore. You can literally stroll across the island from the Atlantic Ocean to the Gulf of Mexico. The realization that you are on

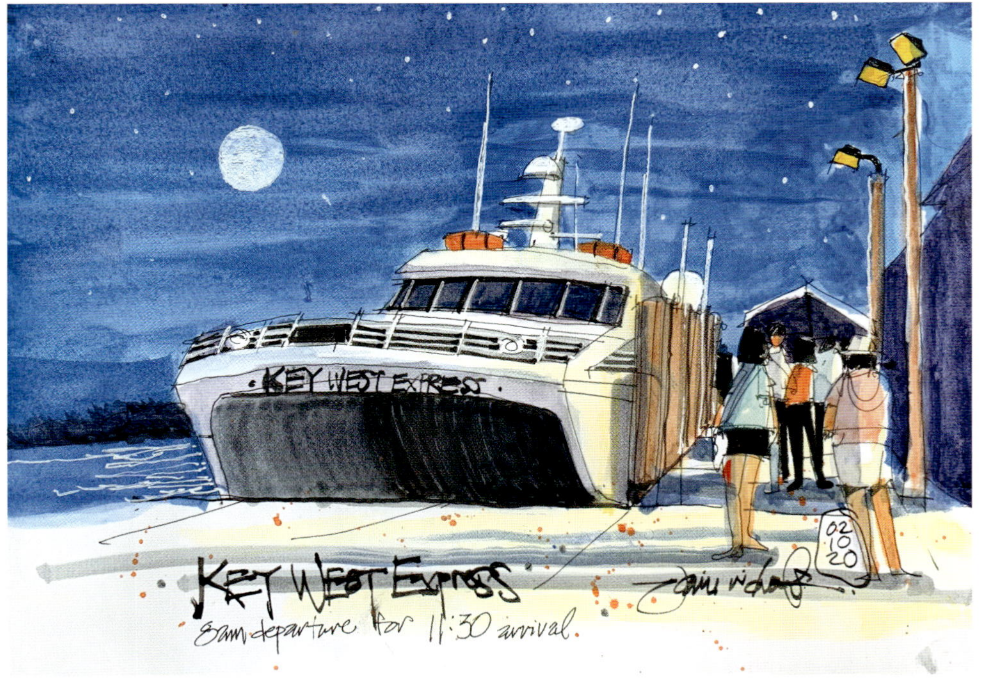

The Key West Express high speed catamarans board around daybreak from docks in Fort Myers Beach and Marco Island, and get us to Key West in time for lunch.

such a small, vulnerable speck of coral surrounded by the high seas heightens the sense of living on the edge of both safety and sanity, a feeling driven home most vividly during hurricane season.

The island's mystique, lore and notoriety are legendary in proportion to its tiny 4.2 square miles of area. There are a handful of "must see" spots—Duval Street, Sloppy Joe's, the Hemingway house, Mallory Square at sunset—that are often overwhelmed with tourists that arrive from the airport and cruise ships, and who rarely make it far from that cluster of attractions. A few with more time and adventurous spirits make the 166- mile drive from Miami through the chain of key islands on the Overseas Highway, the best way to get a sense of the very real remoteness, fragility and genuine weirdness of the Florida Keys.

I came here for a break right after high school 40 years ago...I never went back. After three months, my dad sent my best friend down here to talk some sense into me and bring me home. He never went back either.

Walk a couple of blocks off the party scene on Duval, and you're in the gorgeous, quieter parts of town. It's smallish blocks, filled with late Victorian-era architecture of the 19th and early 20th centuries, much of which was built by shipbuilder-carpenters and furnished with salvage from ships wrecked on the reefs. They're nestled into lush tropical vegetation of palms, giant Ficus trees with dramatic aerial roots, orchids, bougainvillea, papaya, and others. There are very few franchises. Locally owned restaurants, coffee houses, shops, galleries, and lodgings typically reflect the eccentric personalities of their owners. The sidewalks, bar terraces and sidewalk tables are often shared with feral chickens, descendants of roosters raised for cockfighting (only outlawed in the 1970s) who roam every nook and cranny of the town.

Getting out onto the water expands the experience of Key West. At a minimum, there are sunset cruises from Key West Bight, most of which are hour-long parties that stay pretty close to shore. Better are fishing charters. Tarpon, permit, bonefish, snapper, jack crevalle, goliath grouper, and great barracuda are lurking. Sailfish season begins around November and peaks around January, tapering off in April. A low-flying seaplane making the 45-minute flight to Dry Tortugas National Park gives an entirely different perspective. With good weather you can see

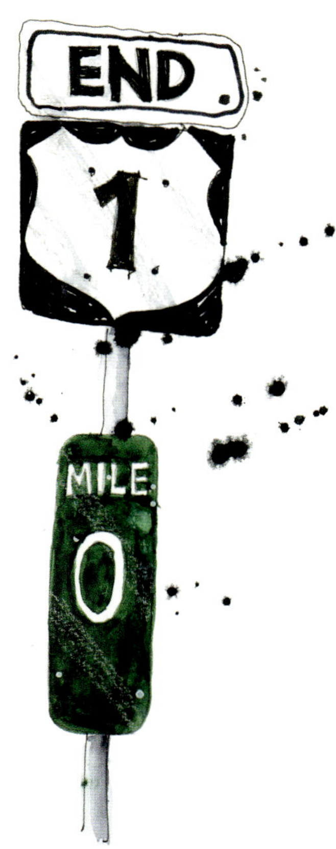

U.S. Highway 1's Mile Marker 0—literally the end of the road.

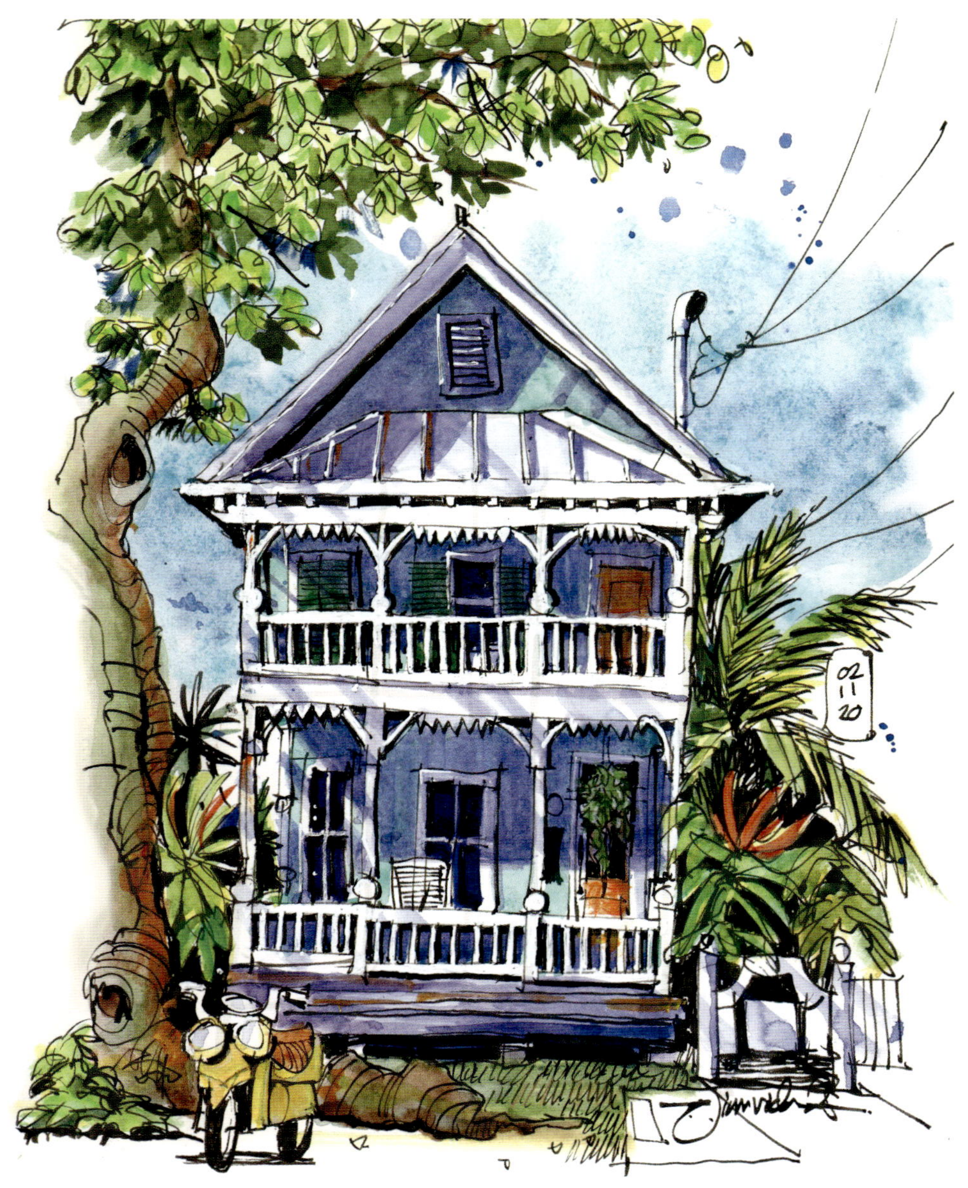

Do yourself a favor. When you've tired of Duval Street, take a break to stroll back through the old residential neighborhoods a couple of blocks off the drag. They're shaded, quiet, and brimming with laid-back tropical character.

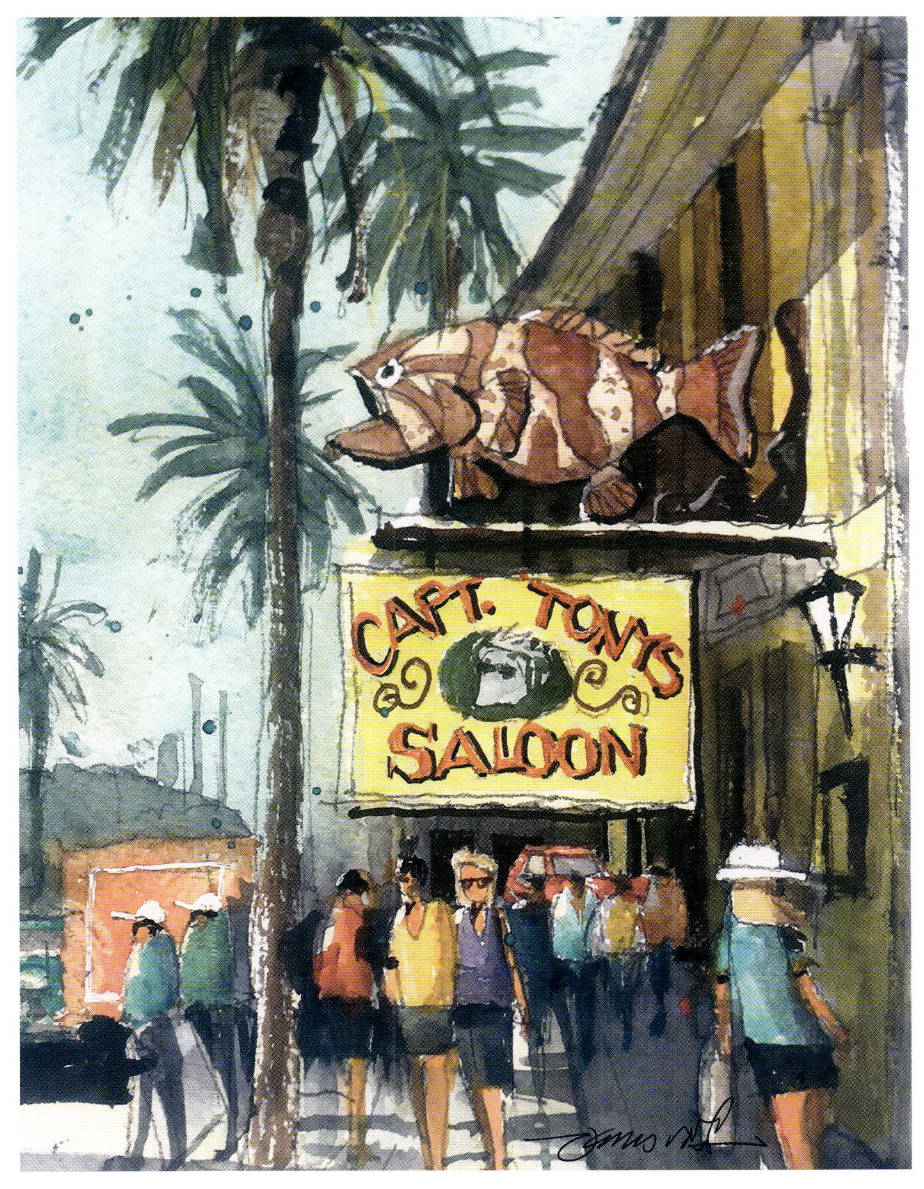

Capt Tony's Saloon—Sloppy Joe's from 1933-1937--has seen Hemingway, Truman Capote, Tennessee Williams, Shel Silverstein, Jimmy Buffet, and the occasional travel artist grace its barstools.

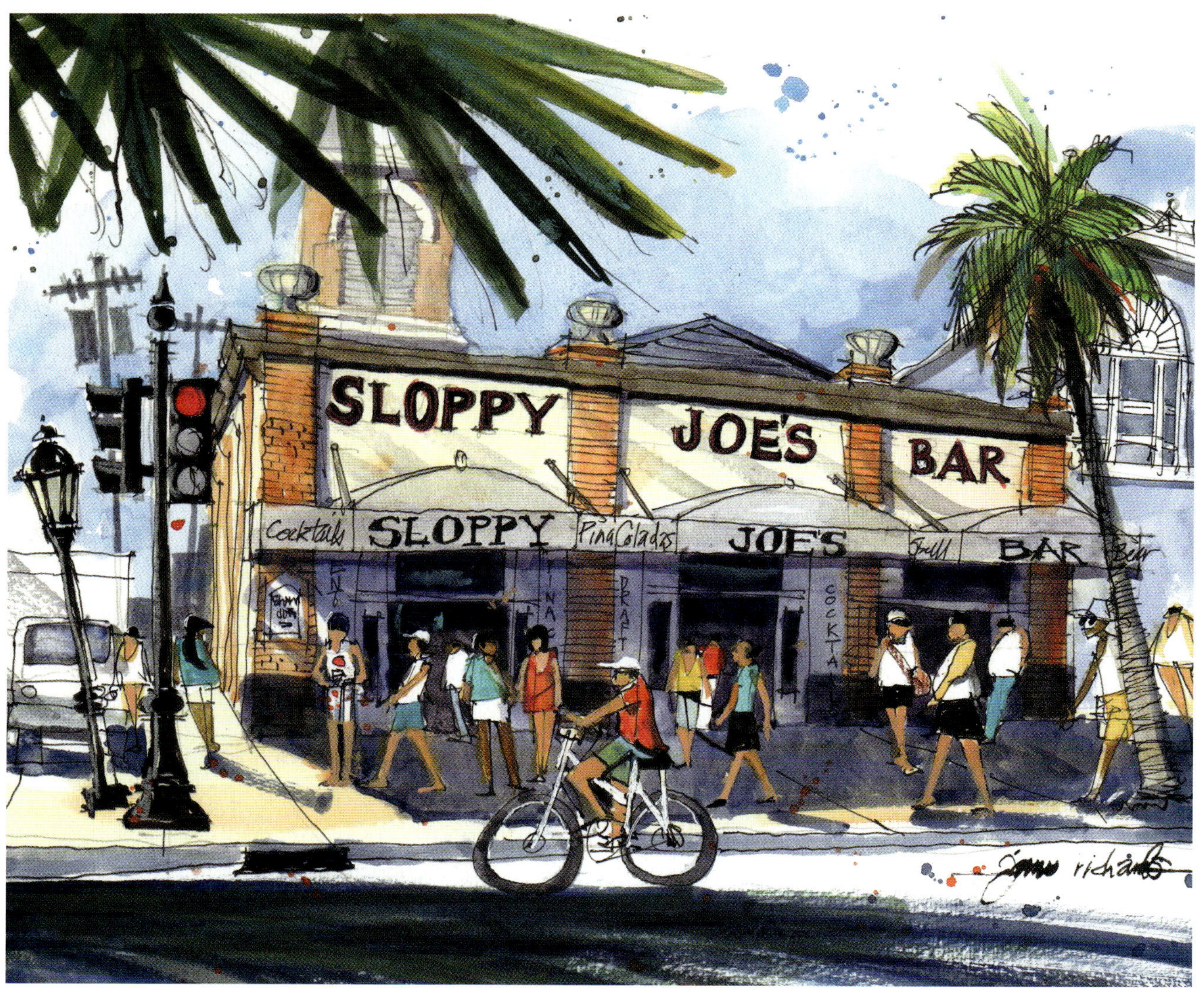

Joe Russell quietly bought this building when the landlord raised the rent from three to four dollars a week for the location that is now Capt Tony's. When the existing lease expired, Joe and a band of Key West drinkers moved the bar from that location to this one in the middle of the night, basically taking everything but the walls with them. It has been Sloppy Joe's ever since.

sharks, sea turtles, and shipwrecks in the clear shallows below. Taking off in the brilliant, clear turquoise water and banking for views of the beaches and the reefs of Garden Key is the top shelf experience for me.

I think Hemingway, Tennessee Williams, Truman Capote, Jim Harrison, Jimmy Buffett, and other creatives who felt pulled there were on to something. Hemingway called it "the St. Tropez of the poor." While the economic demographics have decidedly changed since he lived here, it's still a place I feel drawn to and continually inspired by. When I put my feet up on the balcony porch rail, pour a rum drink, and start drawing or writing, I'm home. Key West is still the real deal.

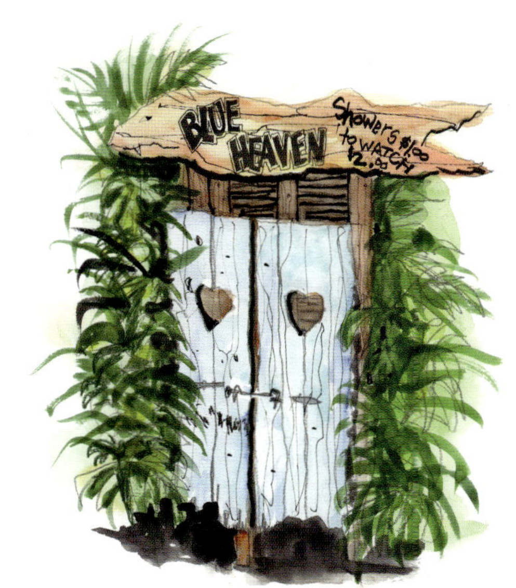

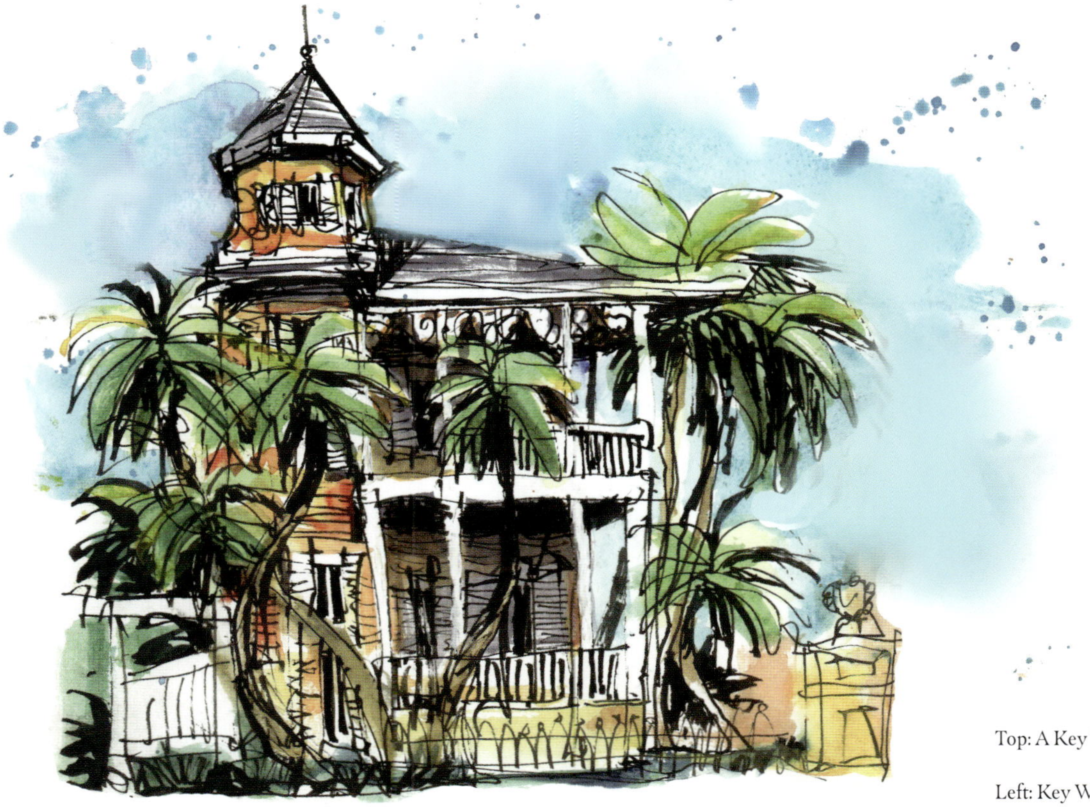

Top: A Key West moment.

Left: Key West character.

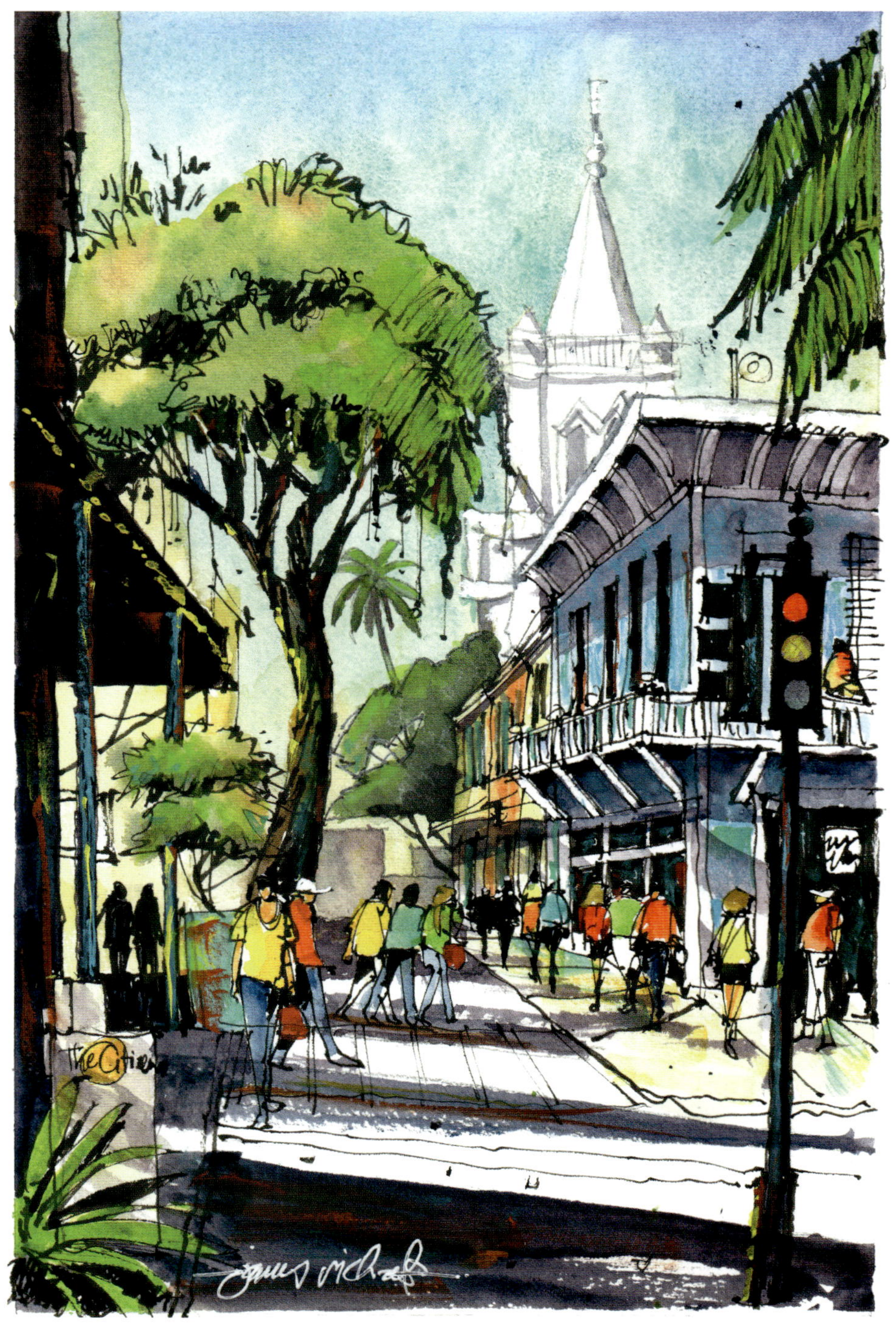

Duval Street on its quieter western side.

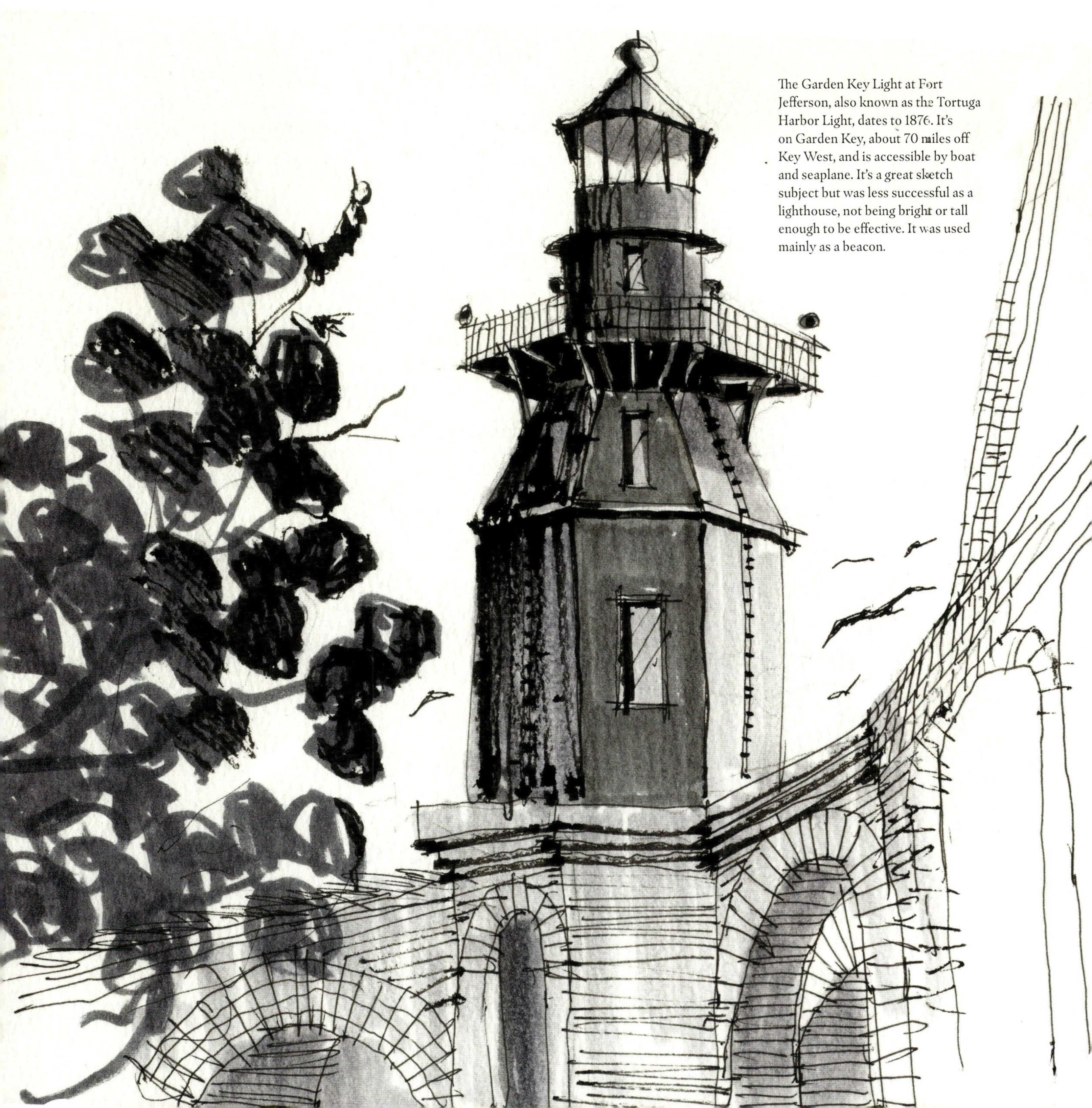

The Garden Key Light at Fort Jefferson, also known as the Tortuga Harbor Light, dates to 1876. It's on Garden Key, about 70 miles off Key West, and is accessible by boat and seaplane. It's a great sketch subject but was less successful as a lighthouse, not being bright or tall enough to be effective. It was used mainly as a beacon.

"We seceeded where others failed"

Another window into Key West's quirky culture is the curious but not really surprising story of the founding of the Conch Republic, when Key West briefly seceded from the United States in protest over a U.S. Border Patrol roadblock on U.S. 1, the single, thin ribbon of roadway connecting the island to the mainland. Vehicles were stopped, occupants questioned, and searches for drugs and illegal aliens ensued, much as would happen at a border crossing into (or out of) another country. These actions, of course, backed up traffic for miles, greatly inconvenienced the residents of the Keys and put a serious dent in Key West's tourism. After repeated complaints from the Key West City Council and failed attempts to get an injunction of the roadblock, the mayor and council reasoned that if they were to be treated as a foreign nation, they might as well become one. Accounts of what happened next vary slightly, as the events occurred some time ago and there was alcohol involved, but this is my favorite version.

In the course of a day, Key West citizens condemned the action, declared the island the independent Conch Republic, and symbolically attacked the U.S. Navy by breaking a loaf of stale Cuban bread over the head of a man in a naval uniform. One minute later, the new Conch Republic surrendered to the same uniformed man and promptly applied for foreign aid. It seemed a perfectly reasonable and appropriate thing to do in 1982 Key West. Come to think of it, it would probably seem so now.

The spirit of the Conch Republic lives on, mostly as a local point of pride and tourism ploy. The secession event is commemorated every year with a festival, and Conch Republic merchandise can be purchased at any number of spots on or near Duval Street. The Grown-up and I are proud holders of official Conch Republic passports—honored in at least one Caribbean nation—and the nation's flag hangs on our living room wall. At the end of the day, it's more a state of mind than sovereign nation, and my mind has a thatch umbrella, hammock and umbrella drink there.

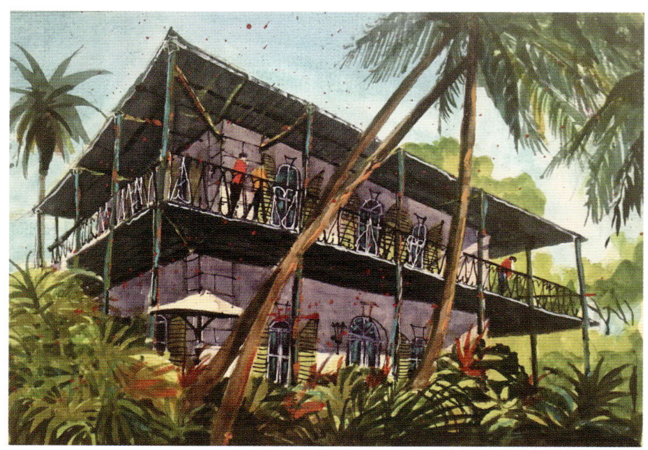

907 Whitehead Street, Ernest Hemingway's residence from 1931 to 1939, where he wrote some of his best novels and short stories.

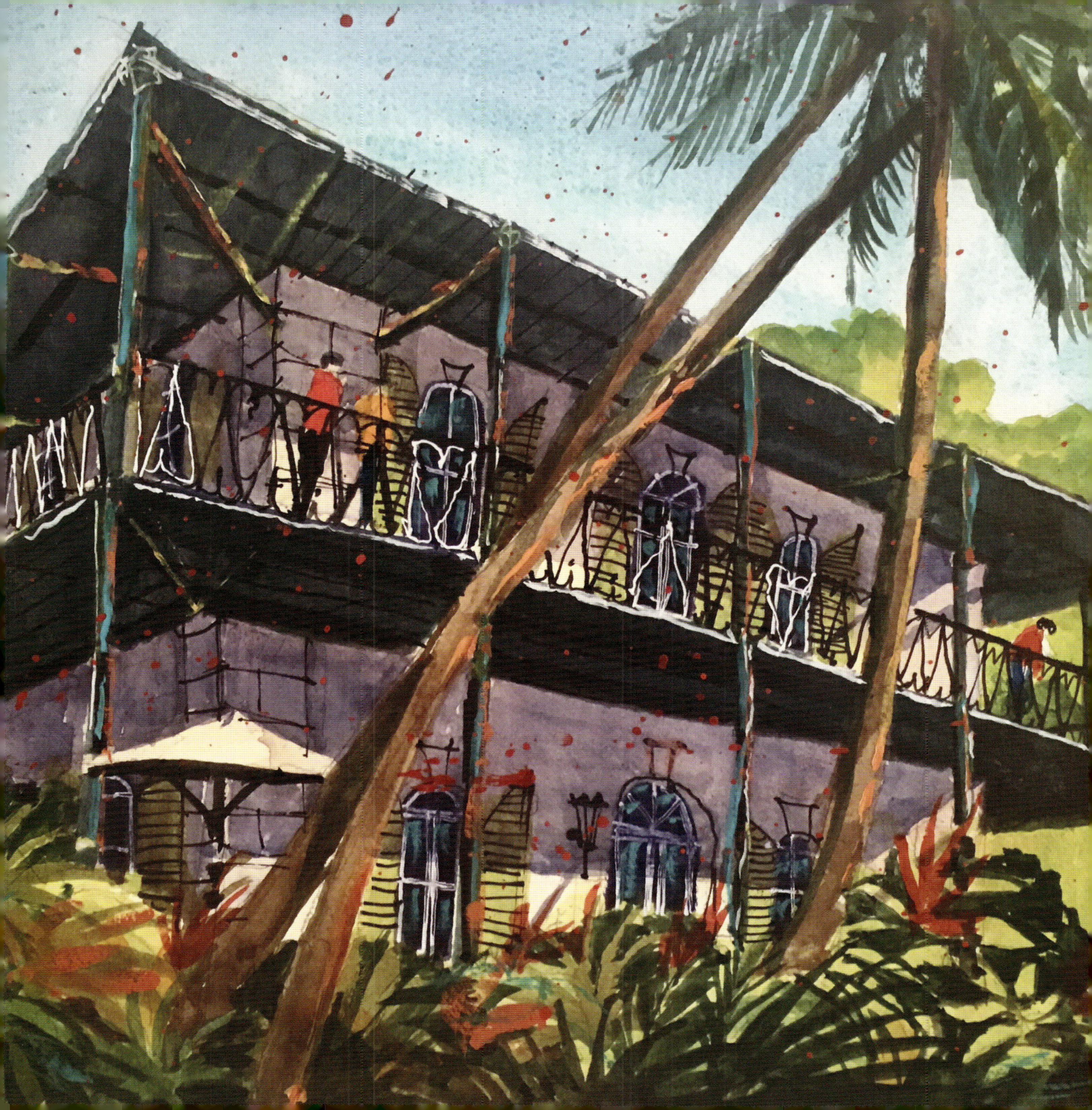

The Sketcher's Code

Finish on the spot. Or not.

Degree of completion of a sketch done on location can be dependent on lots of things: being evicted by security, dire need for a bathroom, sunstroke heat, frostbite cold, being assaulted, and the pace and patience of your travel companions. I always try to finish my ink drawing on the spot, so that color is optional. Work on it. Simplify tools. Try a smaller sketchbook. Edit the scene well. Quicken your pace. Limit color to where it will make the most impact, or simply make color notes and add it later. Don't stress. The sketch police aren't lurking in the bushes. Creating the sketch your own way is your reward for getting out there in the first place.

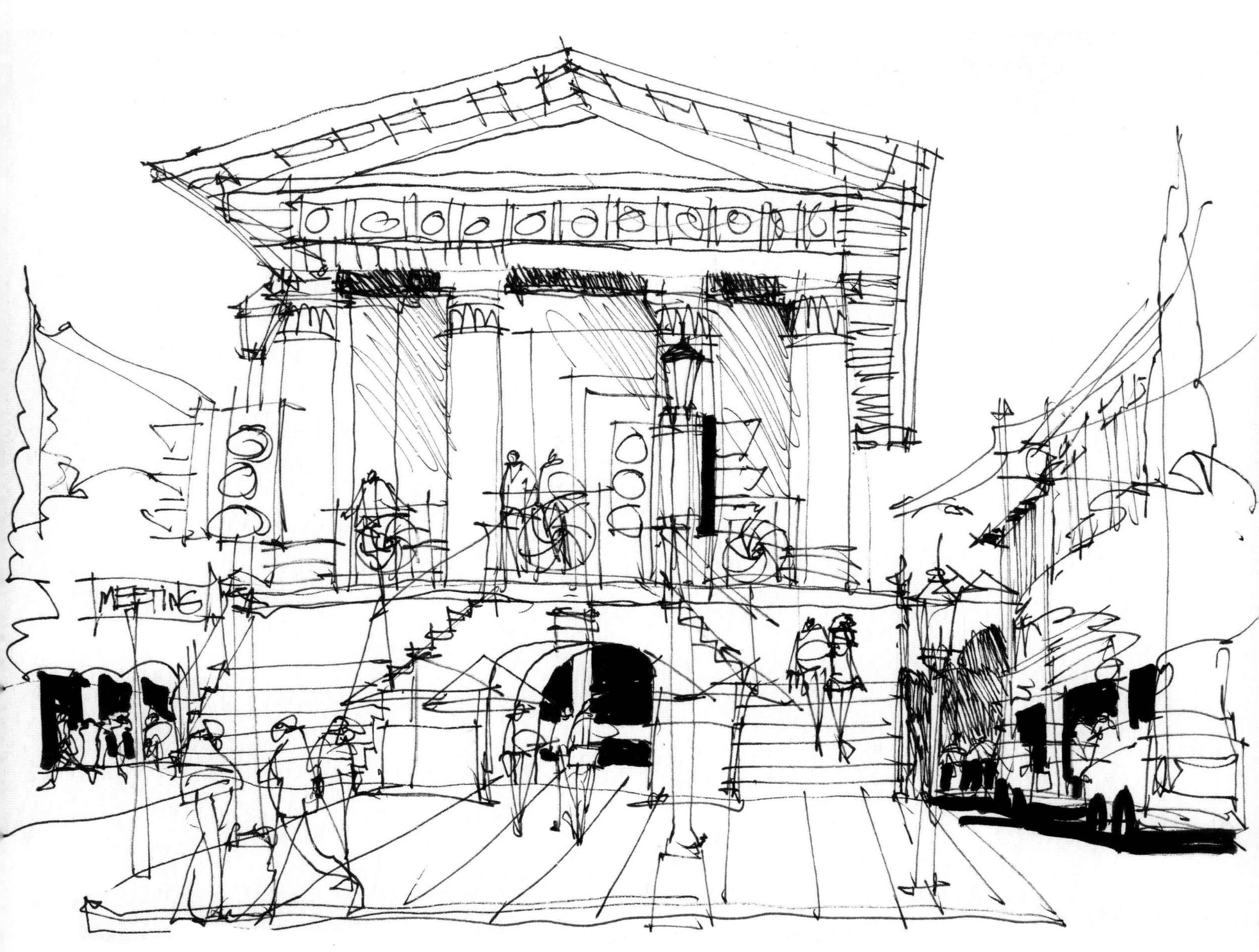

Charleston, South Carolina.

AFTERWORD:
FOLLOWING THE VOICE

I THINK THIS POINT in my life and work can best be summed up by two stories. A few years ago, Patti and I gave an end-of-semester party at our house for my grad students. It was joyful—lots of laughs, stories, even an impromptu "talent show" (no cameras allowed). As people were leaving the house, one stayed, sitting silently on the sofa and looking pensively into the fireplace. Strange. She was my graduate assistant. I knew her pretty well, and this was unusual.

"What's up, Xie?"

She said she was nearing graduation, and as we all knew, the economy was on life support. The job market was in the crapper, and even with an impressive double major, she felt her prospects at that moment looked bleak. After years of study, leadership, and damned hard work, it was tough for her to see what her options—or her future—looked like.

Of course, I got it. In the last bad economic downturn, our award-winning design firm had to close shop, and for a while I felt my career was in free fall. "But once word got around," I told her, "I had 16 different firms express interest within a couple of weeks."

"Yeah, but you used to be the shit."

"Wait. Excuse me? Used to be?" What did I miss? Was I not, still, the shit?

After some stuttering, stammering, awkward apologies and a good laugh, we moved on. But the comment is always in the back of my mind because, like smart humor, it's only funny because it's true (well, mostly).

Story two: fast forward to Tuscany a few years later. It's my first sketching workshop there, and Steve, a talented architectural photographer, has accompanied his father, a longtime sketcher. Steve didn't have a lot of sketching experience, and though shy, was up for wading in.

His sketches were pretty good early in the week. Then they got better. And they continued to get better, like something inside him had opened up. And he was opening up to the group as well, with wry observations, great stories, and perfectly timed, mic drop one-liners. By the end of the week, he was sketching dinner from a balcony overlooking the long dining table below, making a playful but killer drawing of all 13 workshop guests and their food from above. Mic drop. Again.

A couple of weeks later, Steve sent me a note sharing his thoughts on the experience. It's been a while, but basically it said this:

"I expected to learn. I expected to fall in love with the landscapes, hill towns, and seasides. I expected to eat well. What I didn't expect was to rediscover that six-year-old boy who still lived inside me, who loved to draw without judgement."

I know that I'm not a young lion anymore. My body is less forgiving. My passports are full and frayed and my sketching gear shows unmistakable signs of very high mileage. At the same time, my skills are growing, pushing my boundaries into new and exciting directions. I take myself (much) less seriously. I feel like I'm exactly where I'm supposed to be.

And I still hear the voice. My fire for following that voice down a highway or across an ocean has never faded. But the winds are changing. I'm taking off some of my old, worn clothes to put on brighter colors, scarves, and a hat that suits my mood, with paint on my hands and a twinkle in the eye. Patti and I will watch sunrises, dance in the grass, drink spritzes in sidewalk cafes, maybe inspire some who choose to set aside their day-to-day and come along. I'll sketch piazzas, make drawings of characters I see there, write books, tell stories, and as Bob Dylan wrote, "dance beneath the diamond sky with one hand waving free." That's what following the voice looks like to me now.

Xie is a wife, mom and an award-winning star in our profession. Steve is a skillful and passionate urban sketcher, a big part of his full, creative life.

And I'm still the shit.

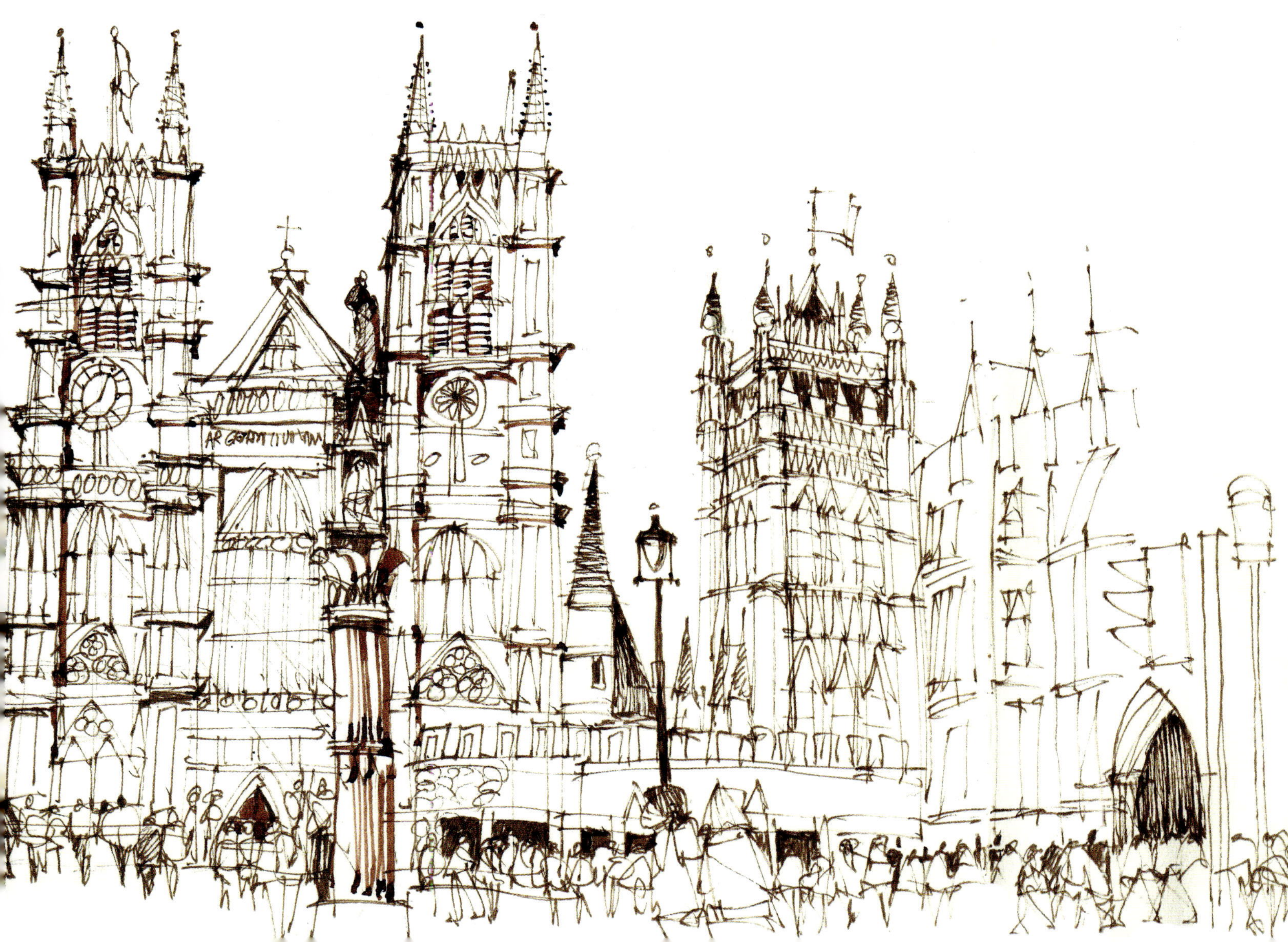

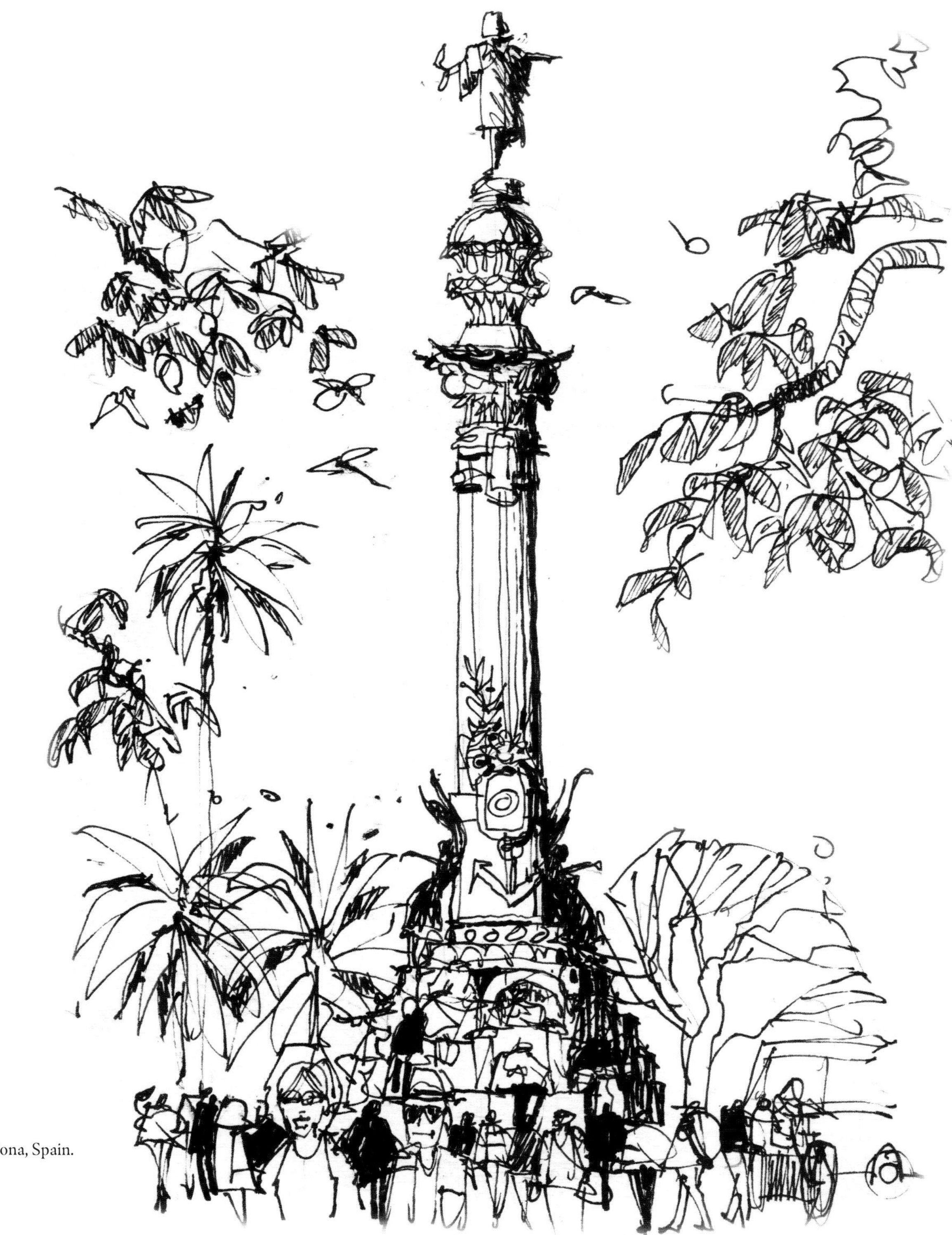

Barcelona, Spain.

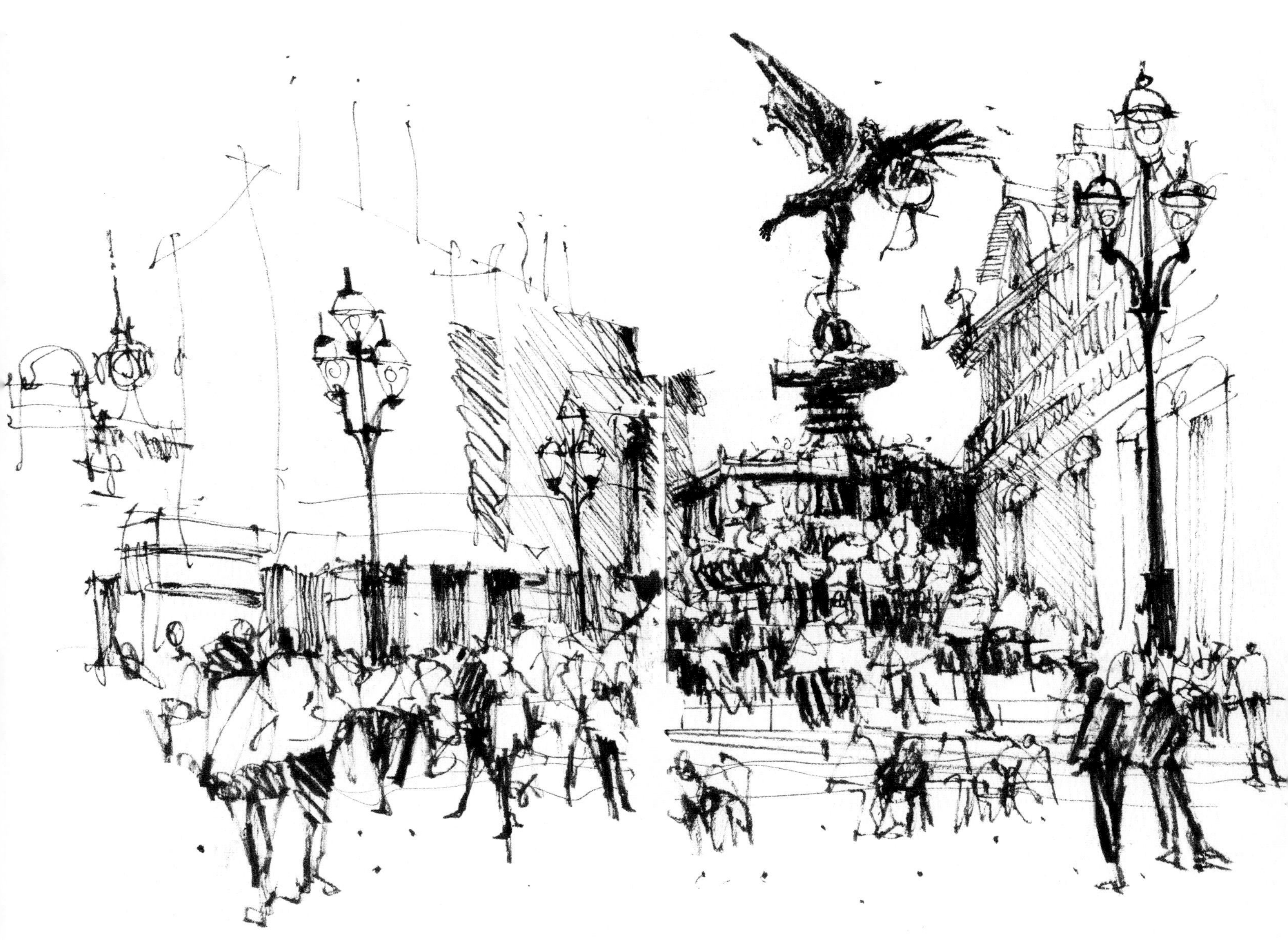

Picadilly Circus, London.

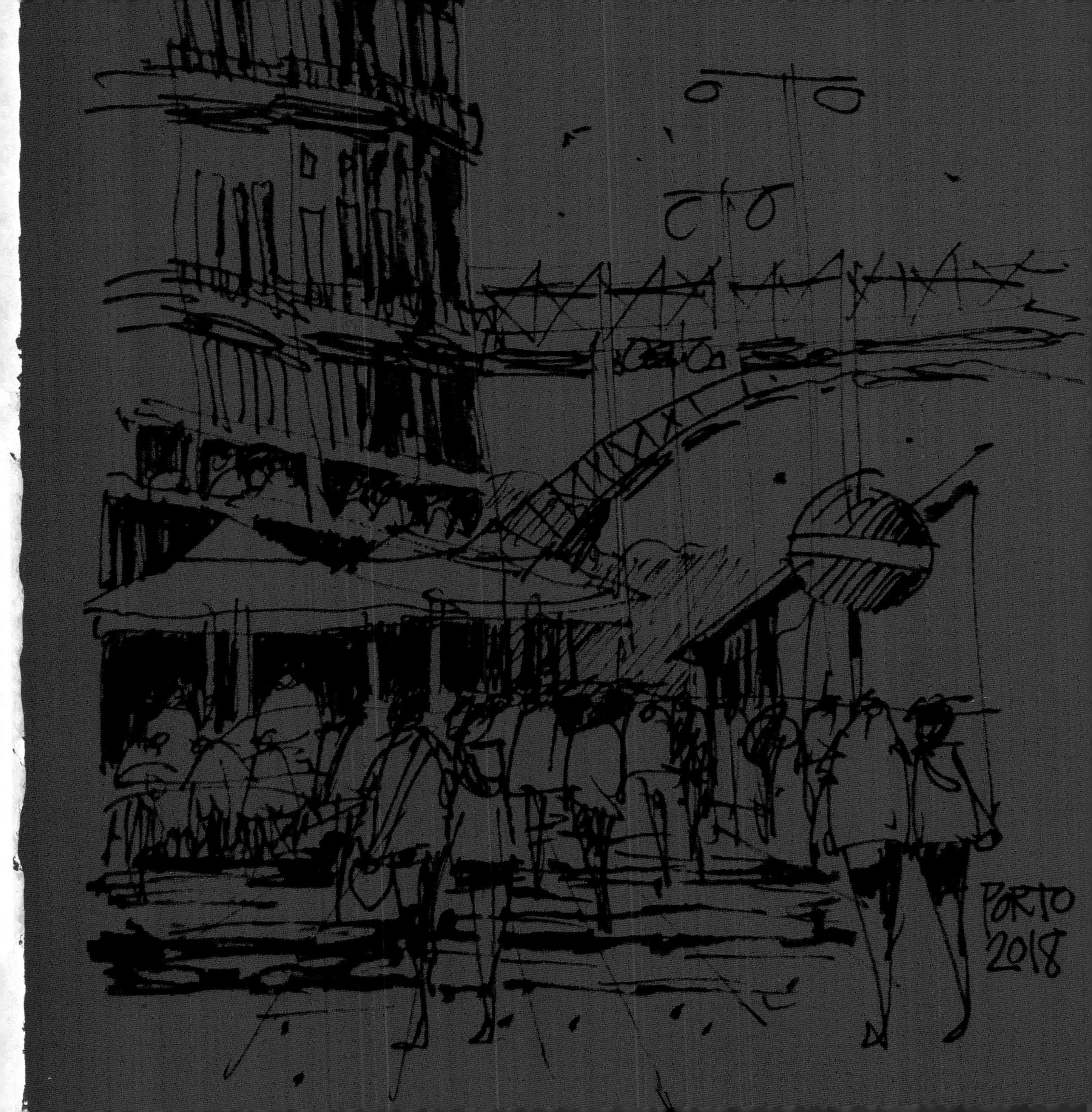
PORTO
2018

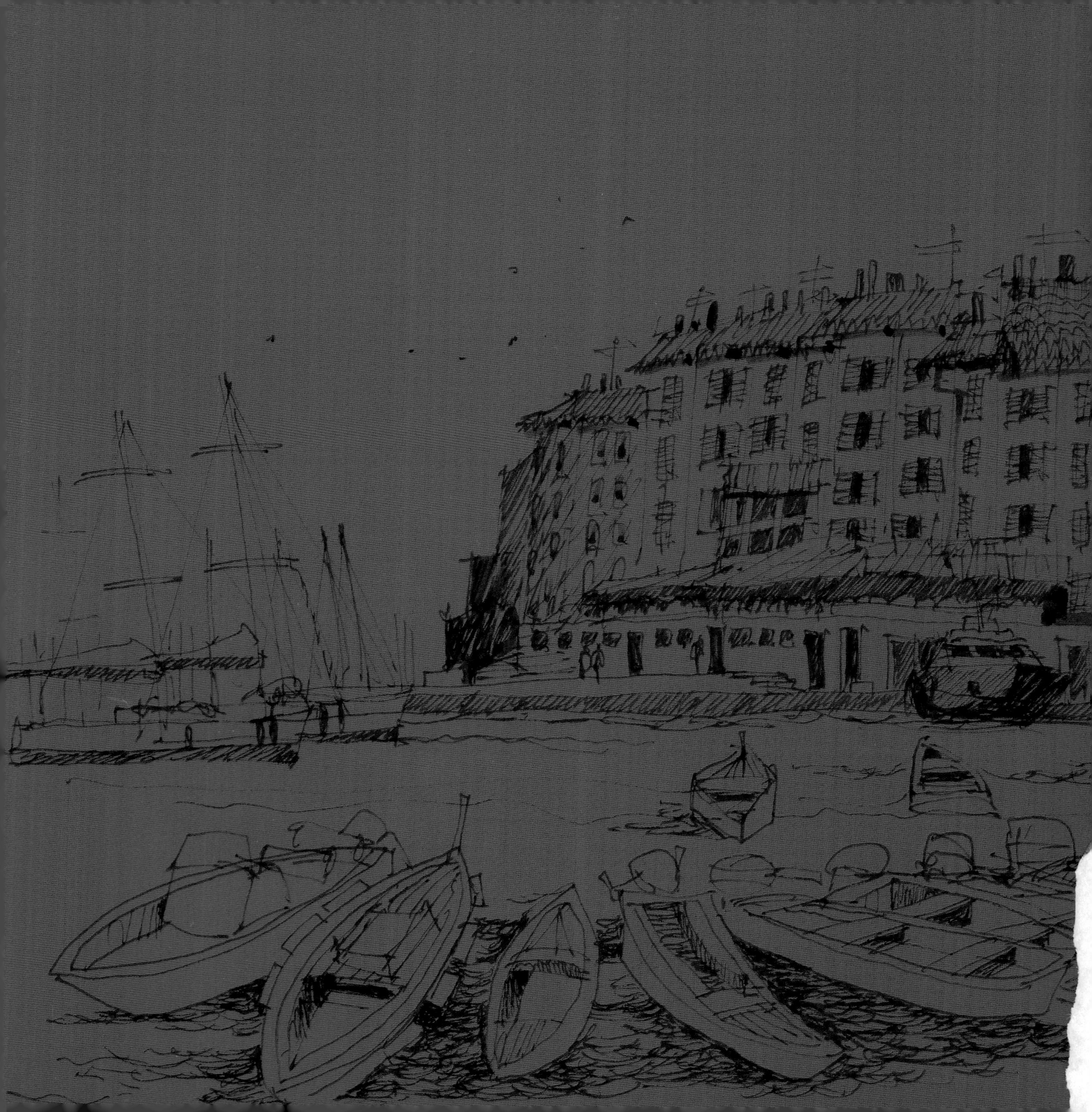